Merry Christmas

Louise, Xmas 98

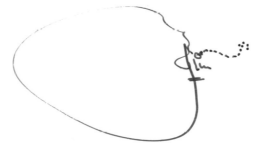

. . . For Emma, Chlöe and Bridie

Working with men for change

Edited by

Jim Wild

UCL PRESS
UCL
PRESS
Taylor & Francis Group

First published in 1999 by UCL Press

UCL Press Limited
1 Gunpowder Square
London EC4A 3DF
UK

and

325 Chestnut Street 8th Floor
Philadelphia
PA 19106
USA

The name of University College London (UCL) is a registered
trade mark used by UCL Press with the consent of the owner.

British Library Cataloguing-in-Publication Data
A catalogue record for this book is available from the British Library.

Library of Congress Cataloging-in-Publication Data are available

ISBNs: 1-85728-860-2 HB
1-85728-861-0 PB

Typeset in Times by Graphicraft Ltd., Hong Kong.
Printed by T. J. International Ltd., Padstow, UK.

Patriarchy has run its course, and now not only fails to serve the real needs of men and women, but with its inalienable racism, militarism, hierarchical structures and rage to dominate and destroy, it threatens the very existence of life on earth.

Rosalind Miles, *The women's history of the world*

Contents

Editor's acknowledgements

Several individuals need mentioning for their influence and support during the process of creating this book on men and change. The ideas behind this volume arose from discussions, almost a decade ago, with John Casson – a therapist in Greater Manchester. These discussions led us to submit proposals to a number of publishing houses but their response was cautious and the project went no further at the time. John's influence is very much present in these pages. I would also like to identify Jock Spence, whom I met in the early 1980s at Birchwood Hall Commune. He introduced me to the agenda of the growing movement of "men against sexism", and together we formed a local men's group, giving us the opportunity to discuss and to clarify our personal and political agendas. In the mid-1980s I began to work in child protection, at a time when connections between child abuse and male violence were first beginning to be understood. Though more than a decade has passed there persists a widespread disbelief that men in domestic situations are capable of such terrible sexual violence and abuse. In this context, two individuals stand out for me – Beatrix Campbell and Judith Jones. Both have stood up with great courage during this time of profound crisis. They have been able and willing to support practitioners with words of clarity that articulated what many of us felt was left unsaid, and they have been a tremendous influence on my own commitment to activism in child protection.

I would like to thank all the contributors to the book for their time and for their ability to keep to deadlines while employed at the sharp end of social care work. The staff at UCL Press/Taylor & Francis have always retained enthusiasm for the project, with Caroline Wintersgill a flexible, creative and vital influence – balancing her willingness to expand the publication with simultaneous concerns that the deadline was constantly moving into the distance!

On a more personal note, I would like to acknowledge my partner, Joan Healey, whose support and love has helped me through several personal struggles and who has never lost faith in our relationship. Finally I would like to pay a special tribute to the Gestalt therapy group in Nottingham, of which I was a member. Over a period of almost four years we all grew and developed – sharing the pains and pleasures of what life unexpectedly brings. Our changes could not have been fully realized without the skill of Ian Greenway, who facilitated the group and played a central part in the healing of my own wounded childhood.

Preface

In the early 1970s, *The male machine*, by Marc Feigen Fasteau, attempted to speak directly to men about the crippling effect of masculinity. Responding to the second wave of feminism it challenged so much about what it is to be a man. We now have a wide range and diverse list of publications that relate to men, and a developing understanding of our impact in the world. However, at times it seems to me this is very limited and marginalized. When we watch the news, read a paper or hear of the latest child abuse horror story, men's "impact", is rarely connected to wider society. Looking through the lens of gender and reflecting objectively about the way we as men relate to others can lead to a profound shift in our understanding of how we are shaped by many notions, ideas and influences that distort or pressure us into ways of being that limit our potential. In reality, there are few men involved in the process of personal change and there is little encouragement to embrace different ways to be a man. Although we have many cultures, religions and belief systems, what holds true is the pervading influence of masculinity, contextualized within power relations that are so profoundly unequal. Much in the shaping of attitudes, personality, relationships and the structures in wider society is taken for granted as everyday reality. The aim of this book is to challenge these notions, and to support men to find courage and explore change. Although initially daunting and frightening, men can find the path to new awareness, and what Susie Orbach calls "emotional literacy".

Working with men for change attempts to bring together for the first time, theory, research and practice – combining these areas in order to equip the reader with knowledge, information and opportunity for personal reflection. The book has a natural divide between theory and practice for wide-ranging use. Whether you are an individual man or a worker in social care wanting to run a men's group, I hope what you find here will be of use. This publication is designed to inspire men (and women) to reflect on what it is to be a man and to consider a different journey – towards a more fully realized awareness of our impact on others and the dreadful consequences of patriarchy. In facing the issues this publication raises there will be opportunities to take the risk of exploring personal and political space that has previously been left uninhabited, avoided or unoccupied for many and complex reasons. Some men will naturally be defensive about this publication. But all we ask is for men to be less dominating and destructive in the world and more empathic – allies of women, children and other men without resorting to any kind of violation or abuse.

JIM WILD

Notes on contributors

Susan Cayouette is the Clinical Director at Emerge: Counselling and Education to Stop Domestic Violence, located in Cambridge, MA, USA. She has worked in the battered women's movement for 15 years and has spent the past 10 years at Emerge. She has a Doctorate in education from Boston University and is a licensed Marriage and Family Therapist.

Malcolm Cowburn is Lecturer in Social Work at Sheffield University, UK. He has extensive experience with groupwork programmes for adult male sex offenders. He works with group workers, helping them develop programmes of work and consider issues of anti-oppressive co-working. His publications have considered issues relating to gender, race, sexuality and groupwork with adult male sex offenders.

Lena Dominelli holds a Chair in the Department of Social Work Studies at the University of Southampton, UK. She came into education from the field and has worked as a community worker, social worker and probation officer. She has taught and undertaken research in social work for the past 20 years and is the author of many books and articles.

Tim Foskett holds a degree in psychology from the University of Wales, College of Cardiff, UK, and a three-year Certificate in person-centred and existential counselling and groupwork from City University, London, UK. He has been employed by PACE since July 1995 and, with Alfred Hurst, has developed a unique approach to HIV prevention with gay men, through the use of therapeutic groupwork.

Jeff Hearn is Professional Research Fellow in the Faculty of Economic and Social Studies, based in the Department of Social Policy and Social Work, University of Manchester, UK, and Visiting Donner Professor in Sociology at Åbo Akademi, Finland with particular reference to gender research. His most recent books are *Men in the public eye* (1992); *Violence and gender relations* (1996); *Men as managers, managers as men* (1996); *Men, gender divisions and welfare* (1998); and *The violences of men* (1998).

Alfred Hurst is a qualified social worker and holds a Masters degree in public service management. He is currently in his final year of a MSc. in family therapy at the Institute of Family Therapy at Birkbeck College, University of London, UK. Alfred offers organizational consultancy to a number of statutory and voluntary sector organizations as well as offering facilitation to groups and organizations.

Luke Daniels is an organizational consultant and an activist and trainer working with violent men. He assists social care professionals in establishing projects relating to male violence in the UK and internationally.

Susie Orbach is a nationally and internationally known psychotherapist and writer. She sees individuals and couples, acts as a consultant to organizations and supervises the work of other psychotherapists. She co-founded The Women's Therapy Centre in London in 1976 and in 1981 the Women's Therapy Institute, a postgraduate training centre for psychotherapists in New York.

Hilary Pengelly is Senior Lecturer in Social Work at Sheffield Hallam University, UK. Her main area of interest is reflective practice in individual and groupwork settings. She teaches anti-oppressive social work methods and is currently interested in the gender issues for women and men co-parenting after separation and divorce.

Victor Jeleniewski Seidler is Senior Lecturer in Social Theory and Philosophy in the Department of Sociology, Goldsmiths' College, University of London, UK.

Tom Shakespeare is Research Fellow at the University of Leeds, UK. He is a member of the disability movement and has written and broadcast on disability issues.

John Stoltenberg has, for over 20 years, been the most influential radical feminist male writer in the United States. Alice Walker said of his first book, *Refusing to be a man*: "I believe this book can change the lives of millions of people . . . a book that can give hope to coming generations". Gloria Steinem said of his next: "John Stoltenberg has always been the foremost theoretician of masculinity as a violence-filled prison for men. Now, in *The end of manhood*, he provides a practical, compassionate, everyday guide for an escape to freedom". John is also the author of *What makes pornography "sexy"*, about an experiential "do-the-pose" workshop he developed for men. He holds a master of divinity degree from Union Theological Seminary in New York City and a master of fine arts in theatre from Columbia University School of the Arts, USA.

Wanda Thomas Bernard is Associate Professor at the Maritime School of Social Work, Dalhousie University, Canada. A graduate of Sheffield University, UK, she is particularly interested in community based research, and research in social work practice. As a social work practitioner and educator, she is committed to engaging in empowerment based research, and bridging the gap between academia and community.

Keith Tudor is a social worker, an accredited counsellor (BAC), a registered independent counsellor (UKKC) and, as a Certified Transactional Analyst, is a registered psychotherapist (UKCP).

Jim Wild is a manager and trainer in child protection and has been an activist/ researcher on men and masculinity since the early 1980s. He presently researches men's issues and retains a working commitment to child protection. He co-facilitates workshops on gender issues and regularly runs groups for men on change and personal development, based on the programme in this publication.

Paul Wolf-Light has worked professionally as a psychotherapist and counsellor since 1989. Between 1992 and 1996 he worked as counsellor and counselling supervisor at the Everyman Centre in Brixton, London, working exclusively with violent men. Since July 1996 he has worked in the same capacity at the Everyman Centre in Stonehouse, Plymouth. A member of the Achilles Heel Collective that has produced *Achilles Heel* magazine since 1992, he has written regular articles on men and masculinity for the magazine.

Chapter One

Introduction

John Stoltenberg

I want to say a few words about why working with men for change is vitally important to us all. Although I have not spoken to each reader of this book, one by one, I suspect that many of us want the world to be completely different. We want the violence men do to stop.

I suspect that at some point in our lives it dawned on many of us – deeply, personally: men have got to stop raping. Men have got to stop beating up on women. Men have got to stop sexually harassing women on the street, in the workplace and in the academy. Men have got to stop sexually abusing children. Men have got to stop violating and degrading women in public and in private. This list goes on. Men have got to stop.

Because, for instance, if any woman is at risk of being physically or psychologically beaten by her husband, boyfriend, or lover, equality and love are impossible. And because, for instance, so long as in any society men can get away with rape, freedom is a joke.

At some point, for many of us, we realized that we want a world where violence is not sexy. We want a world where no one is put down so someone else can get off. We want a world where you do not have to have a certain skin colour or a certain genital in order to live your life in freedom, dignity and justice.

Some of us have that certain genital. And so as adults we are not, generally speaking, the sort of people who get raped. We are not the sort of people whose employment or academic prospects depend on whether we put out. We are not the sort of people whose most intimate partner beats us then demands sex with us or beats us then divorces us and takes away the children. We are not the sort of people who have to live every day trying to avoid being the target of some man's angry and aggressive sexual imagination. We are not that sort, those of us with that certain genital.

So we could sit back and relax. We could take it real easy. We could find other ways to spend our lives. But we noticed something. We noticed there's a war going on. This war is not one you'll see reported as such on television or in the daily newspaper. This is a war waged with hate and rage through sex. It's a war waged with power and control through force, laws and money. It's a war waged episodically with unimaginable malice through racial and sexual violence. It's that kind of a war.

And we – those of us with that certain genital – noticed something else. We noticed that we had been recruited and trained to be foot soldiers in that war. Looking back at how we were raised, and looking around us closely at the society we grew up in, we can see that none of us escaped some basic training for that war.

Each of us can recall, for instance, a time we bullied to avoid being bullied. A time we hurt someone just for the sport of it. A time we saw boys around us, their sexual feelings animated not by affection in equality but by animus in inequality – and we felt in ourselves something similar stirring. Many of us still have bruises and broken bones from that basic training. Some of us are still in a kind of shell shock from that basic training. In many individual ways, those of us with that certain genital – those of us raised to pass in the world as real men – carry with us the training we got to be foot soldiers in men's war of violence.

And we said no. Just simply: no. We each of us said no. First we said it quietly, to ourselves. We said, "I can't. I can't commit that violence. I cannot harbour that hate. No matter how sexually charged the violence or the hate – it is not me". And then we said, a little louder, "I refuse. I refuse to be such a foot soldier. I refuse to fight the war of men's violence. I refuse to fight that war".

Is that true for you as it is for me? If so, pronounce the words: "I refuse to fight that war". Just say to yourself quietly: "I refuse to fight that war".

An extraordinary thing happens whenever that odd individual voice says no inside us separately. We can begin to hear one another murmuring words of dissent. We can begin to hear one another saying no. Once we ourselves say no, we can witness other hearts and minds changing. We can feel other flesh and bone disarming. We can recognize the anguish in other consciences, crying out in desperation, wanting to stop, refusing to fight any longer to defend a world that keeps everybody else underneath, refusing to commit that violence, refusing to harbour that hate.

That's why many of us have committed ourselves to working with men for change. And I want us not to forget it. I want us not to forget who we became when we refused – when we individually and separately decided we could not serve in that war.

For women who are working with men for change, the reason may be different. You may have been in some foot soldier's war zone. You may have been the strategic target. In the war of violence done by men in order to feel like real men, you may have been the quarry, the prey. The butt of the jape. One of the necessary casualties, the body count. The enemy in some man's armed struggle to prove and defend his manhood.

Some of us who were raised to be foot soldiers also caught some of the flak – especially if because of our youth, small stature, stigmatized ethnicity or sexuality, or poverty we did not sufficiently qualify at some point for the infantry. We were put in our place. Or we simply caught friendly fire. Because that certain genital is not armour plate.

I could ask all of you who are the war wounded to describe your injuries. The pain you still remember. The bad thing done to you. The memory that still wakes you up nights. The attack you survived. The time you were pressured, bullied, forced, coerced, hurt; you were hurt, the war happened to you, the war of men's violence found you in its path, like a heat-seeking missile, and you were the warm body, and it got you, the war got to you, it did to you some distress, some humiliation, some pain, some damage. You survived. But you do not want that to happen to you ever again. And you do not want anything like that to happen to *anyone*.

At some point in your precious bodily lifetime, the war of men's violence happened to you. At some point in your life the war found you out. You were in the war zone and you got hit – however physically, emotionally, literally, metaphorically, you got hit.

Some of us – those of us with that certain genital – are working with men for change because we have refused to be foot soldiers in that war. And all of us who are the war wounded are working with men for change because we want the world to be completely different. We want the war of men's violence to end. We want to stop the violence men do in order to experience themselves as real men. We made up our mind. The war machine must be dismantled.

This is an enormous task. And I want to pose a challenge about how, in working with men for change, we select our priority outcome. Because if we want the violence to end but we want there to still be "real men", we may not have selected a priority outcome that is doable. We may not be able to end men's violence and simultaneously maintain a category called "real men" for people with that certain genital to belong to. We may not be able to succeed in working with men for change if the category "real men" remains the boundary beyond which we dare not go.

I want to encourage us to stand outside gender categories. I want to encourage us to see the ways folks raised to be a man are trying to jump through hoops in order to grow up and pass as real men. I want to encourage us to see that the very hoops we keep children with a certain genital jumping through are part of the problem. To end the violence, we may have to get rid of those hoops.

Never forget the reason we are working with men for change. Whether you are a conscientious objector or whether you are among the war wounded or whether you are both – we want, we need, the war to end.

This war is waged to defend the identity of men over and against women, but ending the war does not require us to wear our gender identity like a dog tag around our neck. In fact, I submit, it helps to stay centred, instead, in our moral identity.

This is the choice some of us made when we said no, when we became war resisters. Our moral identity is expressed and made manifest in the choice we all made to keep the war from happening anymore, from hurting anymore.

When we stand outside gender categories, and when we inhabit instead our moral identity, we see the war in a crucially new way. We see the war – being waged to keep men feeling like real men, over and against the bodies of others – and we see it from the standpoint of our human and humane conscience, not our genitalia.

We are working with men for change because of a choice we each made – a choice to stop men's war of violence. Each one comes to that decision from particular circumstances. Each one who makes that choice makes it from a particular life, from a biography of being raised to be a woman or a man, in specific economic circumstances, with a particular family of both blood relations and culture. But we must none of us lose sight of who we became in that moment when we said no to men's war of violence against women and children and other men – no not this time, no not ever.

If we lose sight of who we became in that instant, and who we become each instant we say to that war, "no, never again", we lose sight of who we are most fundamentally. It is our moral selfhood out of which, and only out of which, the possibility for a different world is born.

If we lose sight of who we each become in that moment, if we forget, we lose our chance to solve the problem, we lose our best chance to speak meaningfully to foot soldiers still loyal to the war.

So when we talk to one another in our work with men for change, when we listen to one another full of hope and expectation, let us not forget who we are. Let us not forget why we are doing this work. Let us not forget who we be. And let us help one another to become.

(© John Stoltenberg, 1999)

Chapter Two

It's time for men to change

Jeff Hearn

Introduction

This chapter is about the possibilities and prospects for changing men. First, I look at why we are discussing this question in the first place, and trace the main influences that have brought about this concern. Then I outline what the problem is and some of the major arenas in which men need to change. These include: the family and the care of other people; sexuality; violence and non-violence; and work, organizations and management. Men are likely to face dilemmas, contradictions and ambivalences in facing this challenge, and it is important to acknowledge rather than obscure these. Finally, I relate these issues to men in and around social care, social work and probation – as managers, workers and service users. In each case, there are both general, personal and political principles to be identified in moving men away from power, and local agendas and priorities to be established within particular agency and policy contexts.

Why now?

So what are the possibilities and prospects for changing men? Why are we addressing this question now? First and foremost is the impact of feminism. This has not only problematized what a woman is, but also, sometimes indirectly, has problematized what a man is. This has involved both naming men's general social power, and recognizing differences among men. Indeed just as there are many different accounts of women, so there are of men and what men are.

In addition, there has been the impact of other gender and sexual movements and politics, most obviously the gay political movements. These too have problematized men, especially in terms of heterosexuality not necessarily being the norm. Men become problematized through being recognized as desirable or potentially desirable to each other.

Third, there have developed a rather uneven series of responses by men to feminism, and feminist theory and practice. These have ranged from the anti-feminist to the ambiguous to the pro-feminist. A particularly important development in the last ten years or so has been the increasing professionalization of some of these responses and the debates around them in and around social welfare, state and para-state organizations.

Further political critiques of men have developed from other directions, most obviously around race, ethnicity, racism and anti-racism. These have shown that there is not just one way of being a man, and indeed not just one way of being dominant, even when racism is being experienced by men. For example, some black men, especially black Asian men, have a different attitude to some white men to physical contact with other men. Black Asian Moslem men are likely to have a different relation to physical contact with each other, to the use of alcohol, and the creation of men's spaces to that of many white non-Moslem men. Also, being a black man may suggest a different prioritization of gender to being a black woman.

Then there are the effects of changing patterns of work, employment and unemployment for both women and men. This primarily concerns the decline of "traditional" working-class employment in agriculture, fishing, mining and manufacturing industry. At the same time, many middle-class men have experienced job insecurity and perhaps redundancy. There have been increases in the number of women who are in employment, particularly part-time employment. These trends taken together mean that there are more families and households where women are earning as much as, or more than, men. About 20% of men have women partners who are the main breadwinner – a three-fold increase since the early 1980s. These patterns of work clearly vary greatly by locality, class, age and ethnicity.

Paralleling these public domain changes are equally dramatic changes in the private domains – in the increased rates of separation, divorce and, indeed, recoupling and remarriage; greater mobility and dispersal in family structures; and a greater awareness of children's and young people's rights (e.g. regarding paternal authority and violence).

Meanwhile, global changes are taking place in the relationship of the world powers – in the international economy, in new nationalisms, new technologies, and so on – that are both largely controlled by men and, in turn, construct and reconstruct men.

Interestingly, these changes are often contradictory in their effects on men – both increasing the power and potential power of (some) men, and decreasing and challenging the power of (some) men. Furthermore, these problematizations of men are themselves attracting increasing interest from the press and other media. What all of this produces is an intense set of connections between social changes in everyday life, political movements and media representations, as well as academic commentaries and governmental policies.

The problem of men

So what is the problem of men? The problem is both very simple and rather complex. The main problem is that men and masculinities continue to be associated with power and control. Yet saying that is not to suggest that men are naturally or essentially any one thing. Men and masculinities are just as variable as women are. Another aspect of the problem of men is that, while there are clearly all manner of changes in process, there is also a profound state of no change, in the sense that the many arenas of power remain persistently in the control of men. All this association of men and masculinities with power creates specific problems in the form of pain, damage and distress for women and children. For example, 90–99 per cent of child sexual abuse is by men. Men's association with power also creates problems for men themselves. This perhaps partly helps explain men's life expectancy of six years less than women's. Men who are themselves in social, medical or psychological difficulty may live that experience through a relation, or attempted relation, with power. Indeed the very power and control of both some men and men generally creates problems for other men, for each other (Hearn 1987). These combinations of pain, damage and distress to others, and power and difficulty for men themselves, constitute many of the problems dealt with by social care, social work and probation. Moreover, the agencies that house social care, social work and probation services have their own parallel problems within them. Before looking at these and other implications for social care, social work and probation, it may be useful to spell out the arenas in which men need to change.

Arenas of change

The problem of men takes different forms in different arenas of society. Accordingly, there are different possibilities for changing men, for men to change, within these different arenas (Hearn 1996b). First, there is the arena of the family. One of the main challenges for men here is how to develop appropriate personal relations in families – that is, how to relate to children, women and other men in ways that do not draw on the traditional power of fathers and husbands. These questions are severely complicated with the increasing number of reconstituted families, with all kinds of complex arrangements around childcare and the use of time. There is a particular need for a post-marriage ethics for men, that challenges men's control of women through children after the end of marriage.

A second and related arena is the care of others. Care has been defined as an activity for girls and women, and not for men and boys. Indeed, boys and men learn not to care for others. Changing this is an urgent task. A special challenge is how to encourage boys and young men to become more at ease with the bodily care of others in a way that does not lead to further dominance. This has to be done with great care and caution, perhaps initially through other encouragement of care in their own families, the teaching of safety and first aid, and the care of pets and animals, and then moving on to the care of babies, children, older people and people with disabilities. In so doing, nurture can be redefined as normal for boys and men.

Third, there is the arena of sexuality. For many men there is still a profound interconnection between sexuality and sexism. Men may see sexuality as a given, even as uncontrollable; sex may be reduced to intercourse, ejaculation, orgasm. Anti-gay attitudes may persist, just as do glorifications of sexual violence. Sexuality politics may themselves be diverging – becoming both more reactionary and more progressive. There is a major need to strengthen sex education for boys and young men so that pro-women and gay-affirmative approaches to sexuality are known, understood and appreciated. As men, we need to acknowledge our sexuality without being oppressively sexual or sexually oppressive; we need to move towards non-oppressive, non-violent sexualitities.

Violence, men's violence, is the next arena, and this is itself interconnected with the previous arena of sexuality. There is a need to rename various activities of men as violence; men remain the specialists in the doing of violence. This need for renaming applies especially with regard to crime. About 84 per cent of all recorded crime is by men; about 97 per cent of those in prison are men; a quarter of all men are convicted of an offence by the age of 25; and two-thirds of all male offenders are under 30 (Cordery & Whitehead 1992). Violence takes very many forms – to women, children, each other, ourselves. It also does not bring happiness. There is a need for a national commitment against violence. As the Gulbenkian Foundation Commission report (1995), *Children and violence*, stressed as its first priority recommendation:

> Individuals, communities and government at all levels should adopt a "Commitment to non-violence", of similar standing to existing commitments to "equal opportunities".

The Report continued:

> The aims of the commitment are to work towards a society in which individuals, communities and government share non-violent values and resolve conflict by non-violent means. Building such a society involves, in particular, reducing and preventing violence involving children, by developing:
> – understanding of the factors which interact to increase the potential for violence involving children, and those which prevent children from becoming violent
> – action to prevent violence involving children in all services and work with families and children
> – consistent disavowal of all forms of inter-personal violence – in particular by opinion-leaders.

Governmental and other policies and strategies should tell boys and men not to be violent, should advocate policies that encourage men to behave in ways that facilitate women's equality, and make it clear that the realization of such changes depends partly on men in politics and policy-making, and their own understanding of their gendered actions.

A final arena I want to say something about is that of paid work, organizations and management. This is a key arena for changing men in terms of the structuring of work and organizations, both vertically and horizontally (Collinson & Hearn 1994, 1996). Most obviously men continue to dominate the highest levels of organizations and management. One particularly worrying scenario suggested by the current structuring of work is the increasing separation between those in employment working longer hours and those not in employment staying longer out of work. Work is not just the direct organization of labour, it is also the less direct organization of time. And this brings us back full circle to the family, the domestic, the "private", and the growing concern with how to combine family and work, for both men and women (New Ways to Work 1995).

Changing men: politics, dilemmas, ambivalences and contradictions

Changing men, changing ourselves, necessitates a focus on our politics and practice. It involves clarifying our relationship to feminism, anti-sexism, each other, gay men, children; it involves taking these relations seriously, although not necessarily with seriousness. One early attempt to provide such a statement was produced in about 1980 in the form of "Anti-sexist men's commitments" (Box 2.1). However, such "commitments" can fail to engage with the reality of men's situation.

For men to change may involve facing dilemmas, ambivalences and contradictions. This applies both to men within agencies and men in contact or potential contact with agencies as customers, clients or users. Some of the most significant dilemmas, ambivalences and contradictions are set out in Box 2.2.

Box 2.1 Anti-sexist men's commitments (Commitments Collective 1980)

- Commitment to the (anti-sexist men's) group
- Consciousness-raising done rigorously
- Support for the women's liberation movement
- Support for gay liberation
- Sharing child care
- Learning from gay and feminist culture
- Action on our own behalf
- Propaganda and outreach programmes (linked to action)
- Link-ups with other men against sexism groups
- Renunciation of violence (physical, emotional and verbal)

Box 2.2

Dilemmas and ambivalences
- How important to me is changing myself and other men?
- How much effort should I put into this?
- Do I want this to be a fundamental part of my life?
- In what ways do I like being a man and in what ways do I not like being a man?
- In what ways do I feel ambivalent about change?

Contradictions
- How do I learn from feminism? Which feminism?
- How do I learn from feminism without taking over women's space?
- Do I need to depend more on men, depend more on women, or depend more on both?
- How do I recognize "being a man" without overemphasizing that status?
- How do I recognize "being a man" while stopping being a man?

Changing men in social welfare

All the issues raised so far, are important for changing men in and around social care, social work, probation and social welfare more generally. For example, the long-standing debate on "care and control" can be redrawn in terms of different forms of masculinities. In thinking how to change men in social welfare, there is clearly a need for a general understanding of the position of men in society, in terms of both men's collective power, and the differences between different groups of men and different individual men (Hearn 1998b). There is also a need for a general politics for men that is pro-feminist, gay-affirmative and anti-sexist (see Box 2.1). In addition, each field (social care, social work and probation) has its own particular characteristics and local challenges, in terms of men in agencies and men in contact or potentially in contact. In recent years, social work has become increasingly focused around child protection. This raises the question of whether this is a model that should be extended to other spheres, such as men's violences and abuse to women. Probation has traditionally been a larger employer of men than the social services. It also operates within the context of the criminal justice sector, with its male-dominated culture, and the associated law and order debate. While the probation service may have had more autonomy than social services, it has in recent years been subject to much closer control, with less discretion for individual officers. On the other hand, there are signs of increasing interest in focused work on men, who have been violent to known women in the form of men's programmes.

Box 2.3   Men as workers and practitioners

- Recognizing involvement as men rather than just as "workers" or "professionals"
- Being clear on the work process between men or between men and women
- Recognizing the need to change men and masculinity in general
- Explicitly working on sexism with men who are in favour of sexism
- Working with sympathetic colleagues, managers and other workers and professionals, such as teachers and youth workers, who are against sexism
- Working on the relationship of sexism and other oppressions, such as ageism, classism, disablism and racism
- Raising the priority given to day-care and other social care and social services provisions that may enhance women's opportunities
- Working on their *own* sexism, including their practice outside work
- Joining or starting a men's anti-sexist group or similar initiative, either within or outside the agency

---

In order to change men in social welfare, it is necessary to look carefully at the particular situation within different agencies. It involves working from the existing gender structure of agencies, and developing an analysis of that structure. Different possibilities for changing men exist where, for example, men are in a majority, a minority, or are evenly represented with women. Such basic gender structures affect the possible strategies for changing men. At its simplest, the allocation of work to men is affected very largely by the proportion of men available in a given agency. Similarly, the gender structure of agencies is also a major determinant of relations between women and men there. Men in welfare agencies who are concerned to change need to examine the particular structures, tasks and culture of those agencies, and work with women on a collaborative process of change. Within different agencies, there are many ways for men to change – as workers and practitioners, managers and users. Some of these are summarized in Box 2.3 and 2.4 (Hearn 1990, 1993, 1994).

Men may relate as users (or potential users) to social care, social work and probation agencies in three main ways: as those experiencing problems (needing care), as those creating problems (needing control), or as those avoiding the agency (avoiding care and/or control). Men may experience problems through addiction, ill-health, depression, disability, and so on. These problems may or may not be "caused" by being men, but the experiences of them is likely to be mediated by gender, by being men (Gershick & Miller 1995). Men may cause problems for both others and, in time, themselves by virtue of their power and control, even when they are themselves relatively powerless within the context of societal power. Men may also avoid agency services. They may be reluctant to use services that provide assistance around health, emotional crises and mental well-being. They may be absent from receiving care; they may be absent from agency contact when they directly or indirectly cause problems for others (e.g. child care and child protection).

Box 2.4   Men as managers

- Have less men in management
- Put this change on the agenda for discussion
- Assist the creation of a minimum mass of women in management
- Transform organizations and management
- See changes in organizations as opportunities for challenging men and men managements
- Change dominant models of management and masculinity
- Give greater priority to domestic, "private" and caring responsibilities
- Structure training budgets for men and management in inverse proportion to the number of women/men in management
- Asking how men can assist, not block, equal opportunities policies
- Consider "temporary" solutions to intractable problems
- Attend to the issues of sexuality, sexual harassment and violence through changing policies and practices
- Asking men managers where they stand

Men's involvement with welfare agencies or the creators of problems is most obvious with regard to the question of men's violence and abuse. Men's use of violence and abuse in such ways have often been ignored or even implicitly condoned. This is especially so with regard to men's violence to known women. While Social Services departments have a statutory duty in relation to children in danger of violence, abuse and neglect, this does not apply to women who are in similar danger from men. Men's violence and abuse clearly causes pain, damage and distress to those receiving the violence and abuse. It may also lead to, or be associated with, damage to the man himself, in the form of depression, use of drink or drugs and, occasionally, institutionalization. There has been a considerable debate over the most appropriate stance to be developed in relation to men who are violent and abusive to women (Adams 1988; Caesar & Hamberger 1989; Edleson & Tolman 1992; Dankwort 1992–93). In recent years, there has been a recognition of the importance of both cognitive–behavioural and feminist/pro-feminist approaches that focus on power and control (Pence & Paymar 1986). Intervention is not only about stopping physical violence, as if that is some separate activity, it is about moving away from power and control in all aspects of the man's relations with women. To do that means presenting positive ways of living that do not reinforce power and control. Such programmes can be a significant and effective initiative, especially when linked to wider educational and political change (Dobash et al. 1996). A crucial issue is the placing of such programmes on a formal Court-mandated basis rather than leaving them to voluntary access. Any such development needs to carefully screen out men who have no interest whatsoever in change, and who may even use the programme to learn new forms of violence and control.

Box 2.5 The development of agency policy and practice on men's violence to women

- Educating men on what violence is
- Dealing with the problem as the responsibility of the statutory sector
- Producing clear, general policy statements
- Developing public campaigns
- Changing the conditions that produce and sustain men's violence
- Addressing other oppressions
- Developing appropriate and detailed policy and practice
- Monitoring, maintaining and improving policy and practice
- Working against violence with men in contact in a focused way
- Placing issues of power, control and responsibility as central in focused work with men
- Developing interagency work with men
- Making men, men's power and men's violence explicit in agency and interagency work
- Addressing the need to change men in agencies
- Dealing with the ambiguous issue of men's support for men
- Reaching out to men not in contact with agencies

Most importantly, any innovations for men of this kind have to supplement broader public policy, including: consistent police and prosecution policy and practice; interagency work with women experiencing violence; improved housing provision for women; and state support for women's aid and other projects for women. Men's violence to women represents a clear challenge to the development of agency policy and practice by men and in relation to men (Box 2.5) (Hearn 1996a, 1998a).

Conclusion

In summary, men's relationship with social care, social work and probation is only understandable in the context of men's broader position in society. Similarly, changing men in social welfare hinges on similar principles and politics to changing men more generally throughout society. This has been the focus of some men's, particularly pro-feminist men's, concerns since second-wave feminism. This is not a new question. Changing men does not just involve the simple adoption of principles by men, but also recognizing ambivalences, dilemmas and contradictions and working from that position of reality.

Social care, social work and probation are concerned with the problem of men – as the creators of problems, the sufferers of problems, the avoiders of agency contact. In some cases these three aspects are intimately related to each other.

Men's power, men's oppression of others, men's experiences of their own personal problems, and the avoidance of agency contact (whether from the care of agencies or the control of agencies) can all be connected to each other. Men who are users or potential users of such (social welfare agencies can both maintain) patriarchal power and be the dispensable casualties of patriarchy. Men can need both care and control, and also spend much of their time avoiding both.

Furthermore, parallel issues around the problem of men persist *within* welfare agencies that deal with men. To address these necessitates focused attention by men, the development of an understanding and an analysis of men in the agency, and the formulation of new policies and practices. It's time for men to change.

References

ADAMS, D. (1988) Treatment models of men who batter: a profeminist analysis. In *Feminist perspectives on wife abuse*, K. YLLO & M. BOGRAD (eds). Newbury Park, CA: Sage.

CAESAR, P. L. & L. K. HAMBERGER (eds) (1989) *Treating men who batter.* New York: Springer.

COLLINSON, D. L. & J. HEARN (1994) Naming men as men: implications for work, organisation and management. *Gender, Work and Organization* 1(1), 2–22.

COLLINSON, D. L. & J. HEARN (eds) (1996) *Men as managers, managers as men,* London: Sage.

COMMITMENTS COLLECTIVE (1980) Anti-sexist commitments for men – draught [*sic*] 3. *Anti-Sexist Men's Newsletter* 9, 17. Reprinted in ROWAN, J. (1987) *The homed god.* London: Routledge & Kegan Paul.

CORDERY, J. & A. WHITEHEAD (1992) Boys don't cry. In *Gender, crime and probation practice*, P. SENIOR & D. WOODHILL (eds). Sheffield: Sheffield City Polytechnic PAVIC Publication.

DANKWORT, J. (1992–93) Violence against women: varying perceptions and intervention practices with women abusers. *Intervention* (Canada) 92, 34–48.

DOBASH, R., R. E. DOBASH, K. CAVANAGH & R. LEWIS (1996) *Research evaluation of programmes for violent men.* Edinburgh: Scottish Office.

EDLESON, J. L. & R. M. TOLMAN (1992) *Intervention for men who batter.* Newbury Park, CA: Sage.

GERSHICK, T. J. & A. S. MILLER (1995) Coming to terms. Masculinity and physical disability. In *Men's health and illness*, D. SABO & D. F. GORDON (eds). Thousand Oaks, CA: Sage.

GULBENKIAN FOUNDATION COMMISSION (1995) *Children and violence.* London: Calouste Gulbenkian Foundation.

HEARN, J. (1987) *The gender of oppression: Men, masculinity and the critique of marxism.* Brighton: Wheatsheaf.

HEARN, J. (1990) Child abuse and men's violence. In *Taking child abuse seriously*, Violence Against Children Study Group (ed.). London: Unwin Hyman.

HEARN, J. (1993) Changing men and changing managements: a review of issues and actions. *Women in Management Review* 7(1), 3–8.

HEARN, J. (1994) Changing men, changing managements: social change, social research and social action. In *Women in management – current research issues*, M. J. DAVIDSON & R. BURKE (eds). London: Paul Chapman.

HEARN, J. (1996a) Men's violence to known women: men's accounts and men's policy developments. In *Violence and gender relations: Theories and interventions*, B. FAWCETT, B. FEATHERSTONE, J. HEARN & C. TOFT (eds). London: Sage.

HEARN, J. (1996b) Moving away from power: family, care, sexuality, violence and organisations. In *What next for men?* T. LLOYD & T. WOOD (eds). London: Working with Men.

HEARN, J. (1998a) *The violences of men*. London: Sage.

HEARN, J. (1998b) The welfare of men? In *Men, gender divisions and welfare*, J. POPAY, J. HEARN and J. EDWARDS (eds). London: Routledge.

NEW WAYS TO WORK (1995) *Balanced lives. Changing work patterns for men*. London: New Ways to Work.

PENCE, E. & M. PAYMAR (1986) *Power and control: Tactics of men who batter. An educational curriculum*. Duluth, MN: Minnesota Program Development.

Chapter Three

Working with men from a feminist perspective

Lena Dominelli

Introduction

The question of whether or not to work with men for the purposes of furthering egalitarian relations between men and women has exercised my skills since the early 1970s when I hesitantly sought to introduce feminist insights into work I was doing with a small group of men who wished to stop beating their partners (Dominelli 1981). Although I was keen to have a successful group, the effort did not live up to my expectations. Part of the problem was that I had failed to appreciate the significance of men's socialization processes in their interaction with other men, the psychological significance of their relationships with women and children, and the impact of the broader social culture on men's behaviour and willingness, or even ability, to change it. Lacking such knowledge, I focused instead on feminist methods and feminism's commitment to egalitarian relations to guide my wanderings through what was unknown territory. As I charted my way around the many obstacles I encountered, my feminist friends scrutinized my efforts and constantly asked me to justify using my talents, time and energy in what they saw as an unworthy pursuit, which detracted resources and, most crucially, me from the pressing task of improving women's lot.

My intellect agreed with them. If I spent my time working with men, this could not be used to work with women. And I felt guilty. At the same time, I was not prepared to pack in my activities. My heart said that the work was important and needed to be done. It was not completely irrelevant to women's welfare, for if these men could learn to relate to women in non-violent ways, women would benefit. This feeling has been vindicated in subsequent writings (Stoltenberg 1990) and by recent research which indicates that, even in cases where a particular woman leaves a violent man, if no attempt is made to change the man's behaviour he goes on to form a relationship with another woman and, before long, his violence surfaces there too (Gondolf 1987). Moreover, I knew from my work that imprisonment, a response often advocated by my critics, was no solution. Relations between men in prison are usually abusive. These confirm men's aggression and encourage the use of violence in resolving disputes (Marcus 1971; Priestley 1980). It also provides the locale where those with limited experience in violent techniques gain knowledge and skills from those who are better practised at it than they.

In the intervening two decades, I have become more convinced about the appropriateness of men and women using feminist methods and insights in seeking to change men's behaviour towards others. Yet, the tensions which were present in the beginning remain, except that there is now evidence to show that both positions (for and against women working with men) have their merits. Working with men from a feminist perspective, as we shall see later in this chapter, is intellectually demanding and emotionally difficult. On a more practical level, one of the fears articulated by those who reject women's involvement in such work – that men and women will compete for the same resources with men securing a disproportionate share of them – appears to be holding (Lees & Lloyd 1994; Perrott 1994; Pringle 1994). For example, state funding for men's groups that work with physically violent men has increased, while that going towards women's refuges has declined to the extent that many fear for their survival (Cavanagh & Cree 1995).

The pitting of men's and women's needs for financial resources against each other in this way is deplorable. To begin with, there are few resources for adult women survivors of men's violence (Gray et al. 1995). The state has only ever been a reluctant and miserly funder of feminist initiatives for women. Thus, it does not follow that if the money hadn't gone into men's groups it would have been channelled women's way. Furthermore, women's welfare is also undermined if men don't get the resources they need to change. Recent evidence suggests that women's contributions to work undertaken with violent men have been invaluable (Cavanagh & Cree 1995). Many instances of provisions addressing men's violent behaviour that now exist would not have got underway had it not been for feminists' challenge to men to get their act together (Seidler 1992). Finally, resourcing the needs of both men and women does not *have* to be antagonistic. For example, EMERGE, a men's collective in the USA, deliberately decided early on in its formation not to apply to sources that would fund women's activities, in order to avoid invidious competition between them (Adams 1988). However, refusing such assistance in our current gendered and cash-strapped society is rare, for it has to be endorsed by an explicit political decision supporting such an approach.

Moreover, the controversy around women's involvement remains. A number of feminists continue to be skeptical about the value of either men or women attempting to wean men away from generalized aggression in their relationships with others and change their behaviour in ways that respect women, children and other men who are less powerful than they (Perrott 1994). Hence, despite its excellent analyses of men's aggressive behaviour, much feminist literature has yet to address the question of what to do with the perpetrators of violence against women and children (e.g. Newburn & Stanko, 1994). An exception to this trend is Cree & Cavanagh's (1995) *Working with men from a feminist perspective*. Earlier, Dominelli

& McLeod's (1989) *Feminist social work* argued that feminist principles and methods were relevant to men as well as women.

As a result of this legacy, I have reached the conclusion that, in the short-term, we will have to live with the contradictions and ambiguities inherent in this situation, while simultaneously working to overcome them. In the longer term, let us hope that egalitarian relations will prevail across the gender divide. Meanwhile, for the lives of children, women and men to be enriched, it is important that work which takes on board feminist insights is undertaken with men. However, individual women's wishes about whether or not they personally work with men must be respected, without their being penalized in their career development and prospects. To do otherwise is to abuse women through the exercise of gendered and institutionalized managerialist power (Dominelli 1991).

In this chapter I consider some of the issues that need to be considered when working with men from a feminist perspective. Central to this is the problematic nature of masculinity and the importance of redefining it in more nurturing directions. In addition, I argue that working with men in accordance with feminist principles has an important contribution to make in enhancing the well-being of men, women and children.

Feminism's relevance to men

Feminism's relationship to men has been an ambivalent one in many respects. This is because there is no single definition accepted by all feminists of what this relationship consists of. Moreover, engaging men in a discussion of the relevance of feminist principles and methodologies to them is problematic. Despite the existence of men who are supportive of feminist initiatives and seek to learn from its theory and practice (Snodgrass 1977; Bowl 1985; Hearn 1987; Stoltenberg 1990), many men fear feminism as a political ideology and are anxious about its implementation in everyday life practices (Gairdner 1992; Lyndon 1992; Farrell 1993). These men exaggerate the current impact of feminism, and erroneously emphasize its uniformity. They miss the significance of its diversity in the politics of men and women's interaction with each other. This diversity extends over a range of political positions, and encompasses liberal feminists who argue for changes within the status quo, to radical feminists who seek wide-scale revolutionary changes and the transformation of the current social order (Tong 1989). Thus, feminism offers a variety of answers to the question of how social relations between the genders should be conducted.

However, despite feminism's pluralism, feminists share a common aim of ensuring that men do not have an unfair share of social resources, victimize women or curtail women's access to the public sphere (Phillips 1993). Feminists' starting point, first and foremost, is the realities of women's lives as they experience them. Feminism's determination to improve the quality of life for women has an uncomfortable message for men who desire to hang on to gender-based privileges: men who benefit from these will have to give them up. For, without their doing so, gender equality cannot be achieved. The one option feminism does not leave men is that of "no change". Moreover, many feminists have placed the onus of securing changes in men's behaviour on men themselves (Dworkin 1981; MacKinnon 1987). Thus, feminism encourages both men and women to play their respective parts in establishing a new world order based on egalitarian principles.

Diversity remains a key feature of modern feminism. White middle class feminists in the West began their praxis by arguing the importance of feminism in securing the liberation of women (Firestone 1971; Millet 1972). Men, as oppressors, were either left on the sidelines while women delved into their innermost creativity to develop a range of facilities of use to them, or struggled against as the sources of women's misery by having the finger pointed at them (Solanas 1971). Why then were the antagonistic stances advocated primarily by white radical feminists challenged by feminists themselves, particularly white socialist feminists (Adamson et al. 1976) and black feminists (Davis 1981; Hooks 1984; Bryan et al. 1985; Collins 1990) as well as groups of men who went on to form anti-sexist men's groups which drew on feminist messages and methods to examine the quality of their own lives in capitalist society (Achilles Heel Collective 1983; Metcalf & Humpheries 1985; Seidler 1992)?

Black feminists (Davis 1981) and white socialist feminists (Dominelli 1986b) have argued that capitalism oppresses men through their waged work as well as women. Moreover, since capitalism draws a sharp distinction between private life and the public sphere, it stunts men's growth, particularly their emotional development, short-changes them in their intimate relationships with women, and prevents them from forming affective relationships with their children (Zaretsky 1975). Men also became aware of and began to speak about their "empty" inner core (Rutherford 1992), focusing on the limits of traditional hegemonic masculinity (Festau 1975; Tolson 1977) and its failure to identify the absence of relational bonds between father and son (Rutherford 1992) as well as women (Achilles Heel Collective 1983). For these men, feminism provided tools of analysis and insights that men could use, not only to support women seeking to free themselves from patriarchal domination, but also to challenge men's relationships with other men and develop these on a richer footing. However, men's position *vis-à-vis* feminism has been contradictory. While drawing some optimism and comfort from their deeper understanding of their emotional being, men found women's demands that they give up their privileged status and assume their share of the drudgery of housework and other menial tasks disconcerting (Festau 1975; Snodgrass 1977). Moreover, men's failure to respond to women's agenda in terms that were considered appropriate by feminists left them feeling alienated from women and disheartened about even the possibility of mutually beneficial change (Lyndon 1992; Farrell 1993).

Men felt uneasy about their relationships with women, particularly on the intimate emotional levels (Rutherford 1992). And, they could not easily find ways of avoiding the sexualizing of both their relationships with and feelings about women (Achilles Heel Collective 1983). Moreover, their homophobic beliefs stood in the way of their developing intimacy with their male peers (Snodgrass 1977). These barriers persist despite men's attempts to deal with them in their anti-sexist work (Rutherford 1992). In addition, men have been frightened that they cannot meet the new demands for equality that women have placed upon them at the individual level. And their own socialization processes have prevented them from exposing their own emotional vulnerabilities and psychological need for assurance in the public arena (Snodgrass 1977). Men could also not quite trust themselves to be non-oppressive in situations that placed them on the defensive for the historic privileges which they had enjoyed over women (Rutherford 1992). Feminists were also wary of their relationships with men and sought not to be oppressed in their pursuit of freedom by those who enjoyed structurally endorsed power over them. So, while women grappled with their mistrust, men struggled with their guilt, providing a tension between the sexes/genders that remains to the present day.

Going back to the past was not an option open to women. For some women, the solution to this contradictory situation was to establish separate provisions for women and engage in women-centred and lesbian relationships (Tong 1989). White socialist feminists and black feminists have persisted with their demands for men to become more involved in domestic life and participate in childbirth, child-rearing, elder-care, and other day-to-day domestic chores (Tong 1989). This involvement became increasingly important as women became more active in the waged labour market (Walby 1990). Yet, while many men responded to this call by becoming involved in cooking, minding children in crèches, and other similar activities, women continued to carry a disproportionate share of domestic work, whether or not they also worked for a wage (Walby 1990).

The profound changes brought about by the greater penetration of women in the labour market and the globalization of the economy, with the associated decline in highly paid full-time work for men in the manufacturing trades and the increase in part-time jobs for women in the low-paid public sector (Walby 1990), have proceeded alongside the feminist movement. These changes have heightened men's sense of loss in a known and established role – the Victorian *pater familias*, or head of the family unit. The white middle-class feminist critique of traditional family life and women's willingness to assert their independence in looking after themselves and their children by heading single-parent families and seeking divorce in ever greater numbers have exacerbated men's fears about their insecure position in modern society.

In this complex situation, men have both supported and avoided feminists' calls for new egalitarian relations between men and women. Facing such a fundamental and persistent challenge, men have responded differently to this ambiguity. Some, including Metcalf & Humpheries (1985) and Rutherford (1992), have struggled to create less oppressive ways of behaving as men. They have done this by problematizing masculinity and seeking to deconstruct it so that the new alternatives to the prevailing dominant forms of masculinity could be unleashed. Others, such as Bly (1992), Lyndon (1992) and Farrell (1993), have sought comfort and security in the traditions of their fathers, thereby contributing to the revival of men's mythical pasts and privileged positions.

Feminists' problematizing of masculinity, especially as expressed through men's indifference to domestic work, lack of involvement in child-rearing and the use of violence and aggression to control others, became an important catalyst in getting men to examine themselves. Moreover, given the importance of the three areas noted above on the quality of everyday life, it is not surprising that feminists have devoted considerable energy to studying men's roles in childcare, elder-care, housework and male violence as crucial areas in mapping the context within which relations between men and women occur. These topics have also provided key issues through which women have sought to change men's behaviour and move it in more egalitarian directions.

At the same time, these activities have increased the tensions between men and women. For women have sought to get men to take responsibility for their own behaviour and develop their own initiatives on these fronts. In short, women have refused to be satisfied with men's verbal assurances of doing better. They have demanded that men take *action* that promotes more egalitarian relations between the genders and a greater diversity of lifestyles.

Problematizing masculinity

Men's fears of being unable to meet women's expectations have increased men's feelings of emotional insecurity (Rutherford 1992). Addressing these fears is critical in enabling men to take note of feminist insights in transcending the limitations of traditional masculinity. Feminist perceptions into their emotional life and feminist methodologies are valuable aids that men can draw upon to assist them in this task and the process that advancing it entails (Bowl 1985). Men's self-help groups such as the Achilles Heel Collective and the Working with Men Collective pay testimony to this fact.

As a major subject in feminist theorizing, men's violence and action on how to end it (Brownmiller 1975; Dobash & Dobash 1979; Dworkin 1981; Stanko 1990) has been a hotly contested area. This is so because violence and aggression are central facets of masculine identity (Festau 1975), and feminist struggles around it strike at the heart of men's insecurities. Although women can be violent (a subject that merits study in its own right), men are the main perpetrators of both physical (Dobash & Dobash 1979, 1992) and sexual violence (Finkelhor 1984) against women and children. Violent crimes against the person have been rising inexorably over the years (Lupton and Gillespie 1994), so finding ways of reducing its occurrence will improve the life circumstances of women and children.

Reversing this state of affairs necessitates interventions that change men's behaviour towards others, educate men in non-violent ways of resolving interpersonal conflict, challenge societal norms celebrating masculine violence and aggression, and redefine masculinity in more nurturing directions. Furthermore, the victim–survivors of such violence need adequately funded facilities to get over the trauma they have experienced and learn the skills necessary for resuming control over their lives. Building on the few resources that currently seek to do this work is an urgent matter for the state to pursue. Men, as the key power-holders within the governmental decision-making machinery, can take a lead in releasing the funding for such services. Caring professionals, including social workers and probation officers, have a vital role to play in facilitating this objective and keeping the issue alive in the public arena.

Sadly, it is not only feminists who have exhibited a disinterest in the question of how practitioners can best work to change the behaviour of aggressive men, whether they are situated in a community or custodial setting. Politicians have tended to ignore this matter, as have mainstream academics and practitioners in welfare settings. Even recent key texts for social workers and probation officers (e.g. Raynor et al. 1994; Smith 1995) have neglected this subject. Thus, working with men from a pro-feminist perspective, whether or not they have been convicted of violent offenses, remains a generally neglected area.

Social services departments and other organizations employing social workers rarely respond to the needs of either women who have been physically assaulted or the men who have committed such atrocities. Rather, their organizational structures, legal responsibilities and strategies for practice focus largely on the impact of "domestic violence" on children (Gray et al. 1995). Consequently, the hard-pressed voluntary sector and private agencies have been making most of the running in improving service provision in this area. This means that facilities for both victim–survivors and perpetrators of domestic violence are in short supply, regardless of gender. Similar problems exist in relation to sexual abuse, although social workers may focus on enabling the non-abusing parent (usually the mother) to support abused children and work in conjunction with the police to determine whether or not sufficient evidence can be gathered to press charges in a court of law. But, even here, their concerns do not stretch to doing work with the offender after conviction or even prior to this during an investigation in cases where such action might be deemed appropriate. Even probation officers, who have the opportunity to cover such work once a man has been sentenced, find few facilities devoted directly to interventions on this front.

Feminist and pro-feminist authors have identified the importance of addressing the issue of masculinity when working with men (Bowl 1985; Hudson 1988; Dominelli 1981, 1991, 1992; Pringle 1992; Newburn & Stanko 1994). In some feminist analyses, men's abuse of power is deemed to lie at the heart of their exploitative relations with women and children (Rush 1980; Gordon 1985; Stanko 1985; Dominelli 1986a, 1989; Hanmer et al. 1989). Others hold that part of this problem is men's celebration of an aggressive masculinity and its use as a normalizing activity (Dominelli 1991) carried out within the ambit of their peer group (Hudson 1988; Graef 1992). According to these authors, men's relationships with other men play a crucial role in men utilizing violence to assert control over others and prove their manhood. In other words, violence becomes a means whereby men legitimate their claim to being part of the community of men. While there have been differences of emphasis and views about the targets of intervention amongst the proponents of these two positions, they have contributed to challenging the claim that it is a small group of weak, pathologically oriented men whose activities lie behind the substantial rise in statistics on violent crime. In doing so, they have highlighted the place men's cultural norms, on both the personal and institutional levels, have in endorsing men's aggressive behaviour, thereby implicating all men in the activities of convicted violent men (Brownmiller 1975; Dworkin 1981).

Consequently, these analyses have problematized masculinity more generally and highlighted a "continuum of violence" against women (Kelly 1988). This continuum encompasses a variety of abusive behaviour ranging from verbal abuse to rape, and provides what Brownmiller (1975) has termed a "rape-supportive culture". By implicating all men in controlling women through violent means (Brownmiller 1975; Dworkin 1981), feminist studies have also initiated a debate into hitherto taboo topics – men's use of physical and sexual violence to dominate and control others alongside their self-exclusion from childcare and other forms of domestic labour.

Opposition to this development, because it focuses on the contribution all men make to legitimating a climate in which some men use extreme violence to solve disputes and dominate others, has been virulent. The assault on this analysis and women's limited gains around family life has prompted men to establish a counter-movement that has sought to reaffirm men's patriarchal supremacy and their power to determine the course of social development (Gairdner 1992; Lyndon 1992; Farrell 1993). This reaction has been crucial in legitimizing attempts to claw back feminist advances, limited as they have been, especially in the family arena (Gairdner 1992).

Child welfare considerations and the role of men and women in the family have been at the forefront of this struggle. In the West, men who are actively organizing the backlash against feminist gains through a conservative men's movement ignore the fact that men had previously owned women and children as chattels, that women gained access to children only after a long battle to assert their rights in the matter, and that men had become disinterested in the subject. Instead, these men take no responsibility for their exclusion from fatherhood and blame women for their predicament. Moreover, men have sought to curtail the newfound freedoms and financial independence women have acquired, either through their own labour or through income support accessed by the welfare state, by attacking welfare provisions and single-parent families headed by women (Gilder 1981; Minford 1984; Halsey 1995). The backlash initiated by men has affected the social context within which men's abuses of power occur. This reaction also provides the backdrop within which work with men is undertaken and contributes to the undermining of those efforts. I will now move on to consider the implications of feminist analyses for work that social workers and probation officers might do with men.

Few social workers and probation officers undertake work that is specifically geared to working with men and with the aim of rehabilitating them in ways that enable them to develop non-abusive relationships with women, children and other men less powerful than themselves. Until recently, much of the work done with men in the statutory sector has occurred within the context of the criminal justice system and has been more concerned with punishing men for wrongdoing than with using this as an opportunity to get the men concerned to work on re-orienting their life's direction and priorities. However, since the mid-1980s, some probation services and voluntary agencies have begun to address the question of working with violent men and using feminist insights in their work (Dobash & Dobash 1992). Their efforts have raised a number of questions about how work with men should be undertaken and who should be involved. While recognizing that the answers to these questions are controversial, there is much to be learnt from these attempts. I seek to do this in the discussion that follows.

Treatment for the offender

There is no consensus on what work should be done with convicted violent men, although the disagreements seem to be greatest around one particular group; that is, sex offenders, whether in custodial settings or in the community. Nonetheless, interventions range from medical or drug-based ones seeking to reduce sexual drive to psychosocial techniques such as cognitive behavioural therapies that aim to get men to accept responsibility for their behaviour and gain an understanding of their victim's perspective (for a comprehensive summary of key studies on this subject see Bagley & Thurston (1996)). Commentators have failed to achieve a consensus about what characterizes the profile of an abusive man, including a sex offender. For example, there are many different types of sex offenders, ranging from incestuous offenders and paedophiles to serial rapists. Each of these categories may have several subdivisions (Groth & Birnbaum 1978; Pollard 1994; Waterhouse et al. 1994). This complexity suggests that a plurality of responses is required to make any headway in this work. Thus, there can be no illusions about the enormity of the task before us.

Responses to men involved in programmes countering domestic violence usually treat the men involved as if they constitute a homogeneous group (Cree & Cavanaugh 1995). This approach is likely to mask differences that need to be addressed if ending violence in all its manifestations is our goal. Reducing the problematic nature of such responses requires further research that will enable us to understand more fully the motives and objectives of different groups of men and the role that violence plays in sustaining their sense of themselves as men.

Thus, a key element in our search for an end to male violence is exploring the nature and extent of the link between violence and masculinity. Moreover, the problems to be addressed are exacerbated by the spread of an aggressive masculine culture that has encompassed the globe. This state of affairs has been reached, Connell (1995) claims, because the connection between violence and masculinity has been exported abroad by Europeans.

A direct concern with masculinity and its accompanying cultural norms is rarely expressed in the literature covering the treatment of violent men (Bagley & Thurston 1996). However, it can be implied in the prescriptions that are set. Benjamin

(1995: 288), for example, suggests that to successfully challenge male perpetrators of violence against women the following precepts should be observed:

- Dealing with violent men's denial by holding them accountable for their behaviour.
- Providing alternative ways of viewing the world and relating to other men, women and children by deconstructing their patriarchal and sexist belief systems.
- Responding empathetically to the traumas and wounds that violent men may have experienced in their past.

This list is useful in confronting men's views about themselves and others. However, it needs to be supplemented by actual changes in violent men's behaviour and a reconceptualization of what is considered "normal" masculinity in the broader society. Without this latter addition, responses can individualize a problem that has a collective dimension, and thereby ensure that necessary changes in the cultural and societal norms underpinning masculinity and endorsing abusive relations between a particular man and other people are minimized. Moreover, bringing about cultural and organizational changes of this magnitude requires a reformulation of the concept of violence in order to take on board the complexity of the dynamics encapsulated by it as well as the range of situations in which it is perpetrated.

Men direct violence against others to ensure social control and conformity. Men may, therefore, be at the receiving end of violent acts from other men. In short, violence is the mechanism through which men exercise power over others. Divergence from the acceptable white middle-class heterosexual male norms through social divisions such as "race", age, sexual orientation and disability complicate the picture. "Difference" may, in and of itself, provide the basis for aggressive acts among men. Addressing the broad configuration of violent activity this inspires requires a non-stereotypical view of violence and demands responses capable of tackling it in all its forms – emotional, physical and sexual. Countering it also calls for a redefinition of masculinity in more caring directions.

Considering human relationships in non-rigid and non-hierarchical ways enables workers to explore the multiple forms of oppression that men can experience along the dimensions of "race", sexual orientation, age, disability and other social divisions. And, it allows recognition of the fact that men can oppress others while simultaneously being oppressed themselves. This multiplicity cannot be tackled unless men are held accountable for their behaviour. Women cannot be blamed for the predicament men are in. Dealing with the complexities of men's lives requires the development of models of masculinity that foster social responsibility, social justice and equality (Benjamin 1995). Or, as Dominelli (1992) frames the objective: "Men need to feel OK about themselves without having to put others down in the process". Reorienting masculinity in this way opens up a comprehensive range of roles and behaviours for men to adopt, thereby facilitating their developing more satisfactory relationships with others. It also provides a point of convergence between convicted violent men and men in general.

For these reasons, I am skeptical about the usefulness of drug-oriented treatment as *the* answer to the question of what should be done when seeking to rehabilitate violent men. While acknowledging that some men may need drugs to control their violence, I do not adhere to the view that drugs will provide the solution to curtailing the problem of widespread male aggression in this society. Nor do I think that psychosocial approaches, including anger management and cognitive behavioural therapy, which focus solely on individual change, will do so on their own. What is likely to be needed is a complex combination of approaches that is tailored to the specific needs of an individual man while at the same time doing something about the ways in which social and cultural values endorse masculine aggression and male violence. Thus, eliminating men's violence in their relationship with others requires practitioners to engage in bringing about both individual and societal changes that will enable people to obtain personal fulfilment and find ways of resolving disputes with others through non-violent means. This is a tall order, and requires consciousness raising and re-education regarding the conduct of interpersonal social relations on a massive scale. In addition, it calls on all individuals in society to play their part in bringing about this change. It also requires welfare authorities to consider how they will address the needs of practitioners directly engaged in working with men.

Issues to be considered when working with men

Professionals who work with men usually do so with men who have been *convicted* of violent offences. However, there is an unknown number of *unconvicted* men who nonetheless have committed acts of violence against others. While in this section I focus largely on work with those who have been found guilty in a court of law, I acknowledge the contradiction inherent in the situation: *many* violent offenders remain hidden (i.e. they are located outside the realm of public knowledge). However, by addressing men in general, work aimed at delegitimating the use of violence in conflict resolution and promoting efforts aimed at redefining masculinity in more nurturing directions should go some way to reducing the overall pool of potentially violent men.

Given that the gist of my argument is that men need rehabilitative intervention aimed at terminating their abusive behaviour, the question arises of who should do this work and under what conditions. First, I will consider the issues that are relevant to women working with men, and then address those of men working with men.

Women working with men

The first topic to be considered in relation to women working with men is that of compulsion. Women may be required by their employers to work with men,

27

regardless of whether they wish to or not. Being compelled to work with men is a matter of particular importance to women employed within the criminal justice system. Women probation officers, for example, have found that a refusal to work with men, particularly violent men, has been interpreted by their line managers as incompetence, or as an inability to work with all clients and held against them for the purposes of promotion (Dominelli 1991). Such responses indicate the need to institute a policy where women are, as a matter of course, given a choice about whether or not to work with men *without being penalized* for not doing so.

Women should not be coerced into doing such work. There are a number of valid reasons for their refusal to consider taking it on. The woman may be objecting out of principle, feeling that women should not work with men. Her refusal would, therefore, have nothing to do with her competence or skill levels. Given women's generalized fear about male violence, she may be responding out of concern for her safety – an issue which should not be ignored by her line manager. She may be reacting out of the bitter experience of having been a victim–survivor of male violence in the past, or may even be dealing with it in her current living arrangements.

Women should not be asked to re-live traumatic events. These reasons may well apply to men. They, too, should be accorded the right to say no to working with violent men. Employers have a responsibility as part of good employment practice to safeguard the welfare of all their employees in all circumstances. This includes an unfettered right for employees to progress, in their chosen career on the basis of their capacity to perform well in the work they do. Having "specialist" options so that only those with the necessary training, inclination, aptitudes and skills undertake work with violent men is one way of dealing with the dilemmas faced by employers with employees claiming exemption from working with such clients. And, it enables employers to contribute to a collective responsibility to end men's abusive behaviour.

Women working with men will find the task emotionally draining and exhausting. Line managers will need to be sensitive to this and ensure that workers are not overloaded. Limiting the number of cases or groups that these workers undertake, particularly with violent men offenders, is one way of dealing with this problem. Line managers should also assist in the creation of support groups capable of responding to workers' needs during work time. These groups should be developed as safe havens or confidential environments for exploring issues of concern to the workers in supportive ways. Workers should also have recourse to their support groups during work time.

Although they constitute part of good employment practice, support groups for this purpose require resourcing if they are to function as intended. They will compete against other priorities as well as with different types of support group in their demands for resourcing at a point in time when budgets, particularly those in the public sector, are being severely restricted. Securing scarce resources in this area may exacerbate tensions already present in the workplace. If it is only women who are accessing these facilities, it may well prompt misogynist colleagues to perceive such measures as women getting an unfair share of limited resources, thus undermining the conceptualization of these provisions as part of an effort aimed at ensuring that a job is being done under the appropriate conditions; that is, securing women's safety and ability to perform the task to the highest possible standards.

Women who decide that they want to undertake work with violent male offenders have to take other precautions. To begin with, a woman's sense of self will have to be strong and her confidence in her abilities high, to protect her from the client's attempts to undermine her in various ways. Included among his endeavours in this regard are the games he plays to get her to sympathize with him and blame his victim. He also seeks to attack the way she works with him and undermine her sense of self, her person, her dress. Additionally, she will need training in how to: work effectively with a violent man; become aware of his resistance to changing his behaviour; and recognize the ploys he will use to get her to collude with him.

Women also have to address issues concerning their own safety – both physical and emotional. Their doing so becomes particularly relevant in a situation in which their clients are men who have been *convicted* of crimes of violence against women. The women workers' safety has to be taken seriously for, as Scully (1990) suggests, these men's contempt for and hatred of women is a key aspect of their behaviour. Tackling such attitudes with the intention of reversing them is a major aspect of the work women workers will be undertaking with these men. It is a purpose that creates a tension between the worker and the client from the start. Moreover, this work is being conducted in a social context rooted in misogynist caricatures of women's lives and which devalues women's contributions to society (Rutherford 1992). This in turn feeds into these men's negative views about women. Hence, the potential for violence against women workers is high.

Moreover, violent men tend to minimize the impact of their coercive behaviour on women (Cowburn 1993). Consequently, such men lack awareness of the effect of their behaviour on women. A recent survey of convicted rapists in Britain, for example, has revealed that they have very little compassion for their victim–survivors; nor did these rapists understand the significance of their assaults on women's lives (the *Guardian* 5 March 1991). If they operate within such a mindset, violent men may resent attempts aimed at focusing on these dynamics. A woman worker who does so may unintentionally exacerbate the likelihood of abusive behaviour emerging in her professional interactions with violent men. Again, managers subscribing to good employment practice have no option but to support women workers in dealing with the effects of these men's attitudes on the work that is done with them.

Men will also seek to control the woman worker in a variety of ways (Edley & Wetherell 1995). Violence against women is a key instrument in their repertoire of controlling behaviour (Dobash & Dobash 1979). Controlling women through "everyday" forms of violence (Stanko 1990) is a common method men use to get their own way. Little is known about the specific conditions in which men use violence to control women workers. However, the possibility of a violent man resorting to violence is more likely to surface if the woman worker is being "difficult"; that is, if she is trying to get him to confront his oppressive behaviour against women by making him own it, deal with it, and think about its impact on his victim–survivors.

While research on this subject is scarce, we know that violence against caring professionals has risen dramatically in recent years (Lupton & Gillespie 1994). Moreover, a disproportionate number of its victims are women. Examining this evidence will be critical in revealing the extent to which attempts to change men's behaviour underpins violent responses to them.

Women's safety is also compromised by a set of dynamics around displaced anger, which is inherent in the work women workers do with violent men. Displacing their anger onto women features prominently among violent men. Research has exposed how men who have been humiliated by other men take it out on women because they feel feminized; that is, their identity as *men* has been undermined and they blame women for their predicament. This raises the significance of masculinity and their subscription to masculine ideals in both precipitating and explaining their behaviour. As Rutherford (1992) puts it:

> ... it is to women that they (men) turn for support in their struggle to regain their masculine status and place amongst other men. It is women who bear witness to his humiliation and it is they who are deemed as robbing him of his self in their demands for his love. (Rutherford 1992: 181)

Interaction with women, therefore, offers men a refuge from other men, while simultaneously threatening them with losing their manhood (Kimmel 1995). Thus, a woman worker may be in danger of "copping it" for someone else's behaviour or for a sequence of events that is entirely beyond her control.

The centrality of men's sense of self in intergender dynamics (Kimmel 1995) means that women may be placed under considerable risk when working with men, whether the men are violent or not. Hence, whether male clients have been convicted of violent offences or not, women should not be compelled to undertake such work without their explicit or freely given consent. If women volunteer to do such work, the necessary support infrastructure and training should be in place before they start such work.

Men working with men

Working with men is also difficult for men workers. To begin with, men find it hard to expose their vulnerabilities, especially their emotional weakness and dependency to others. They have had little experience of sharing innermost feelings with either men or women (Rutherford 1992). This makes it difficult for men to overcome emotional distance in their relationships with others. Yet, understanding their inner needs is crucial to getting men to assess their disatisfaction with their way of life and to opening the door to seeking alternatives. Some of the difficulties men workers face are similar to those encountered by women. In the context of working with violent men, these include being concerned about their safety, ensuring they are sufficiently trained for the job, having self-knowledge about their own sexuality, and being able to act confidently and competently.

Having men working with men raises other problematic issues. I will consider these next. Men who work with men, even those drawing on feminist principles and methods, need to be on their guard if they are to avoid colluding with male client's derogatory views about and contempt for women. Resisting this may be hard, because the perpetrator of abusive behaviour will seek to draw on unquestioned shared assumptions regarding how they conduct their relationships with women (Snowdon 1980). This strategy is used in the hope of securing the men workers' sometimes unwitting acquiescence to their refusal to mend their ways and unwillingness to explore their behaviour, its meaning for them and its impact on their victims.

The men workers will also have to feel confident and secure in their own masculinity. If they show a fear of the man they are working with, he may seek to take advantage of this and get the man worker to compromise his position. Men's fear of other men is an important feature of the dynamics among men and must be addressed explicitly by both workers and managers. Fear of being considered un-manly and stigmatized or bullied as a result may make men workers reluctant to own up to these feelings in public. For, in expressing them, they may be labelled as unmanly. Their reluctance to speak out is likely to be heightened if the attack upon them is one involving sexual rather than physical violence (Stanko 1990; *The Observer* 4 April 1993). This is because men are expected to initiate sexual encounters, not to be victimized through them. Also, the dynamics of "hegemonic" masculin-ity (Connell 1995) exclude men who have indulged in sexual violence from their fraternity (Priestley 1980) for exposing the myth of men as protectors of the weak (Dominelli 1989). Once their activities become public knowledge, these men lose their place in the community of men and the protection of other men that this implies.

Those men engaging in physical violence are not deemed to have taken advan-tage of their victims in the same way. Moreover, most physical violence is of men against other men. In these circumstances, a closer matching of the differentials between the victim and attacker is presumed. Thus sexual violence is stigmatized and its perpetrators are brutalized, while physical violence is glamourized and the strong fearless fighter is admired by other men (Dominelli 1991). If, on the other hand, the perpetrator is afraid of the man worker, perhaps because he holds power over him, the man worker will have to ensure he does not abuse the power he holds over him, as this may model inappropriate behaviour that the 'client' may sub-sequently try to emulate and use to justify his own abusive behaviour. Men can use feminist theories to help them gain insight into these dynamics and assist them in dealing with them in their practice.

Colluding with other men's sexism is a key issue to be addressed by men working with offenders (Snowdon 1980). Collusion makes confronting men with the enormity of what they have done, particularly in cases of physical or sexual violence, extremely difficult. Violent men may exploit such collusion to minimize the impact of their behaviour on victim–survivors and avoid taking responsibility for their action. As Benjamin (1995) warns, collusion is not the same as empathiz-ing with the issues men need to deal with if they are to become anti-sexist in their behaviour towards women. The former devalues women's experience, the latter does not.

Thus men working with violent men share with women workers concerns about safety and a desire to end men's violence. However, as indicated above, men working with men, whether violent or not, have issues about their own gender and masculinity that they need to acknowledge and attend to.

Men and women co-working together

Co-working, that is, men and women working together as a team, is popular among probation officers undertaking work with violent men (Cowburn 1993). They see working with women as a device that prevents men from colluding with each other, or at least as a check against their doing so. A danger to be guarded against in such arrangements is the view that the mere presence of women colleagues suffices in averting this becoming a reality. Women can unintentionally collude with dynamics aimed at keeping them in their place. Moreover, expecting *one* woman in a group dominated by violent men to challenge such collusion on her own is setting a difficult goal for her to achieve. Thus, while this approach to the problem may be advantageous for men, it carries several risks for the woman involved, and sets her up to fail.

The woman will also have to desist from colluding with male supremacist notions about women. The pressures on her to go along with collusive dynamics will be great, regardless of whether they are co-working with a group of violent male offenders or young male burglars. Her acquiescence with sexist norms is often difficult to identify because they are based on normalizing assumptions that are hard to question and expose. But she will sense her complicity intuitively and feel uncomfortable about her position. It is vital that she acknowledges these feelings and checks them out to uncover their empirical basis. Women's support groups provide safe spaces that can be very useful for exploring her views and working out strategies for dealing with a range of situations that may arise.

Men workers need to ensure that they are not dumping the responsibility for changing the perpetrator's negative views of women on their women colleagues. Additionally, men workers who co-work with women have to take care to ensure that neither what they say nor what they do replicates sexist relations that undermine the woman's position or skills. Such reactions would endorse notions of male supremacy and confirm men's negative beliefs about and contempt for women.

The woman co-worker also has to take steps to avoid being dumped upon in sexist ways. She has to draw on her assertion skills to withstand being placed in the role of acting as the guarantor of men's non-sexist behaviour. Were this to happen, she would find her position untenable. If she feels herself approaching this predicament, she needs to call on management for support in protecting her interests and resolving the issue. The agency should, therefore, have a policy and procedures that can be activated rapidly in such instances. The task then to be undertaken is that of facilitating men workers to take their responsibilities seriously and put the non-dumping policy into practice by not undermining women workers. At this point, managers should also authorize and facilitate the woman worker's use of the support networks she chooses during worktime.

Co-working can be a useful way of working with men, provided that the women involved in such arrangements are not dumped upon by being made to feel responsible for turning sexist abusive men into non-sexist and non-abusive ones. Fulfilling this goal requires personal changes in men and structural changes in society, including a realignment of gendered power relations in egalitarian directions.

A further set of issues arise when men and women are co-working around childcare issues. Here, women's ambiguities about *how* to involve men so that this arena does not become colonized by men usurping power in the one sphere in which women have traditionally exercised some authority come to the fore. Women's feared loss of power in the domain of childcare is greater than in that of working with violent men. For, in the latter case, women have not been dominant power-holders and they share with men the limited objective of making society safer by reducing male violence. There is an empirical basis for women's anxieties. If men follow the same path in the private realm as they have done in the public one, women will lose out. In the public sector (e.g. in medicine and social work), men engaged in "women's work" have collared the higher paid managerial echelons and left women to occupy the lower paid subordinate ranks (Ehrenreich & English 1979; Grimwood & Popplestone 1993). Men are also ambivalent about their participation in caring work. While they are willing co-workers in the development of affective relationships, they have proven less keen to engage in cleaning the messy bottoms of babies, sick children or incontinent adults.

Additionally, there is the question of whether men can be trusted to work with vulnerable others, particularly dependent children, when they constitute the main source of sexual and physical violence against them. Some men have indicated that caution is necessary in this respect (Box 1971; Frosh 1988; Frosh & Glaser 1988). They concur with feminist insights which have exposed men's abuse of power within intimate or family relationships and worked against the privileging of men's traditional interests. Yet, if feminists' aim of getting men and women as equal participants in childcare and other forms of domestic labour is to be achieved, this contradiction has to be resolved. Feminism does offer some grounds for optimism in this respect, as in calling for a redefinition of masculinity in more nurturing directions, violence and aggression will not remain as socially sanctioned norms. Once this aspiration becomes operationalized, men may be more readily trusted to work with dependent and powerless others without abusing them for their own purposes.

Black feminist insights into working with men

So far, this chapter has concentrated primarily on the usefulness of feminist perspectives in working with men in Western countries such as England. It is also largely about white men and women working with white men, particularly violent ones. Black women have other considerations, alongside safety concerns, that differ from those occupying the energies of white women.

Key among these is racism, which compels black women to unite with black men to seek their liberation as black people. Thus, black women's struggles for gender equality have to occur within the context of their obtaining racial equality. Their struggles are both different from white women's and overlap at some points. For example, black women, like white women, want their men to play a greater role in housework, childcare and elder-care. However, when it comes to questions of violence, black women are aware of a contextuality that is absent for white women. Violence against black women draws on racist stereotypes of both black men and black women. In these, white people paint black men as sexually predatory, while portraying black women as sexually promiscuous. Many black women in Britain have refused to report sexual violence because they fear racist stereotypes about black men as violent sexual predators will exacerbate the difficulties they will encounter at the hands of white professionals, including the police and others involved in the criminal justice system (Wilson 1993).

Fear of deportation is another major disincentive for black women to report sexual and physical assaults against them (Mama 1989; Wilson 1993). Racist depictions of their position, therefore, need challenging. Doing so may, at times, pit black women's interests against those of white women. When it comes to working with individual black men, black women's approach to working with violent men is more collective and less likely to centre on the individual perpetrator as the target for change. For example, in Britain, black feminists have challenged racist immigration laws by campaigning against them and rejected inappropriate service provisions by setting up their own facilities (Mama 1989; Wilson 1993), thus highlighting the need for organizational change in dealing with violence against them.

Similar points about organizational change have been made by black feminists in other countries. Women in Vanuatu, for instance, see collective social responses as essential in addressing domestic violence in that country. As they have said, the feminism of Pacific women places emphasis on:

> . . . the values of collectivity and on connecting women's movements to broader sociopolitical struggles for self-determination where the self is a collectivity rather than an individual. (Jolly 1996: 183)

Black feminist approaches, however, are also relevant to white women in the West. They have implications for the ways in which black women might wish white authorities to respond to the issue of violence so that the racism inherent in judicial processes and societal views about black people are taken on board (Bhatti-Sinclair 1994). Thus, they have identified the necessity for anti-racist structural changes as well as changes in individual behaviour. Black feminist insights are also relevant to white women in challenging the dominant view of masculinity represented as aggressive man. Underpinned by sexist social norms and values, it has to be questioned and changed at the social or collective level, and not just at that of the individual man. Black feminists' conceptualization of relationships between men and women is also useful in interrogating the worldwide spread of Euro-pean formulations of masculinity, rejecting the violence that is inherent in them and holding forth the promise that men and women can work together for a better world.

Conclusions

Working with men is a demanding task. Men will attempt to include caring profes-sionals in their collusive sexist behaviour unless these workers consciously take steps to ensure that this does not occur. Working with violent men carries addi-tional risks that need to be confronted, for such men will seek to minimize their offences and blame their victims for what has happened. In addition, working with violent men is fraught with physical danger.

Both men and women workers will have to ensure that they do not collude with either the men's denial about having perpetrated violence or their minimiza-tion of its impact on victim survivors. Workers will also have to protect themselves from threats of violence against them and prepare for the emotional turmoil they will encounter in such work. It is, therefore, crucial that management supports workers in order to enforce good practice with violent men and safeguard their well-being.

Finally, working with men requires us to work in anti-racist ways to address the needs of black women and black men and incorporate the insights proffered by black feminists to ensure that change in anti-racist egalitarian directions is embarked upon at both individual and collective levels, thereby encompassing the personal as well as structural elements in our social relations. Hence, eradicating sexism and racism in their various manifestions from our social relations is a task that involves us all.

Working with men from a feminist perspective provides a crucial means of proceeding along these lines. And, it is central in reformulating definitions of mascu-linity such that they promote the dignity and well-being of all people, regardless of gender or other social division. Men have everything to gain from using feminist theories and principles of practice in constructing a future as fully developed men human beings relating to women human beings on an egalitarian basis.

References

ACHILLES HEEL COLLECTIVE (1983) Special issue on masculinity. *Achilles Heel* **5**.
ADAMS, D. (1988) Treatment models for men who batter: a profeminist analysis. In *Feminist perspectives on wife abuse*, K. YLLO & M. BOGRAD (eds). Newbury Park, CA: Sage.

ADAMSON, O., C. BROWN, J. HANISON, J. PRICE (1976) Women's oppression under capitalism. *Revolutionary Communist* **5**, 1–48.

BAGLEY, C. & W. THURSTON (1996) *Child sexual abuse*. Aldershot: Gower.

BENJAMIN, O. (1995) Healing, community and justice in the men's movement: toward a socially responsible model of masculinity. In *The politics of manhood*, J. RUTHERFORD (ed.), 286–91. Philadelphia: Temple University Press.

BHATTI-SINCLAIR, K. (1994) Asian women and violence from male partners. In *Working with violence*, C. LUPTON & T. GILLESPIE (eds), 75–95. Basingstoke: BASW/Macmillan.

BLY, R. (1992) *Iron John: A book about men*. New York: Vintage.

BOWL, R. (1985) *Changing the nature of masculinity – a task for social work*. Norwich: University of East Anglia.

BOX, S. (1971) *Deviance, reality and society*. New York: Holt, Rinehart & Winston.

BROWNMILLER, S. (1975) *Against our will: Men, women and rape*. New York: Bantam.

BRYAN, B., S. DADZIE, S. SCAFE (1985) *The heart of the race: Black women's lives in Britain*. London: Virago.

CAVANAGH, K. & V. E. CREE (1995) *Working with men: Feminism and social work*. London: Routledge.

COLLINS, P. H. (1990) *Black feminist thought*. London: Routledge.

CONNELL, R. W. (1995) *Masculinities*. Cambridge: Polity.

COWBURN, M. (1993) Groupwork programme for male sex offenders: establishing principles for practice. In *Groupwork with offenders*, A. BROWN & B. CADDICK (eds), 218–30. London: Whiting and Birch.

CREE, V. & K. CAVANAGH (1995) *Working with men from a feminist perspective*. London: Routledge.

DAVIS, A. (1981) *Women, class and race*. London: Women's Press.

DOBASH, R. E. & R. P. DOBASH (1979) *Violence against wives: A case against patriarchy*. New York: Free Press.

DOBASH, R. E. & R. P. DOBASH (1992) *Women, violence and social change*. London: Routledge.

DOMINELLI, L. (1981) Violence: a family affair. *Community Care* 12 March, 14–17.

DOMINELLI, L. (1986a) Father–daughter incest: patriarchy's shameful secret. *Critical Social Policy* **16**, 8–22.

DOMINELLI, L. (1986b) *Love and wages*. Norwich: Novata.

DOMINELLI, L. (1989) Betrayal of trust: a feminist analysis of power relationships in incest abuse. *British Journal of Social Work* **19**(4), 291–307.

DOMINELLI, L. (1991) *Gender, sex offenders and probation practice*. Norwich: Novata.

DOMINELLI, L. (1992) Masculinity, sex offenders and probation practice. In *Gender, crime and probation practice*, P. SENIOR & D. WOODHILL (eds), 13–23. Sheffield: PAVIC.

DOMINELLI, L. & E. McLEOD. (1989) *Feminist social work*. London: Macmillan.

DWORKIN, A. (1981) *Pornography: Men possessing women*. London: Women's Press.

EDLEY, N. & M. WETHERELL (1995) *Men in perspective: Practice, power and identity*. London: Prentice Hall/Harvester Wheatsheaf.

EHRENREICH, D. & B. ENGLISH (1979) *For her own good*. London: Pluto.

FARRELL, W. (1993) *The myth of male power*. New York: Simon & Schuster.

FESTAU, M. B. (1975) *The male machine*. New York: Delta.

FINKELHOR, D. (1984) *Child sexual abuse: New theory and research*. New York: Free Press.

FIRESTONE, S. (1971) *The dialectic of sex: The feminist revolution*. New York: Cape.

FROSH, S. (1988) No man's land? The role of men working with sexually abused children. *British Journal of Guidance and Counselling* **16**, 1–10.

FROSH, S. & D. GLASER (1988) *Child sexual abuse*. London: BASW/Macmillan.

GAIRDNER, W. D. (1992) *The war against the family: A parent speaks out on the political, economic and social policies that threaten us all*. Toronto: Stoddart.

GILDER, G. (1981) *Wealth and poverty*. New York: Basic Books.

GONDOLF, E. (1987) Evaluating programmes for men who batter: problems and prospects. *Journal of Family Violence* **2**(1), 95–108.

GORDON, L. (1985) Child abuse, gender and the myth of family independence: a historical critique. *Child Welfare* **64**(3), 213–14.

GRAEF, R. (1992) *Living dangerously: Young offenders in their own words*. London: HarperCollins.

GRAY, S., M. HIGGS, K. PRINGLE (1995) Services for people who have been sexually abused. In *Researching women's health: Methods and process*, L. MCKIE (ed.). London: Mark Allen.

GRIMWOOD, C. & POPPLESTONE, R. (1993) *Women*. London: BASW/Macmillan.

GROTH, A. N. & H. J. BIRNBAUM (1978) Adult sexual orientation and attraction to underage persons. *Archives of Sexual Behaviour* **7**, 175–81.

HALSEY, A. H. (1995) *Change in British society*. Oxford: Oxford University Press.

HANMER, J., J. RADFORD, E. A. STANKO (1989) *Women, policing and male violence. International perspectives*. London: Routledge.

HEARN, J. (1987) *The gender of oppression: Men, masculinity and the critique of marxism*. Brighton: Wheatsheaf.

HOOKS, B. (1984) *Feminist theory: From margins to centre*. Boston, MA: South End Press.

HUDSON, A (1988) Boys will be boys: masculinities and the juvenile justice system. *Critical Social Policy*, Spring, 30–48.

JOLLY, M. (1996) Woman Ikat Raet Long Human Raet O No? Women's rights, human rights and domestic violence in Vanuatu. *Feminist Review* **52**, 169–90.

KELLY, L. (1988) *Surviving sexual violence*. Cambridge: Polity.

KIMMEL, M. S. (1995) *The politics of manhood: Profeminist men respond to the mythopoetic men's movement (and the mythopoetic leaders answer)*. Philadelphia: Temple University Press.

LEES, J. & T. LLOYD (1994) *Working with men who batter their partners: An introductory text*. London: Working with Men/The B Team.

LUPTON, C. & T. GILLESPIE (eds) (1994) *Working with violence*. Basingstoke: BASW/Macmillan.

LYNDON, N. (1992) *No more sex wars: The failures of feminism*. London: Sinclair Stevenson.

MACKINNON, C. (1987) *Feminism unmodified: Discourses on life and law*. Cambridge, MA: Harvard University Press.

MAMA, A. (1989) *The hidden struggle: Statutory and voluntary responses to violence against black women in the home*. London: London Race and Housing Unit.

MARCUS, A. M. (1971) *Nothing is my number: An exploratory study with a group of dangerous sexual offenders in Canada*. Toronto: General Publishing.

METCALFE, A. & M. HUMPHERIES (1985) *The sexuality of men*. London: Pluto.

MILLET, K. (1972) *Sexual politics*. London: Abacus/Sphere.

MINFORD, P. (1984) State expenditure: a study in waste. *Economic Affairs* April–June. XIV.

NEWBURN, T. & E. A. STANKO (1994) *Just boys doing business: Men, masculinities and crime*. London: Routledge.

PERROTT, S. (1994) Working with men who abuse women and children. In *Working with violence* C. LUPTON & T. GILLESPIE (eds), 135–52. Basingstoke: BASW/Macmillan.

PHILLIPS, A. (1993) *The trouble with boys: Parenting the men of the future*. London: Pandora.

POLLARD, P. (1994) Sexual violence against women: characteristics of typical perpetrators. In *Male violence*, J. ARCHER (ed.). London: Routledge.

PRIESTLEY, P. (1980) *Community of scapegoats: The segregation of sex offenders and informants*. Oxford: Pergammon Press.

PRINGLE, K. (1992) Child sexual abuse perpetrated by welfare personnel and the problem of men. *Critical Social Policy* **36**, 4–19.

PRINGLE, K. (1994) The problem of men revisited. *Working with Men* **2**, 5–8.

RAYNOR, P., D. SMITH, M. VANSTONE (1994) *Effective probation practice*. London: DASW/Macmillan.

RUSH, F. (1980) *The best kept secret: Sexual abuse of children*. New York: McGraw-Hill.

RUTHERFORD, J. (1992) *Men's silences: Predicaments in masculinity*. London: Routledge.

SCULLY, D. (1990) *Understanding sexual violence*. London: HarperCollins.

SEIDLER, V. (1992) *The Achilles heel reader: Men, sexual politics and socialism*. London: Routledge.

SMITH, D. (1995) *Criminology for social work*. London: BASW/Macmillan.

SNODGRASS, J. (ed.) (1977) *A book of readings for men against sexism*. New York: Times Change.

SNOWDON, R. (1980) Working with incest offenders: excuses, excuses, excuses. *Aegis: Issues on Child Sexual Assault* **29**, 20.

SOLANAS, V. (1971) *The society for cutting up men manifesto*. New York: Olympia.

STANKO, E. A. (1985) *Intimate intrusions: Women's experience of male violence*. London: Routledge.

STANKO, E. A. (1990) *Everyday violence: How men and women experience sexual and physical danger*. London: Pandora.

STOLTENBERG, J. (1990) *Refusing to be a man*. New York: Meridan.

TOLSON, A. (1977) *The limits of masculinity*. London: Tavistock.

TONG, R. (1989) *Feminist thought: A comprehensive introduction*. San Francisco: Westview.

WALBY, S. (1990) *Theorising patriarchy*. Oxford: Blackwell.

WATERHOUSE, L., R. DOBASH, J. CARNIE (1994) *Child sexual abusers*. Edinburgh: Central Research Unit/Scottish Office.

WILSON, M. (1993) *Crossing the boundary: Black women survive incest*. London: Virago.

ZARETSKY, E. (1975) *Capitalism, the family and personal life*. London: Pluto.

Chapter Four

Making the links: gender, oppression and change

An interview with Susie Orbach

Jim Wild

Jim Wild: You've been interested in gender issues for over thirty years and many of your publications have reflected this. Can you tell me what you think the major changes have been over that period, some of the key changes that you've seen in relation to gender, men and women?

Susie Orbach: Well, I think there *are* changes at the level of consciousness. At a conscious level, some men wish to relate to their kids, to have some gentleness, to have a full range of emotions, and this corresponds in shifts of consciousness where women now feel that they're entitled to be in the world, to be regarded, to have some kind of personal authority, to be taken seriously. But I don't think those changes have necessarily happened, either in society or inside of people, and I think the sort of emotional and political struggles that we're faced with are much more complex, and from where I sit I see boys struggling desperately with attitudes to violence, well they're not even struggling. When we look at young boys or at the process of unculturation it's very, very hard for boys to feel that anything except being hard, being violent, being tough, making money, being interested in naked bodies is a legitimate form of identity for them. It sounds so crude, but there is a very polarized position for boys going into manhood at the moment. I don't necessarily think men want this, but I think in the transition period, there's still a tremendous difficulty if not more difficulty for boys. Unlike for girls, where something exciting is opening up and girls are feeling more entitled and deserving.

I don't think it's actually happened for the generation of women who are out in the world of work, I still think they feel it's quite a difficult place and very abrasive, and women can feel inconsistent about what they can do in the world and they struggle under this mad yoke of being "superwoman" when nobody ever fought for that and all of this nonsense around being multi-people. So women are expected to be the perfect mother, the perfect wife, the perfect person and have the perfect body. That kind of stuff does weigh very heavily on the generation of women in their twenties and thirties.

Jim Wild: In terms of young boys and the messages they're still getting, those messages are really hard to undo aren't they?

Susie Orbach: I think what's so painful is how difficult it is for boys to express themselves more widely than the gender stereotypes. For example my son has a circle time in school which is a period where you're supposed to be able to talk about and reflect on your feelings. He says, "Oh mum, my teacher's really great she lets us have a rumble instead of having to do feelings". So there definitely is a preference among the boys about having a fight rather than having to talk about their feelings. Of course it is easy enough to understand this if there is just one thirty-minute opportunity a week to exchange feelings in the midst of a school culture which has an ethos of competition and toughness. It takes much more of a commitment to emotional literacy to challenge boys limited and limiting views of themselves. Now what I find with men that I see in therapy (which is a very self-selective population) is that they come in very distressed by their inability to have an emotional repertoire that's of value to them and they're very interested in changing it. They are terribly open to change, but there are enormous difficulties in being able to expand their repertoire, and to not immediately become fearful, because they don't know, can't describe, can't access different aspects of themselves. It's not so much because they don't want to but because they are inexperienced. As a consequence they find it hard to hang in with their fear and find new responses. The fear propels them, I think, to dispense their discomfort and they do so in the ways they are accustomed to, by aggression; whether it's sexual, or physical aggression, or aggression towards themselves.

Jim Wild: One of the interesting things that I notice for example relates to divorced men and how they lose contact with their children, that's often reflected on by people saying "well, they were never good fathers anyway". But I have a view that there's often too much pain for them to face.

Susie Orbach: Yes, I think that's a really good point, men may not know how to make contact with that pain. Instead of pain being a motivating force for them to have their vulnerability and to connect from that basis, on top of the pain there's guilt, shame and very often a withdrawal. Out is the only route in the absence of any support or understanding for the difficulties one might face in making a direct relationship with a child when a mother has previously managed, mediated or been in between that relationship. And then of course there are the economic difficulties if fathers have nowhere to take their children, no child-friendly places to hang out with them.

But I don't want to be only gloomy because I also have the experience of divorced fathers who would never have become active fathers if they'd stayed with their partners, but because they've separated, these men have a separate and sustaining relationship with those children. Now these may be men whose economic circumstances allow them to have the children at their house. I have really noticed that there are divorced fathers, who are actually fathers, who would have been the guys who would have done nothing at the level of relating to those kids. So I think that's an interesting other twist.

Jim Wild: One of the other issues we both know about, is that of the silence being broken around sexual abuse of girls and boys and I'm wondering how much this information impacts on people's understanding of what men do in the wider society. I have a hunch that it's leaking out and people are starting to realize in the wider society that some men are actually quite dangerous.

Susie Orbach: Yes, I think it's a problem. But the less men have to do with babies and children, the more fearful they become of them. The less they understand their own vulnerabilities, the less they understand their own childhood, and with reference to abuse, if a man was abused himself as a child and unable to work any of that through the more likely he will be to then act it out. So from my perspective, since I don't think sexual abuse is about sex at all, but I think it is about fear and terror, aggression and violence, the more that men do engage with babies and children regularly and in a supported way the better. Some might say that this view is excessively naïve or generous as there are men who are a danger to children and should be excluded. Of course I don't want to underestimate the horror of sexual abuse but I don't necessarily want to remove men from contact with children as a way to address it. We need to understand what sexual abuse is about, how to treat offenders, how to protect children but not terrify ourselves with the view that says all men can/will/might offend. I don't believe that.

Jim Wild: You use the phrase "emotional literacy" and I know that you've used it a lot in talking about men. Can you again reiterate what you mean by emotional literacy and how much you've developed these ideas.

Susie Orbach: Well, I just think it's a phrase that can be stretched in a million different directions. For me it means the capacity to be able to recognize the complexity of what you're feeling, above all, to hold on to what you're feeling, not to sort of bash it out and expel it without understanding, but to be able to reflect upon it, to feel it, and hopefully to be done with it. I think there's a real problem in our interpersonal and social relations. Distressing feelings don't ever get digested, so they are for ever at the ready, available for manipulation by politicians, or the family, or at work, etc., etc., and I think emotional literacy means being able to recognize your emotions and then finding a way to digest them.

Jim Wild: There almost seems to be a conspiracy to stop that, would you say that's true?

Susie Orbach: Well, I certainly don't think that we arrange our public affairs in such a way that we're interested in developing emotional literacy, and I think we miss a great chance in education. We know what makes it possible for people to be active participating citizens. They need to know who they are, and what they think and have confidence to act. Our education isn't geared that way. On two fronts the lack of attention to emotional issues in the classroom is damaging. We prevent a certain amount of learning going on where emotional difficulties block learning and by leaving emotional literacy out of the curriculum. We undervalue people and their contribution and we create the conditions in which we our public services and political system fail us. What we do is we exploit emotions in our culture rather than either address the emotional constituents and emotional fallout of public policy or the emotions that galvanize public policy.

If you take the Europe debate, it has little to do with economics, at least I don't think most people can muster the economic arguments, rather it is an "emotional" debate which is misplaced. A lot of it seems to me to do with Britain not having ever assimilated post-imperialism and it's playing out of all of the psychological dynamics on the political stage instead of playing out the political dynamics. It's very curious. We are "emotional" where we need to be political and political where we need to be emotional.

Jim Wild: I think it's also about men arguing a lot of the time.

Susie Orbach: Well, I think one way to look at it is that men defining themselves in opposition to one another, that because so much of male psychology has been to know oneself via one's difference. Men don't get the opportunity to know themselves in the connection, but in their opposition, one to another. This can be seen in a political structure that requires this adversarial practice. Now I'm not somebody who doesn't believe in having severe distinctions in political positions, but I think the compulsion to adversarial politics has an awful lot to do with a push to define oneself by going up against who the other is, rather than actually pushing authoritatively, rather than in an authoritarian manner, but pushing authoritatively for a position that a person believes to be correct.

Jim Wild: So to help men understand what's going on, is there any sort of psychotherapeutic theory about the conditioning and representation of men in families and the gender dynamics that produce these issues?

Susie Orbach: Well Luise Fichenbraum and I wrote something about this in *What do women want?*; *Exploring the myth of dependency*. When we raise children in a society that's so unequal, that has had gender oppression as central, inevitably women who mother, are going to have a set of very complicated feelings about their daughters and a set of very complicated feelings about their sons. And one of the things they're going to feel about their daughters, is that in some way they have to prepare them for the social structure, they have to make it possible for them to fit in, which means reproducing a psychology of oppression, even at the same time as they might wish their daughters to be challenging it. In the case of boys, mothers unconsciously project onto boys that they are other, they are different, they have a whole range of entitlement to be in the world, but also that they're potentially contemptible and damaging because they can hurt women. Luise and I would argue that boys are related to as other from the beginning, and it is with their recognition of gender difference which comes along at 18 months, precisely the same moment when the toddler is crystallizing his or herself as a person in relation to others, that the boy may have a subjective experience of displacement, I'm not like her (mum). Into this gap, into this recognition there is a question or perhaps a feeling by the boy of the way I will get my identity is through difference. Difference and competition being unalike becomes a way of holding together a young boy's identity at a moment of his recognition of his gender difference and psychological difference from his mother. Paradoxically, difference becomes what glues him together physically, and I think that's how it then operates in the political structure.

Jim Wild: But all around them they see that don't they, on television, everywhere?

Susie Orbach: Absolutely. What I admire about boys actually is the ease with which they can disagree with one another, without it causing them tremendous guilt and rifts. For men of my generation that is a fantastic skill. What's painful for boys and men is if it's driven, if you can't agree but can only feel that you know yourself in opposition or in difference. In its worst manifestation this can mean men seek to fight as a way to confirm themselves. From a girl's perspective, to differentiate yourself has been scary, an act of selfhood often outside of what has been possible because of the constraints of femininity. So a boy's capacity to say no, that's rubbish, or I don't belong there, is impressive, I think it's something girls need to learn about.

Jim Wild: I sometimes feel, certainly in the past ten years, that there seems to be a developing understanding that there are issues or policies that need to develop around men and change and women and change. As the millennium approaches, do you feel that may be the case?

Susie Orbach: Well, I wish I felt it was the case. I think there's tremendous upset in society around Dunblane, the Wests, or the Belgium child abuse cases. I'm not sure that what that then creates is a political response. That's what's very, very problematic in our society at the moment. There are all these horrors and people will struggle on an anti-gun legislation, but the somehow essential piece – the fact that we might be able to understand these terrible happenings, we might be able to link child abuse, adult rampaging to a broader picture of how we raise children, the politics of the family, gender relations and so on is lost. Instead of a highly textured political response these phenomena enter public consciousness, a bit like Hollywood, "ah so this is a horror, so this is what it is".

Jim Wild: So it's put in a little compartment, and it's not really unpacked?

Susie Orbach: Our social critics unpack it. Our mothers fear for their children, our fathers fear for their children. But then we seem unable to muster more than a moral campaign when much more is required. We require a more substantial analysis and response that understands why these things are happening and what it says about the kind of interpersonal cultural patterns that are endemic. Because we're now talking about more than a one off. We cannot be talking about the scandal in the children's homes, Dunblane, Belgium and think these are just isolated events, they're linked in complex ways.

Jim Wild: They're happening in every town, in every city in some sort of way.

Susie Orbach: So I think we can have an awareness of terrible happenings and yet in a funny way feel not empowered to act on it collectively, or think about these events as signifying something about our culture.

Jim Wild: What do you think the process is that's happening, that stops people making those links, that's a really important question?

Susie Orbach: I think it's very hard for us to explain the gap between these phenomena, and people's desire to change but not somehow being able to activate substantial change. I think there's tremendous fear in our society at this point, tremendous fear that you can't have an impact on things, except your individual life. I think one of the legacies of Thatcherism is, the good piece of Thatcherism if you like was that people felt that they could do things in their own way, the absolutely terrible and much more devastating piece is that people forgot that there was society and that the only thing that you could do is something in your own life, which of course we know you can't, because you cannot protect your child from this and you cannot make decent schools when you have no social cohesion and only the individual. There is something about the loss of faith in collective action and if it is collective action, it's collective action to keep things out. I mean neighbourhood watch is not really about increasing neighbourhood relationships, it's about protecting the neighbourhood against potential marauders.

Jim Wild: Who are usually men. So do you see any political agenda, a glimmer from any politician who is actually exploring the issue of masculinity and destructiveness?

Susie Orbach: I wish I could say yes, but I think that in the tiny bit of the education debate, there is a little discussion about boys difficulties at school. There's an awareness about the fact that our boys are experiencing difficulty in schools, but I don't think there's a profound enough understanding of why or what pressures they experience. I don't think that masculinity is on the agenda as something that we need to contest, think about, deconstruct, I think we are a long way from that. Tony Blair has to play being a very macho politician, even though I think he would like to have much more of a conversation, but I think he's strategically decided that's not the way to win over the country.

Jim Wild: Okay, so you say you think it's a long way off, and I'm sure that a lot of people would agree with you on that, but in *What do women want?*, your final chapter looked at a future possible vision of what gender relations could look like. How could we get there, and do you think we will?

Susie Orbach: I'm deeply optimistic. Because we do see all around us the cost of how gender hurts us all, and I do also see around me lots of initiatives, personal and private initiatives where people are transforming their interpersonal relations and where people are trying very, very hard. My son's friends say, "Oh Joe, you're not like other dads, you're around, you cook for us, you talk to us". Now that has some meaning for children, it gives them another model to construct themselves from as they grow up, and I do think that there are real changes in sexual politics, and we will have examples from other countries. I think England at this point, or Britain, is not in good shape where gender relations are concerned, but if you were to look at Scandinavia, you'd be incredibly impressed with how they take for granted male and female engagement in child-rearing, how work ought to be distributed, and in the States, I think there is an entitlement to work for women, and a validity to much more emotional agendas that have to be brought into the gender struggles. So I don't think we can look to Britain for best practice, I think we've had it for the moment, but I do think that there are all sorts of initiatives going on in the rest of the world.

Jim Wild: So you're optimistic?

Susie Orbach: I am optimistic, because I think there are a lot of agendas that need to come together at this point. I think that the sustainable economy agenda, the challenge of green politics to the way we constitute our world needs to be linked to a notion of how we can sustain gender relations, how we can sustain families, cultures and also how we can have an emotional life that can sustain all sorts of difficulties within it. So yes, I do feel optimistic.

Jim Wild: I have a feeling if we can make those links, we can also be very kind to the Earth.

Susie Orbach: Absolutely, I think the critiques about the Earth are very hooked up with gender and our economic arrangements. I think what late modernity has shown us, or what the end of the century has shown us, is that mastery of the Earth is not possible and what we have to do is to begin to recognize the modesty of our position, and once you think in terms of that kind of respect towards the planet, you can link up with a kind of respect interpersonally, and the gender agenda can link up from its respect for people to a kind of much more friendly attitude towards the Earth. So I think they are complementary agendas.

Chapter Five

When is a man not a man?
When he's disabled

Tom Shakespeare

Background

Walter Benjamin apparently said that people write books because they are unable to find existing books with which they are completely happy. That certainly explains this chapter, because in years of researching disability I have only ever read one article concerning disabled men. Given that we are a substantial minority – perhaps 5 per cent of the population (approximately equivalent to the proportion of lesbians and gays or of black people in Britain) – this is surprising, not to say unfortunate. I hope this fact will enable the reader to condone the superficiality of the discussion: there's a lot to talk about, not much space, and even less research evidence.

The chapter is divided in three parts. In the first section I review the existing literature on disability and gender, and make some broad comparisons and suggestions. It's largely generalization, but it might make you reconsider some assumptions. The second section draws mainly on research conducted by myself and my colleagues for the book *The sexual politics of disability*, and will introduce you to some real disabled people in order to develop some more ideas, which may or may not be representative of the rest of the three million or so disabled men. In the final section I attempt to draw conclusions and link issues of disabled masculinity to broader concerns about men in general.

Review of the literature

Looking for the disabled man

Disability studies is a new approach to understanding disability, arising out of the social movement of disabled people. It explores disability as a form of social oppression, defining disabled people in terms of discrimination and prejudice, not in terms of medical tragedy: people with impairment are disabled by society, not by their bodies. There is a parallel with feminism, which originated as the intellectual and academic dimension of the women's movement, and was based on a distinction between biological sex and socio-cultural gender. Thus the disability movement distinguishes impairment (medical condition) from disability (social relation). Disability studies replaces the negative, clinical and individualist literature on people with impairment with a problematization of the process of disablement itself.

The political and academic priorities of this new disability radicalism have been to challenge social restrictions, and campaign for equal rights: access to employment, education, and to all aspects of society and polity. However, it has been argued that these priorities for change have contributed to a focus on the public, at the cost of the private. Thus campaigns and research have investigated structures and barriers in society at large, but perhaps have neglected individual and personal dimensions of oppression, among them the experience of impairment, sexuality, family and identity. To some extent, there has been a failure to take seriously the feminist concept that "the personal is political".

This imbalance has led to a claim by disabled feminists that disability studies has neglected the experience of disabled women: that when writers talk about "disabled people", they are in fact talking about disabled men. Morris (1993: 90) provides evidence that some publications have presented a false generic. Others have, I think with justice, pointed to the absence of marginal voices from minority sexual and ethnic communities. These criticisms have been tacitly conceded by some leading male theorists: for instance, Oliver (1991) highlights the following comment:

> Despite the attention given to disability in general and certain impairments in particular, one category within the disabled population has received little recognition or study: women. Like many social change movements, the disability movement has often directed its energies towards primarily male experiences. (Deegan & Brooks 1985: 1)

My reading of the literature, and observation of the disabled movement, in which women have always played a key part, often in leadership roles, leads me to a different conclusion. The problem we face is not so much that a male-dominated literature has constructed a "false generic", saying "people" when they mean "men". Rather, it is that a literature initially dominated by marxists and other structuralists, albeit mainly men, has focused on the public at the cost of the private. Thus we learn much about the public lives of men and women, but next to nothing about the private and personal lives of men or women, and nothing at all about sexual minority or ethnic minoriy disabled people.

As a consequence of this absence, feminists have rightly developed research and analysis of disabled women's experience. In fact, there are now about a dozen books and articles specifically about disabled women (Shakespeare et al. 1996: 7). However, there is still only one research-based article on disabled men (Gerschick

& Miller 1995). Therefore, I conclude that the disabled man is largely absent as a subject of research, both in the traditional clinical and psychological research, and in the radical disability studies literature which has developed over the last ten years.

Gendering disability

As I have suggested, work on the relation of gender to disability is scarce. Too often disabled people are taken as being asexual, or a third gender: this is familiar from the typical row of toilets (ladies, gentlemen, disabled people), but it is alarming to find that most of the traditional and progressive literature fails to explore the differences inherent in disability, and the way that oppression variously impacts on identity and opportunity for women and men, straights and gays, black and white people.

Where the gendering of disability is explored, generalizations take the place of analysis, as for example in the following quotation:

> Whereas disabled men are obliged to fight the social stigma of disability, they can aspire to fill socially powerful male roles. Disabled women do not have this option. Disabled women are perceived as inadequate for economically productive roles (traditionally considered appropriate for males) and for the nurturant, reproductive roles considered appropriate for females. (Fine & Asch 1985: 6)

Disabled people's gender identity is more complex and more varied than this stereotyped view indicates. Some women feel liberated from social expectation as a result of impairment; some men feel doubly inferior. The tendency to highlight the particular problems of disabled women obscures the strength and resistance of disabled women, especially those women who have become leaders of the disability movement: Jenny Morris writes that this notion of "double disadvantage" has the effect of making her feel like a victim (Morris 1996: 2). Masculinity and femininity are in a process of transitional change within Western societies, which makes it difficult to generalize about the strategies of individual disabled men and women.

However, I want to make two observations about the image of disabled women which may be useful. First, it seems that there is a synergy – a reinforcement – between the traditional notion of women and the traditional notion of disability. Adjectives apply such as innocent, vulnerable, sexually passive or asexual, dependent and objectified. We might conclude that, in the case of disabled women, gender and disability often reinforce a second-class status, and potentially undermine independence and agency. Second, disabled women fail the traditional female stereotype because social restrictions and bodily impairments may undermine the capacity to fulfil the caring role as housewife and mother. Moreover, disabled women may not conform to expectation: it has been suggested that physical appearance is a more significant attribute for women than for men in a sexist society. As Chapkiss argues:

> Man believes he survives through his enduring achievements. Woman is her mortal body. A man's relationship to his body, then, appears to be less fraught with tension than a woman's. The male mind can afford to be a more lenient master over the body, indulging in the appetites of the flesh. A man may sweat, scar and age; none of these indications of physicality and mortality are seen to define the male self. (Chapkis 1986: 15)

What, then, of disabled men? Well, immediately Chapkis' comment seems dated, when the objectification and sexualization of the male body in contemporary advertising is considered. While it is true that women are still more likely to be judged on their bodies than men – and older women certainly lose the sexual status that older men often retain – there is a process of equalization between women and men, in which men are now expected to use bodycare products, be well groomed and well dressed, and indeed men are beginning to become victims of traditionally "female" diseases such as anorexia.

And this should not be any surprise. Men's bodies have always been an issue, at least in terms of concepts such as strength, potency and physical activity. Connell reminds us of this:

> True masculinity is almost always thought to proceed from men's bodies – to be inherent in a male body or to express something about a male body. (Connell 1995: 44)

Morris suggests:

> The social definition of masculinity is inextricably bound with a celebration of strength, of perfect bodies. At the same time, to be masculine is not to be vulnerable. It is also linked to a celebration of youth and of taking bodily functions for granted. (Morris 1991: 93)

The idea that masculinity involves a denial of weakness, of emotions, and of frailty is very common in cultural criticism. A typical theme in films about disabled people is of the man, often a war veteran, coming to terms with loss of masculinity through impairment – and this is usually characterized or crystallized in the context of impotency or sexual incapacity. Thus films such as *The Men*, *Born on the Fourth of July* and *Waterdance* all centre on the disabled man and his difficulties in adjusting. The messages here are about stereotyped male heterosexuality, and stereotyped disabled people's dependency. Prevailing images of masculinity, and of disability, offer conflicting roles and identities. The disabled anthropologist Robert Murphy supports these assumptions:

The sex lives of most paralysed men, however, remain symbolic of a more general passivity and dependency that touches every aspect of their exist- ence and is the antithesis of the male values of direction, activity, initiative and control. (Murphy 1987: 83)

The traditional account, such as it is, of disabled masculinity rests therefore on the notion of contradiction: feminity and disability reinforce each other, masculin- ity and disability conflict with each other. As Connell suggests,

The constitution of masculinity through bodily performance means that gender is vulnerable when the performance cannot be sustained – for instance, as a result of physical disability. (Connell 1995: 54)

However, care needs to be exercised: the lives of real disabled men, involving negotiation and redefinition and continuity as well as change, offer a more complex and sophisticated reality than assumptions may imply. Neither masculinity, nor disability, should be reduced to the level of physical determination, and it is neces- sary to be open to the variety of strategies employed by different disabled men.

Disabling sex

One of the problems, for disabled men, and for men in general, is that male sexu- ality is conceived traditionally in a phallocentric and oppressive way. The quotation above from Robert Murphy gives a clue to the way that this affects disabled men. He argues that men are more affected by the effects of paraplegia or tetraplegia on sexual function than are women. He talks of impotence as akin to castration, and views alternative forms of sexual expression as inferior to penetrative sex:

Whatever the alternative, his standing as a man has been compromised far more than has been the woman's status. He has been effectively emascu- lated. (Murphy 1987: 83)

Murphy seems here to be making certain assumptions, based on perceived gender roles and expectations, which are highly subjective, and in many cases sexist. Murphy's view of male sexuality seems particularly prevalent. Popular notions of disabled masculinity focus obsessively on perceived impotence and lack of man- hood. *Lady Chatterly's lover*, and films such as *Waterdance* and *Forrest Gump* reinforce the idea of disabled men being excluded from sexual activity because of erectile failure, and consequently of being less than men.

The medicalization of male sexual dysfunction and the reification of human sexuality has been wittily described by Tiefer (1995). She argues that much sex- ology is more to do with patriarchal and heterosexual ideology than any actual appropriate or effective sexual functioning. This narrow notion of normal sexuality

51

– which is focused primarily on the male erection – is detrimental to the sexual and psychological health of both men and women. My point here is that it is particularly oppressive and undermining of disabled men.

A recognition of the continuum of sexual practices – of which penetrative sex is only a part – and a greater willingness to embrace diversity, experimentation and the use of sexual toys and other alternative techniques would be of value to all sexually active people, not just to those who happen to have impairments. Don Smith writes, in an American collection:

> I felt asexual for a long time because a man's sex was supposed to be in his penis, and I couldn't feel my penis. So that contributed to my feelings of being asexual; it didn't occur to me that it felt good to have the back of my neck licked, or that it felt good to have my arms stroked lightly. Stroking the wrists, then to the arms, then up the arms, is a sequence that I've since learned can be very exciting. (Bullard & Knight 1981: 16)

Sexologist Milton Diamond writes about the importance of doing away with false expectations:

> . . . do away with the "myth", which, in essence, states that the only satisfactory means of expressing oneself sexually and achieving satisfaction is with an erect penis in a well-lubricated vagina. For the able-bodied as well as the handicapped, sexual satisfaction is possible without these practices and, in fact, may even be more satisfying. (Diamond 1984: 217)

Disabling masculinity

I have been concerned to make connections between disability and masculinity and sexuality. Before engaging with the practical interplay of these ideas, I want to make another conceptual suggestion, which is that masculinity as an ideological and psychological process is connected to prejudice against disabled people in general. The idea has been explored more fully elsewhere (Shakespeare 1994), but in essence relies on the commonplace argument that male identity rests on separation from, and superiority to, "the other". The theory originates with Simone de Beauvoir and has been elaborated by Susan Griffin and other feminist thinkers. It is that suggested white heterosexual men construct themselves in opposition to: women, nature, children, black people and gay men. Masculine ideology rests on a negation of vulnerability, weakness, and ultimately even of the body itself. Such elements are denied, and projected onto the other, who is subsequently denigrated and rejected. Misogyny, racism and homophobia are examples of this process.

I suggest that disabled people can be conceived of as "others". In films and other cultural forms, disabled characters act as vehicles for the feelings and anxieties of the non-disabled viewer: disability is used as a metaphor for tragedy, or heroism, or evil. Western thought since Descartes has been based on the separation of mind and body, the distinction between rationality and irrationality, and the distinction between humans and animals; disabled people challenge these distinctions. Because disabled people can represent lack of control, frailty, mortality and the restrictions of the physical, they serve as the opposite, or the other, to the Western rational order, which Seidler and others have identified with masculinity. If there is accuracy in this suggestion, then it becomes clear that what Connell (1995) calls "hegemonic masculinity" does not only undermine disabled men's subjectivity, but also has a role in the generation and maintenance of prejudice against disabled people in general.

Research findings

Gerschick & Miller (1995) investigated the clash between hegemonic masculinity and social perceptions of disability as weakness through interviews with ten disabled men. They found three dominant strategies employed: reformulation, which entailed men redefining masculinity according to their own terms; reliance, which entailed men internalizing traditional meanings of masculinity and attempting to continue to meet these expectations; and rejection, which was about creating alternative masculine identities and subcultures. Those who followed the second strategy encountered the most problems, due to their inability to meet social standards of masculinity. Often this resulted in anger, frustration and depression. The first group, through altering their ways of thinking, and adapting masculine ideals to their own lifestyle possibilities, achieved considerable success by departing from tradition. The third group went further in letting go of conventional gender identity and rejecting the ideology of masculinity: often this was linked to membership of the disability rights movement, with its alternative value system and support structures. The authors argue:

> Thus, men with disabilities who rejected or renounced masculinity did so as a process of deviance disavowal. They realised it was societal conceptions of masculinity, rather than themselves, that were problematic. In doing so, they were able to create alternative gender practices. (Gerschick & Miller 1995: 202)

This research highlights the range of disabled masculinities, and the variations in disabled male identity and experience. These variations were also found in the research I conducted with colleagues for the book *The sexual politics of disability*. We interviewed twenty-one disabled men and gathered responses that challenged stereotypes of both masculinity and disability. Our research suggests not just that disabled men differ from one another, but that individual disabled men receive and embody contradictory and confusing messages:

> I get mixed messages. As a disabled person I am told to be meek and mild, childlike. Yet as a man I am meant to be masterful, a leader, get angry. (Nigel)

In some ways, disabled men are not "real men", they do not have access to physical strength or social status in the conventional way, as these respondents reveal:

> Because my disability means that most women are stronger than me, like when it comes to opening a train door, so I would like to think I am not as sexist as an able-bodied man is, because if, like, I couldn't open a bottle, I would get who ever was with me, a woman or male friend to do it. So the strength thing doesn't relate to me, most women are stronger than me. I never actually thought about the masculinity thing, it's never to come into it, because I just assume that most people are stronger than me anyway. (Jeremy)

> So I suppose I grew up with the feeling of not being very physically strong and even now I feel like that. Walking down a dark street at night I don't like . . . if someone was to jump from the shadows and attack me, I don't feel like I could defend myself. Society doesn't expect you to be physically strong if you are disabled. (Patrick)

> . . . you know, if you go to a restaurant with somebody, it's always the man's place to pay the bill and stuff like that, whereas I find if you're disabled it's not necessarily your place to pay the bill, because you're the poor little disabled person that presumably hasn't got much money . . . I find it highly frustrating when I go in with another able-bodied person, and they automatically present the bill to the able-bodied person instead of me, and I have on occasions said "Actually, I'm paying the bill", they have said "OOPS, sorry!" and got rather embarrassed. (Michael)

> The general stereotype of a man is of a strong person, a person who is able, and can take command. Now because of the number of friends who actually accept that I am dominant and fairly able, I do tend to take control in situations like that, but in a lot of society I am treated as this rather wimpish person who can't make their own decisions. Unfortunately this means that I am unable to put over to some people the fact that I am male. (Zebedee)

Disabled men do not automatically enjoy the power and privileges of non-disabled men, and cannot be assumed to have access to the same physical resources. Moreover, masculinity may be experienced negatively in a way which is rare for heterosexual non-disabled men, although it could be argued that many non-disabled men also cannot attain, or actively reject, the assertive and physically dominant style of conventional masculinity.

By focusing on one disabled man, Eddie, a heterosexual, white, working-class man in his late twenties, we can develop a picture of the complexity of disabled masculinity, which bears out the previous assertion:

> One of the interesting things, I feel, is that with the exception of gays, males don't get hassle, whereas you suffer a form of sexual oppression as a disabled man. I very much see myself as a disabled man, not as a heterosexual man.

Clearly, gay men develop a masculinity that often diverges from the norm. The testimony of Eddie and other heterosexual disabled men seemed somewhat reminiscent of gay non-disabled men:

> I was always a good listener, and I was like a big brother figure for those girls who I fancied. When I fancied a girl, I wouldn't tell her. I was seen as a really good guy, you had a good laugh, I would always listen. Most women saw me as a big brother, rather than a boyfriend, and certainly safe.

Equally, there was a suggestion by some gay men that their sexuality was related to the impact of disability on their masculinity. Others had submerged their feelings of physical difference in being sexually different: they were "out" gay men, but had not come to terms with their impairment.

The benefits of better relations with the opposite sex, albeit achieved at the cost of being seen as potential sexual partners, is paralleled with a self-image and attitude to dress that could be associated with traditional female stereotypes. Eddie felt his image did not measure up to the desirable masculinity to which he aspired:

> There is this thing which I believed for a while, that I was ugly, but it had nothing to do with my facial features, it was because I was disabled . . . But some people can feel kind of okay about themselves, well I find it very hard to do, I feel like this idea of good looking would be quite handsome, not overweight, muscular . . .

He made a specific comparison with women's experience:

> . . . I see a shirt on some people, some youngster's wearing it, and I think, wow, I want that shirt, and I wear it and I think, "God you look awful". Women have that, they see a beautiful dress and they put it on and they think, "God I'm ugly".

Like many disabled men, and women, Eddie had particular issues about looking at himself in a mirror. In this context it is important to observe that disabled people often experience the unwanted attentions, intrusions and stares with which non-disabled women are familiar.

The assumption, mentioned by a number of male respondents, that because of their impairment disabled men are perceived as safe, is an example of biological reductionism. There is certainly evidence that disabled men are capable of violence and abuse towards women, children and other men. Paradoxically, despite the assumptions of his women friends, for Eddie his working-class background meant that "being a man" involved physical strength, and his impairment was no obstacle to expressing this aspect of masculinity:

> I was involved in a lot of fights outside school, although I would never fight a disabled person. A lot of people took the piss out of me, and my brothers had taught me from an early age about fighting. I was in a posi-tion where people would take the piss out of me and I would fight back ... I gave people good hidings! It wasn't a problem that I was in a wheelchair, in fact it was an advantage. I couldn't do anything, and then they would come closer, and then I would smack them in. I would put myself into a position where I knew someone would attack me, and then I would hit them, and feel justified in hitting them ... I had all these problems at school, they thought my dad was abusing me, I would go in with a black eye and I had been fighting in the streets, and they couldn't accept a disabled person had been fighting.

The complexities and contradictions revealed in Eddie's identity and history seen endemic to disabled masculinity, and probably to masculinity in general.

Clearly, there are differences between disabled men due to sexuality, ethnicity and class, as well as factors such as the type of impairment (visible, invisible, con-genital, acquired). As Gershick & Miller (1995) have recorded, different disabled men employ different strategies of rejecting, reformulating or reaffirming traditional masculinity. Some disabled men are hypermasculine, often those involved in sports, while others are "new men". Most are a mixture of various elements. While some have problems with body image, or self-identity, or sexuality, others have success-fully adapted or redefined their practices in ways of which many non-disabled men might be envious. Perhaps it would be appropriate to conclude this section with the testimony of one of our female respondents:

> I just think that, actually the two probably most successful sexual relation-ships I have had have been with wheelchair users. Often disabled men are more erotic and caring. The two men that I have had sexual relationships with who were wheelchair users gave me the most mind blowing sexual experiences that I have ever had in my life. (Paula)

Conclusion

This overview of the relationship between masculinity and disability challenges some of the things that we may take for granted about disability, and reinforces an increasing body of work on the variability of the former. It is necessary to deconstruct and decode masculinities, including disabled versions. I think that non-disabled men have things to learn from disabled men, and could profitably share insights into gender relations, sexuality and, in particular, issues of physicality and the body.

The experiences of disabled men remind us of what we know from the testimony of gay men: that men can be victims, as well as oppressors. Disabled men face social exclusion, poverty, violence and abuse. Disabled people are twice as likely to experience physical and sexual abuse as non-disabled people, and this abuse affects both men and women. This testimony will stand for the many disabled men who described such experiences to us:

> I was sexually abused when aged 6. It often happened, if I tried to resist I was hit very hard. Even these days I still have nightmares. (Mark)

But it would be wrong to conclude from this that disabled men were always victims. Some politicized disabled men link their own experiences to those of other oppressed groups, and develop better ways of relating to people. Others do not. It is clear that disabled men sometimes use pornography and prostitution, and are capable of oppressive behaviour towards women, children and other men. Several respondents told us about their exploitative behaviour towards women. Men can be victims and oppressors at the same time.

Much of what is traditionally associated with masculinity is in fact generative of impairment: fast cars, violence and war, excessive consumption, recklessness and risk, sport, and work, all contribute towards injury and illness. It is important to bear in mind the Canadian term for non-disabled people, "temporarily able-bodied". For many men, impairment and disability will become a personal reality later in life, perhaps even in youth. It can be a particular crisis for the able-bodied man when he loses physical prowess, because so much of his identity is constructed on the basis of strength and invulnerability. A poignant reminder of the frailty that is at the heart of male bodily power is represented by the experience of Christopher Reeve, the American actor who played the role of Superman. Injured in a riding accident, he is now tetraplegic. With other screen idols, such as Steve MacQueen, Montgomery Clift and, of course, James Dean, the image of masculinity has proved all too fragile. It's no coincidence that the latter two are also highly sexually ambiguous. Binary oppositions between straight and gay, disabled and non-disabled are inaccurate and oppressive ideologies, which obscure the continuities of disability and sexuality. Rather than "normal" and "other", we should instead offer "difference".

It is vital not to buy into screen myths and models of masculinity, which are inapplicable to the majority of men, let alone disabled men. It is time to redefine masculinity in less oppressive, more open, more acceptable ways, which draw on the lived experience of men and the potentiality of men for change and self-improvement. The models for such masculinity may well prove to exist on the margins, in the lives of disabled men, gay men, "new men" and others who have had the foresight and courage to reject hegemonic masculinity. It is my belief that this process will involve not only redefinitions of gender relations, but will also have significant implications for the concept and experience of disability itself.

References

BULLARD, D. & S. KNIGHT (eds) (1981) *Sexuality and physical disability*. St Louis, MI: C. V. MOSBY.

CHAPKIS, W. (1986) *Beauty secrets: Women and the politics of appearance*. London: Women's Press.

CONNELL, R. W. (1995) *Masculinities*. Cambridge: Polity.

DEEGAN, M. J. & N. A. BROOKS (eds) (1985) *Women and disability: The double handicap*. New Brunswick NJ: Transaction Books.

DIAMOND, M. (1984) Sexuality and the handicapped. In *The psychological and social impact of physical disability*, R. P. MARINELLI & A. DELL ORTO, (eds). New York: Springer.

FINE, M. & A. ASCH (1985) Disabled women: sexism without the pedestal. In *Women and disability: The double handicap*, M. J. DEEGAN & N. A. BROOKS (eds), 6–22. New Brunswick NJ: Transaction Books.

GERSCHICK, T. J. & A. S. MILLER (1995) Coming to terms. In *Men's health and illness*, D. SABO & D. GORDON (eds), 183–204. London: Sage.

MORRIS, J. (1991) *Pride against prejudice*. London: Women's Press.

MORRIS, J. (1993) Gender and disability. In *Disabling barriers, enabling environments*, J. SWAIN. V. FINKELSTEIN, S. FRENCH & M. OLIVER (eds), 85–92. London: Sage.

MORRIS, J. (1996) *Encounters with strangers: Feminism and disability*. London: Women's Press.

MURPHY, R. (1987) *The body silent*. London: Phoenix House.

OLIVER, M. (1990) *The politics of disablement*. Basingstoke: Macmillan.

SHAKESPEARE, T. (1994) Cultural representation of disabled people: dustbins for disavowal? *Disability and Society* **9**(3), 283–99.

SHAKESPEARE, T., K. GILLESPIE-SELLS, D. DAVIES (1996) *The sexual politics of disability: Untold desires*. London: Cassell.

TIEFER, L. (1995) *Sex is not a natural act*. Oxford: Westview.

Chapter Six

Working with black men for change: the use of participatory research as an empowerment tool

Wanda Thomas Bernard

Introduction

Black men of African heritage are one of the most devalued groups in Western society. Shortly before his untimely death, the world-renowned tennis player Arthur Ashe was interviewed by Charlie Rose on NBC. Rose began by asking Ashe "What was more difficult . . . being a black man, or having AIDS?" Without a moment of hesitation, Arthur Ashe simply responded "Being a black man, because everyday of my life I have had to face racism as a black man". This statement, by a powerful, rich African American man, who was dying of a dreaded disease, aptly sets the social content in which black men of African descent must struggle to survive. The negative statistics about black men can be overwhelming. The overrepresentation in prison populations. The underrepresentation in further education. The "significantly" smaller pool of "marriageable" brothers. I could go on. The goal of this chapter is to examine the effectiveness of participatory research as a tool for working with black men for change.

Black men and change

Generally, in Western society, for black men failure gets defined in terms of how they compare with white men in relation to "success" indicators such as education, employment and social class position. Failure is perceived as their "underrepresentation" in "successful" positions, and their "overrepresentation" in negative, stereotypical roles and positions. Reflecting on the notion of working with black men for change, it is imperative that we unpack the meaning of change. I think it is important

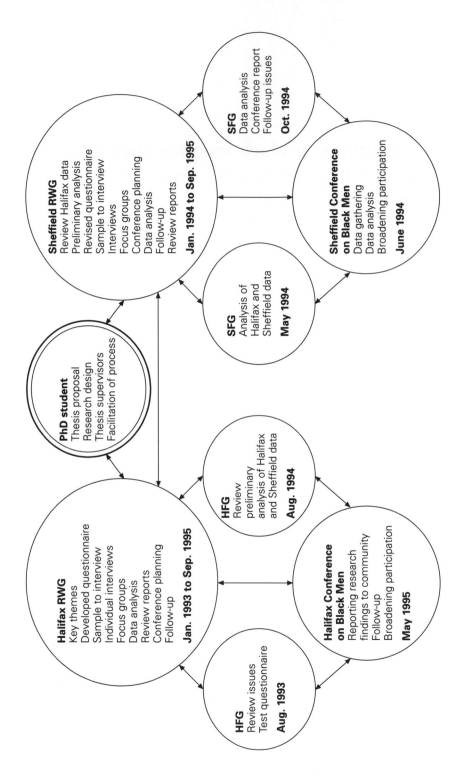

Figure 6.1 The research process used in the study.

to first examine what we mean by change, before going on to the critical subject of this chapter.

Black men have been described as an endangered species. Their overrepresentation in many negative statistics and underrepresentation in high-profile positions in society have been largely interpreted as a problem with black men. The structural barriers imposed by a system of racism and domination rooted in patriarchy are rarely examined as the root causes of "the black men problem". Unfortunately, many black men internalize such negative stereotyping, and work to fulfill those ascribed roles. However, as Hunter & Davis (1994: 37) argue, although black males may be at risk for a number of social and economic ills, within this context of risk there is also survival. The context here, working with black men for change, is referring to that element of survival. Many black men survive, using successful strategies, overcoming numerous barriers to do so. This chapter focuses on how participatory research was used as an effective tool to engage black men in a process of working for change, as defined by them.

Participatory research

Research is the production of knowledge about a given subject matter, and people who produce and control such knowledge increase their "power" to deal with the particular issues involved. Participatory research includes an educational process, action, community involvement and participation. It facilitates the production of knowledge and action directly useful to the community; and facilitates empowerment through the process of people constructing and using their own knowledge. Rarely used in academic settings, for academic credit, Ralph (1988) says that if social workers are truly committed to empowering those we study, then participatory action research is an essential tool to master. Participatory action research is a methodology that has the potential to empower participants to effect positive change in their own lives, because of the new knowledge they produce.

The research project

This participatory research project was conducted from December 1992 to September 1995 (Fig. 6.1). The arrows on the chart, indicate the interactive nature of the research. A total of ten men from Sheffield, UK, and Halifax, Canada, participated in a research working group (RWG) in their home location, and the two groups came together on two occasions. The RWGs directed the entire research: they designed, administered and transcribed the questionnaires used in individual interviews; participated in the data analysis; and edited the final report. They also helped to organize a conference in their own locale.

Forty individual interviews were conducted, twenty in each site, with black men aged 19 to over 65 years, the majority being aged between 26 and 45. In addition, two focus groups were held in Halifax and three in Sheffield. The RWG members were also interviewed, and worked collectively as two focus groups, as well as a joint group on two occasions.

The data were analyzed using a qualitative data analysis program (**Text based Alpha**) and the grounded theory method. The focus groups, the conferences and the joint RWG meetings served as multiple opportunities to conduct member checks to test the accuracy of the data and analysis. Triangulation of data collection and data analysis helps to establish trustworthiness, face validity and catalytic validity (Lather 1991).

The use of the participatory research methodology, with an Africentric theory base, has been an effective tool for this exploratory research with black men of African descent. (For a more detailed discussion on Africentric theory, see Akbar (1984), Asante (1988), Collins (1990), Schiele (1994, 1996) and Bernard (1995).) Participatory research emphasizes the active involvement of "subjects" as key in the study and resolution of their perceived problems. Ownership of the problems and proposed action strategies rests with the subjects themselves. Through this research, black men engaged in an exploration of the successful strategies used to survive in an often hostile and unfriendly terrain. Furthermore, they began a process of redefining masculinity and success from an Africentric perspective.

The social construction of masculinities

The need to theorize men and masculinity (Hearn & Morgan 1990) is becoming more widely accepted. Recent discourses have focused on the social construction of masculinities (Frank 1987; Stolenberg 1989; Kimmel 1989; Hearn & Morgan 1990). Stolenberg (1989) says that one identifies oneself in relation to other men, using some imaginary scale of masculinity. For African descended men, that scale of masculinity is imposed by the ruling class and is socially constructed. Various men's movements have begun to deconstruct masculinities; however, the issues of oppression, dominance and power continue to frame all our lives. For black men, normative definitions of masculinty have historically been outside their grasp. Harris (1992) states that African American men are in multiple jeopardy, and have historically been under attack. As a result many have argued that black men have developed highly exaggerated expressions of masculinity in order to compensate (Gary 1981; Staples 1982, 1987; Majors & Mancini Billson 1992). Few studies have actually asked black men to define themselves or to assess their strengths. In this exploratory study with "successful" (the concept of success as defined in this study is discussed in more detail later in the chapter) black men, those things which helped them to survive and succeed with their dignity intact, in an often hostile environment, were critically examined in two very different locations in the Diaspora.

Black masculinity redefined

Through this research, black men have debunked normative definitions of masculinity, and have challenged many of the pervasive negative stereotypes that have historically characterized black masculinity. The process was an identification of the survival strategies they use and their definition of success for black men. Eight survival strategies were identified through the data gathered. These are each briefly discussed below:

The survival strategies

Positive racial identity

Seventy-five per cent of the research participants from the two sites indicated that the development of a positive racial identity, through connecting with African principles and beliefs, and with others in the Diaspora, was a survival strategy that black men use. This includes: the development of love and respect for oneself and others; a positive value system; and a connection with a black African community culture.

Positive role models and mentors

The presence of positive role models and mentors was identified by ninety per cent of the participants. Role models can come from all walks of life; however, the critical point is that they must be visible and accessible. Black men want role models whom they can emulate. Mentors are considered special role models who provide a positive, caring influence and standard of conduct for young people (Wilson 1991). Mentors usually have a special relationship with the understudy.

Strong political consciousness

The development of a strong and political consciousness was also named as a survival strategy by the majority of participants. African people in Western societies have had to develop a strong political and racial consciousness and ideology to effectively combat the destruction of colonialism, slavery, racism and discrimination. This awareness is used to develop strategies for individual and collective action to challenge and change their position *vis-à-vis* the rest of society. This is evidenced in individual acts of resistance, as well as in local and more broad-based collective action and community organizing.

Positive personal values and supportive relationships

The development of positive personal values and supportive relationships with family and friends was identified by all participants as an important survival strategy. The men who were interviewed stressed the significance of displaying positive values in all aspects of one's life. In addition, the role of the family was probably identified as the most important source of strength that aided their survival. Participants named all family members as contributing to their survival, including extended family. However, the role of the mother was undoubtedly the most highly valued by most participants in both sites. As one participant said "my family has been my survival. I would not have made it without them".

Setting and working towards goals

The ability to set and work towards goals was seen as a vital component of black men's survival. The ability to dream, to set realistic goals and to work at attaining those was seen as key to survival and success. One of the most damaging effects of racism is that it inhibits our ability to dream and to set goals; it often leads to dreams deferred or lost. The men in the study have stated that in order to survive, they have first to have a dream, an ambition, a goal, and then work to realize it, breaking through many barriers to do so.

Attaining education and skills

Attaining education and marketable skills were identified by ninety per cent of the participants as key to survival. However, all participants described their educational experiences as negative in some way, and most have achieved against the odds. Self-motivation has been identified as the most significant factor in these "individual" experiences. The participants identified many blocks and barriers that they had to overcome in order to achieve a quality education and marketable skills. Many are overqualified for the jobs they are doing, and many have trained in more than one area. This was more likely to be the experience in Sheffield than in Halifax.

Employment

Finding and maintaining employment or creating self-employment were identified as elements of survival for black men. Having a job and being able to stay in employment were seen as very important. Self-employment was seen as a positive alternative in this economic climate; however, participants also recognized the costs associated with this. Participants also talked of the pressures that black men have to deal with in employment settings. So, while maintaining employment was seen as a survival strategy, participants also identified the barriers to getting employment, those faced when there, the blocks to advancement, and the stress that these create as issues that need to be addressed.

Spirituality

Spirituality was identified by approximately twenty-four per cent of our sample as a survival strategy. At the conference in Sheffield and in the RWG meetings, the role of spirituality in the survival of black men was seen as more significant than this. However, participants also expressed concern that spirituality was becoming lost in the next generation. The older respondents were more likely to name spirituality as a source of strength than were the younger men.

Summary

Clearly, the survival strategies named by black men who participated in this research, reflect a caring, sensitive, goal-oriented focus towards life. These values and qualities reflect a much different view from the normative one of black men and black masculinity. The emphasis is on positive identity, values, and responsibility for self, family and community, rather than on competition and domination. Such values are rooted in the definition of success that emerged in the research.

The Africentric definition of success

One of the most significant findings in this research has been the way in which success has been redefined by these black men. At the outset, a successful black man was defined as: one who had achieved, or was working towards a set goal(s), using positive, constructive means and was maintaining these. He was considered to be a man who managed to overcome the barriers in a racist society, and to survive. In this research, through the interviews, the focus groups and the Sheffield conference, black men described success and successful black men in terms of values, and not in terms of the material possessions usually associated with success in white society, particularly the standards set by white men.

The men who participated in this study have adopted a set of positive strategies for survival and have redefined success. They have debunked the normative definition of success, and the perception that black people have to assimilate in order to succeed. David Divine summed it up nicely at his keynote speech at the Sheffield conference "Black Men Surviving the 90s", when he said: "keys to success are not related to money or influence or sexual conquest, but to common, taken for granted values such as respect, time for self and others, integrity, being open to others, and loving oneself and others". The way in which black men have redefined success, by placing themselves in the centre of the discussion, is consistent with the theory of Africentricity (Asante 1988), and the Africentric value system as developed by Karenga (1978). Examination of the data from an Africentric feminist perspective reveals that black men's definitions of success reflect the practice of Africentricity through their lived experiences of the Africentric value system, Nugzo Saba, and the survival strategies that have been identified. These values are based on the principle of collective struggle, shared history, resistance and unity. These are the models of success that African descended people should aspire to!

We need to let go of class-based divisions and categories in our society, and focus attention on those aspects of ourselves that we have ultimate control of: self-respect, identity and self-image. We have to create filters that are positive and alternatives to those offered in society at large. What I am talking about can be compared with what we have done with racial identity, in the shedding of white society's definitions of beauty and cultural ethos. The movements that have brought us to where we are today enable us to discard those externally imposed definitions of who we are. The findings in this research suggest that we have to go through a similar process regarding how we define success. The process must begin with discarding those externally imposed indicators and measurements of success, and create a new image of what success means for African people. An Africentric definition of success, that is not just about self-achievement and attainment, but is also a recognition that many contribute to one's success and one is only successful if one is contributing to someone else's success. The African proverb "I am because you are; you are therefore I am" aptly sums up this concept. This definition of success is rooted in the Africentric values of collectivity, harmony, unity and interdependence.

Implications

This research is an example of the power of research in working with black men for change. Through this work we learned that some of the key components of change – resistance, hope and empowerment – are present among this group of black men, whom many have written off as an endangered species. I want to conclude this piece with first voice illustrations of resistance, hope and empowerment, which emerged through this participatory research.

Resistance

The Oxford dictionary defines **resistance** as "the power to resist something" or "an influence that hinders or stops something". In a review of relevant literature, Forbes

(1990) concluded that historically the African American response to colonization has been visibly characterized by a determined commitment to organized resistance to enslavement and disenfranchisement. The first step in our liberation is to resist oppression and to stop colluding with our own oppression. The evidence in these findings suggests that this resistance is viable through in the Africentric value of *Kujichaqulia*, which means self-determination. Proponents of *Kujichaqulia* argue that we define ourselves, speak for ourselves and advocate for ourselves. Asante (1987) states that the entire history of Africans in the Diaspora is marked by resistance to colonization and slavery. Such self-determination and self-definition comprise an act of resistance, and are illuminated in the following quotations:

> In future I would hope that black men would look at themselves in a different light; to be more respectful of each other; to shed feelings of inferiority; to deal more positively with all the negative messages. I hope they feel more positive about themselves, instead of falling into the trap of thinking they cannot accomplish things. I would like to see black men get together to talk about real issues, like family values, community and economic development, as well as the fun things. I would like to see more of an interest in helping each other, and more serious involvement as partners, fathers, brothers, uncles, mentors and role models, promoting family values, commitment and spirituality. That is where our strength as a people comes from. We have to stop trying to impress white society and do more to bring all black people strength. (SRWG)

> I hope that readers of this research will have a better understanding of what it is like to grow to and try to attain education, have good values and morals as a black man, given all the obstacles that are put before us. We are not on a level playing field with our white counterparts. I want people to understand this. Black people reading this must understand that there are obstacles before us, and to survive, we must develop strategies to overcome these. For white society, I want you to understand that the barriers are there, and you have some responsibility for helping to break these down, if you want to be part of a more egalitarian society. It is time for all of society to stop pretending that these problems do not exist, and to stop blaming the victims. We must face the problems, and confront them if we want to make a difference. (HRWG)

Hope

Equally important to resistance, is the reclaiming of hope, much of which rests with the next generation. The Africentric value *Nia* (purpose) means to make our collective vocation the building and developing of our community in order to restore our people to their traditional greatness. Oliver (1989) states that this value encourages a commitment to eradicating structural oppression that impedes the progress of African people. *Nia* (purpose) is not possible without a living hope that things will and can change. Fulfilling our purpose will ensure that our hopes are fulfilled. Bishop (1994) says that hope is something we should build into social-change organizations, because our recovery of hope is key to our liberation.

> In the future I hope that we will come up with specific action plans regarding how the black community can benefit from this research. I hope that people will take the opportunity to re-evaluate their priorities and their way of life, to see how they may influence their family, so that the community will survive and perhaps prosper more than they are today. I hope we take real ownership of the research and do something with it. We have to learn to mobilize our own resources to put them in motion. (HRWG)

> I hope that young people will benefit from this work. They need to know that they can do things, and that we will help in any way we can. We may not always agree, but we understand what they are going through. Things will have to change in the future, especially in the area of education. We need more skills based training, especially for young black men who have left the school system. Many of these guys have talents and skills that have not been recognized or developed. Progress has been made, but there is still more to be done. I see progress in collectivity; our children are making a difference. (SRWG)

Empowerment

Finally, with resistance and hope, there is empowerment. Empowerment is defined as an increase in interpersonal, traditional and political power, which enables people to take action to improve their situation (Gutierrez 1990). On an individual or intrapersonal level, empowerment is a process whereby subordinated individuals or group members increase their skills to exercise influence and perform social roles (Solomon 1976, cited in Swigonski 1995). Empowerment is the healing of individual and collective wounds, enabling individuals and groups to self-define, name oppression, and challenge the social structure and social order. This participatory research has engaged men in a social change process. It is an excellent example of empowerment in action. The following quotations are illustrative of the "empowerment" gained by the black men in this research:

> As people read this report, I want them to know that black men worked together on this research in a way that respected other people's feelings, and that we did this work in support of a black sister. The struggles for

black men and the black communities are real; we cannot change things overnight, but we can make positive steps for future generations. It is important for people to realize the amount of work that has gone into this research, to achieve this goal. I want people to realize that during the three years we worked on this project, Wanda was able to motivate people to get things done through her positive agenda of giving back to the black community. We have received a lot of education from being involved in this project. Most important, it gave us the opportunity to be educated about ourselves, our struggles, and academia, both in Halifax and Sheffield. There are many black men and women out there struggling on their own. We can teach these survival strategies that have worked for us. (HRWG)

I hope that those who read this report will get a better understanding of black men and see that we are not these ebony statues or figurines without emotions, thoughts, feelings or ideas; that we do have goals, and potential, and we can define what ultimately makes us happy. During and after reading this report, readers will receive notice that we are taking ourselves off the endangered species list. (HRWG)

This concurs with Blake & Darling's (1994) assertion that African men must be their own liberators.

Conclusions

Through this research, black men have become more aware of their collective power to change some of what they experience. The ability to self-define masculinity and success is an act of resistance (Collins 1990) and a tool for empowerment.

Working with black men for change requires a process of de-colonization, and a reclaiming of Africentric values and traditions. The interconnectedness and interdependence will help facilitate the successful transition into manhood, as defined by black men, for young black men. This calls for mobilization of resources, both human and material, to develop and implement action strategies that will help to develop more positive choices for the critical mass of black men of African descent throughout the Diaspora. As a Halifax RWG member stated "We must get rid of personal agendas. We have a framework, and need resources to put them into motion". And another voice in Sheffield said "Some of what we are experiencing has been conditioned into us for hundreds of years, but some of us are already working on it within ourselves and with our children". Many of these men now recognize their collective responsibility to also do this within our communities. As Roberts (1994: 38) states, "[African American] men should find support and insight for overcoming societal obstacles within their all-male groups and friendships". Our research findings suggest that, in addition to support, insight and understanding of effective survival strategies, the collective voice of black men is a potential vehicle for creative social action and social change.

The use of participatory research has been an effective tool in mobilizing black men to work collectively for change; that is, change which is managed and directed by black men themselves. This work is illustrative of empowerment in action. (As a result of their involvement in this research and the Halifax conference, black men in Nova Scotia have held two follow-up events: a retreat in March 1996, and a convention in October 1996. These gatherings have led to the organization of a provincial network, provisionally named the Congress of Black Men.)

References

AKBAR, N. (1984) Africentric social sciences for human liberation. *Journal of Black Studies* **14**, 395–414.

ASANTE, M. K. (1988) *Afrocentricity*. Africa World Press Inc: New Jersey.

ASANTE, M. (1987) *The Afrocentric idea*. Temple University Press: Philadelphia.

BERNARD, W. T. (1995) *Survival and success: as defined by black men in Sheffield, England and Halifax, Canada*. PhD thesis, Sheffield University, UK.

BISHOP, A. (1994) *Becoming an ally*. Halifax: Fernwood.

BLAKE, W. M. & C. A. DARLING (1994) The dilemmas of the African American male. *Journal of Black Studies* **24**(4), 402–15.

COLLINS, P. H. (1990) *Black feminist thought*. New York: Routledge.

FORBES, E. (1990) African American resistance to colonization. *Journal of Black Studies* **21**(2), 210–23.

FRANK, B. (1987) Hegemonic heterosexual masculinity *Studies in political economy*, Vol. 24, Autumn, 159–70.

GARY, L. E. (1981) (ed.) *Black men*. Sage: California.

GUTIERREZ, L. M. (1990) Working with women of color: an empowerment perspective. *Social Work*, March, 149–53.

HARRIS, S. M. (1992) Black male masculinity and same-sex friendships. *The Western Journal of Black Studies* **16**(2), 4–81.

HEARN, J. & MORGAN, D. (1990) *Men, masculinities and social theory*. London: Unwin Hyman.

HOOKS, B. (1988) *Talking back, thinking feminist, thinking black*. Between the Lines. Toronto: Canada.

HUNTER, A. G. & DAVIS, J. E. (1994) Hidden voices of black men: The meaning, structure, and complexity of manhood. *Journal of Black Studies* **25**(1), Sept. 1994, 20–40.

KARENGA, M. (1978) *Essays on struggle: Position and analysis*. San Diego: Kawaida Publications.

KIMMEL, M. S. (1987) Rethinking "masculinity": New directions in research, in Kimmel (ed.) *Changing men*, Ch. I, 9–24. California: Sage Publications.

LATHER, P. (1991) Getting smart: Feminist research & pedagogy within the post modern. New York: Routledge.

MAJORS, R. and MANCINI, B. (1992) *Cool pose: The dilemmas of black manhood in America*. New York: Touchstone, Simone and Schuster.

OLIVER, W. (1989) Black males and social problems, prevention through Afrocentric socialization. *Journal of Black Studies* **20**(1), 15–39.

RALPH, D. (1988) Research from the bottom. Lessons participatory research has for feminists. *Canadian Review of Social Policy* **22**, 36–40.

ROBERTS, G. W. (1994) Brother to brother. African American modes of relating among men. *Journal of Black Studies* **24**(4), June 1994, 379–90.

SCHIELE, J. (1994) Afrocentricity –, implications for higher education. *Journal of Black Studies* **25**(2), 150–69.

SCHIELE, J. (1996) Afrocentricity: an emerging paradigm in social work. *Journal of Black Studies* **41**(3), 284–94.

STAPLES, R. (1982). Black masculinity. The black male's role in American society. San Francisco, California: The Black Scholar Press.

STOLENBERG, J. (1989) *Refusing to be a man. Essays on sex and justice*. New York: Penguin Books Ltd.

SWIGONSKI, M. (1995) Claiming a lesbian identity as an act of empowerment. *Affilia* **10**(4), 413–25.

WILSON, A. N. (1991) *Understanding black adolescent male violence: Its remediation and prevention*. New York: Afrikan World InfoSystems.

Chapter Seven

Men in therapy: opportunity and change

Keith Tudor

Introduction

It is a commonplace claim that men are in crisis about their physical and psycho-logical health. The existence and nature of this crisis may be deduced from the following statistics on health and illness:

- Fetal mortality is higher in males during early and late stages of fetal development (Waldron 1986).
- Life-expectancy is lower in men than in women: 72.4 compared with 78.1 years (Office of Health Economics 1992).
- The number of deaths through diseases of the circulatory system (heart attacks and strokes) and through external injury and poisoning (accidents and suicides) is higher in men than in women (Department of Health 1993).
- Acquired immune deficiency syndrome (AIDS) affects nine times as many men as women.
- More than ten times as many men than women are found in surveys of homelessness (Department of Health 1993).
- Men have more unhealthy lifestyles compared with women (Department of Health 1993).
- Of opiod addicts notified to the Home Office, 75 per cent are men (National Audit of Drug Misuse Statistics 1990).
- Although women are more likely than men to get depressed or to harm themselves, suicide rates among men are increasing (and are decreasing amongst women) (Charlton et al. 1993).

The intention of citing such statistics is *not* to claim that men are victims of circumstances or of their "nature"; indeed, perhaps the most significant fact is about men's attitude to their health. Generally, men do not go to see their doctor about health matters, waiting until there is a crisis and then getting admitted to hospital in an emergency; this is also reflected in statistics about dental check-ups (Office for Population Censuses and Surveys 1991). Those men who do go to their GP are less likely than women to tell them that they feel anxious or depressed (Corney 1990).

This represents a level of discounting on the part of men of the existence of any problems and of the significance of the stimulus ("No, I feel fine, I've always had a pain there"). Such discounting is expressed by men in various ways: not minding (as in "I don't mind . . ."); being addicted to alcohol, drugs, pornography, sex, television, etc.; working hard, keeping busy; being violent towards others, particularly women; talking and doing rather than being and feeling – even talking about the crisis of masculinity!

Danger? – men at work

There are ways out of such crises – indeed, *through* crisis. In Chinese calligraphy the characters that comprise the word "crisis" translate as "danger" and "opportunity". Thus the crises of health identified above involve danger to men and others and at the same time offer opportunities – specifically, for the present discussion, opportunities to change. Of course, the solutions to some crises require structural change at a societal level. The impact of patriarchy and capitalism on people is not diminished or overthrown by good intentions or even good analysis. Homelessness and unemployment are not "cured" simply by a change of mind; they may be viewed as crises that require a change of mind, heart, soul and policy, backed up by some redistribution of economic resources. The focus of other solutions is more personal, requiring, as it were, structral change at a personal or psychological level. While the stimulus for personal change takes many forms, such as life experiences and life events, a crisis, the influence of others, or a desire to develop, one solution, at least over the last hundred years, is seen to be in therapy; which, literally, means healing (Gk *therapia*, healing) (*psych*otherapy means "soul healing" – (Gk) *psyche*, soul; later taken to mean "mind"). In this chapter I use the generic term "therapy" to include forms of psychotherapy, counselling and psychological counselling.

For as long as therapy has existed, so too have its critics, claiming, variously, that it is elitist, individualizing, not proven and even dangerous. In the field of working with men who are violent, for instance, there is a lot of suspicion of programmes involved with helping men to change; indeed, some view such an enterprise in itself as dangerous in the sense that, through therapy or some form of psychosocial (re-)education, men may become more adept at being abusive. Such views are based on certain underlying assumptions and theories about human nature, motivation and change – and, in my view, deterministic views (Tudor, 1995a) – which focus more on danger than opportunity. Therapy may be seen as the means of change: taking the opportunity of crisis rather than staying with the danger and dangerousness. Secondly, the social (*extra-psychic*) and the personal (*intra-psychic*) worlds are intimately interrelated: our internal world is shaped by external environmental, cultural factors; our ability to impact on and change our external world is affected by our internal sense and understanding of ourselves, others and life in general. Thus therapy does not take place in a social or political vacuum and does not provide an excuse for past or present dangerous behaviour; it is personal, social and political. Moreover, genuine and lasting personal change affects social change (Tudor 1997). Men "at work" in therapy are not thereby dangerous or made more dangerous, if they are then the underlying assumptions of both the therapy and the therapist should be investigated.

In this chapter, which focuses on therapy as opportunity and change, following a discussion of how men get to therapy (how men make contact), I consider what crises men present when they come to therapy, and how these crises are understood (i.e. how the different therapeutic traditions understand the crises of men and masculinity). These three questions are illustrated by examples (duly disguised) from my practice over a number of years as a counsellor, psychotherapist and supervisor. Following these examples of men in individual therapy, I discuss the importance of working with men in group therapy, and conclude by discussing a number of features of change and how men take, and do not take, the opportunity of therapy to effect change in their lives.

How do men make contact?

Men's attitude to consulting their doctor appears to extend to initiating contact with a therapist. Heppner & Gonzales (1987) suggest several gender issues that affect men seeking therapy: it is unacceptable to have problems; it is unmanly to seek help; and it is embarrassing to reveal inadequacies – and doubly so to another man. My own experience both as a client and as a therapist supports this: men appear to find more difficulty than women in getting to therapy, an ambivalence expressed through cancelled or missed first appointments and early withdrawal from therapy. Kupers (1993) describes a series of transactions with a prospective client over his availability for therapy as a struggle for power. Drawing on the work of Habermas (1971), Bennett (1995) offers some speculative theories as to why men do not come to counselling:

> Instrumental reason has not only become the dominant ideology, but it has also become a common, almost defining, characteristic of the male psyche. Consequently . . . a consciousness and form of action that is dominated by instrumentality, will produce forms of alienation that are predominantly found in men. (Bennett 1995: 310)

Bennett identifies the types of instrumental reason summarized, with some additions, in Table 7.1.

Of course, on the other side of the client/therapist equation, such "reason" also influences male therapists. Heppner & Gonzales (1987) identify a number of issues

Table 7.1 Types of instrumental reason and their implications for men not coming to therapy (based on Bennett 1995)

Type of instrumental reason	Attitudes/key issues	Implications for therapy/not coming to therapy
Domination	You exist for my purpose. Narcissism, aggression	The therapist is seen as powerful and therefore threatening
Distance	Objectification of the other. Lack of empathy, schizoid personality	Therapy is seen as an intimate activity and therefore as threatening
Control	Control in order to minimize difference. Narcissism, symbiosis	Therapy is seen as a situation in which the client may "lose" control
Attitude of success and failure	Dualistic, "either/or" views on life. Bipolar disorders	Therapy is seen as an unknown (organic) process in which ambiguity and doubt are tolerated, even encouraged and therefore as dangerous

for male therapists – sexism, lack of acceptance, inhibition of expression, detachedness, homophobia/heterosexism – any or all of which may inhibit potential clients either from coming to therapy or from staying in therapy. These may also be factors in inhibiting men coming into therapy as practitioners: of nearly 2500 counsellors listed in the British Association for Counselling's (BAC) *Counselling and Psychotherapy Resources Directory 1997* (Palmer 1996), less than 25 per cent are men (I. Palmer, personal communication, 11 October 1996).

Although the discussion here is about change in therapy, it is important for therapists to remind themselves that therapy is not the only forum or motivating force for change. Scher et al. (1987) believe "that the psychotherapeutic encounter, although a significant format for effecting change, is not the only means available. We are committed to the belief that a variety of remediative experiences are available for changing the contemporary situation of men" (Scher et al. 1987: 15). Thus, in practice, when assessing clients, I ask the question "Why psychotherapy?" I am interested in what interest and motivation people have to come to *therapy* (as distinct from any other forum for change) at this point in their lives. This often leads to a discussion about their existing sources of social support as well as to consideration of options other than formal therapy. What distinguishes therapy from, on the one hand, personal growth or, on the other, men's groups (apart from the training and professional status of the practitioner and the organization of the group) is a clear conceptual view on the part of the therapist of the individual's development, level of disturbance and of functioning and, therefore, of their problems and the possibility of therapeutic progress and/or "cure".

What's the matter . . . ?

As far as the reasons for which men do seek help are concerned, Pleck (1987) highlights three findings from research concerning men's increasing time in family roles, men's increasing rates of psychological distress, and the nature and correlates of traditional attitudes about men's roles. In my experience, these findings are certainly represented as issues by the men with whom I have worked, as the following vignettes reflect.

Family roles
- Adam, who presented as a man with traditional values, came to therapy having been violent to his partner who had subsequently left him; he did not know where she or their three-year-old son was. He was in shock because he was not "that kind of man" and wanted to understand what had happened to him.
- Ben and Chris came to couples therapy with the "presenting problem" that their relationship was virtually non-sexual. It soon emerged that, while Ben did his "fair share" with the children, Chris felt that she was ultimately responsible for them.
- David lived in a shared house. He looked after the children of the couple with whom he lived. He had a relationship with a woman who did not live in the house. David came into therapy because he was feeling anxious, worried about his relationship, and generally "run down".

Psychological (dis)stress
- Eamon, a social worker, came across as a very pleasing person, although somewhat passive and unsure of himself. He appeared very "feminine" in his manner and style of dress. A close female friend had recently "fallen out" with him which he did not understand and about which he felt puzzled, hurt and distressed.
- Fergus came into therapy, reporting various physical complaints and signs of stress at work. Although he had recently left his partner of some years' standing, he reported feeling abandoned and isolated.

Traditional attitudes
- Gil was a successful marketing executive. He worked hard – and even harder when under stress. He was outgoing, attractive and apparently had a happy and successful marriage. Then, having worked particularly hard on one contract, he lost it, becoming quite agitated. A friend suggested that he see a therapist.
- Harold came to therapy because he was finding it difficult to cope with the revelation that his wife had been abused. He said he found it hard to believe her. He was sad and angry that she had withdrawn from him sexually, but did not express this for fear of being violent.
- In therapy, Iain, who had been diagnosed as depressed, revealed very traditional (and stereotypical) attitudes towards women – and about men.

A note on the nature of change

Each school of therapy has its own view(s) about the nature of change, in addition to which there are a number of specific models of change. Based on their studies of change outside of treatment, Prochaska & DiClemente (1992) describe a cycle of change: pre-contemplation, contemplation, determination, action, maintenance, relapse, contemplation, etc. Hay (1992) identifies a competency model of change that involves a process from immobilization, through denial, frustration, acceptance, development and application to completion – which Jim Wild applies in Chapter 14 of this book. More generally, change has been described as a turning point, or *metanoia*, which represents both the moment of change as well as change as a continuing process. West (1990), for instance, describes the moment of change and the spiritual quality of metanoia or "repentance, a change of heart, a new direction" (West 1990: 51). Emphasizing the process or dialectical praxis of therapeutic interaction, Esterson (1970) connotes metanoia with "dialectical rationality . . . an enterprise of continual and continuing reappraisal and renewal" (Esterson 1970: 240). Similarly, Clarkson, one of the founders of the metanoia Psychotherapy Training Institute in London (now Metanoia Institute), describes metanoia as a process of transformation and as a unifying (integrating) concept for describing change in life as well as in psychotherapy. Drawing on transdisciplinary sources across ancient and modern literature, she identifies various features of metanoia: intensity, despair, surrender (of a previous frame of reference), (experience of the) void, the importance of relationship, (and of) community validation, a sense of mission, and the appearance of archetypal images of transformation (Clarkson 1989) – features to which I return in the conclusion of this chapter.

Pleck (1987) identifies three broad social (and psychological) trends about men and change: continued traditionalism, superficial change, and genuine, positive change.

Social trends
- At the end of therapy, neither Jim or his therapist felt that it had touched him. Although ostensibly open to change, Jim had come into therapy because his partner had put him under some pressure to come. He was uncomfortable with the attention of individual therapy and did not want to join a group. He maintained his traditional beliefs about men and women and "nature": "I'm happy about the ways things are; in any case I'm too old to change".
- Ken, a successful businessman, came into therapy feeling low and lacking in energy. During the course of his therapy he worked through a number of issues, changing his beliefs and attitudes as well as some of his primary relationships. He and his therapist began to identify some of the blocks (historical and developmental) to his making more fundamental changes, soon after which Ken decided to end therapy: "I've looked into the abyss, I know it's there and I don't want to go into it". (Transactional analysis (see below) makes a distinction between different types of cure: social

control, symptomatic relief, transference cure and script cure (Berne 1961, 1975). Ken is an example of someone making genuine but limited changes in terms of taking charge of his actions (social control) and freely solving problems (symptomatic relief), while not making structural psychological change (transference and script cure).)

- Leroy had come into therapy wanting and needing to make changes in his life, specifically as regards his behaviour. He was isolated, he harmed himself (abusing alcohol and drugs) and others (dangerous driving), and had fixed beliefs about himself ("I'm worthless"), others ("Other people can't handle me") and life ("Life's a bitch and then you die"). He took time to trust his therapist, but then began to make changes, first making decisions about his behaviour and then changing his belief systems. Having worked in individual therapy for a couple of years, he joined a mixed therapy group, as a result of which he was further confronted about his behaviour and attitudes, particularly towards women. He continued changing: choosing a healthy lifestyle, driving within speed limits, developing new, positive beliefs, expressing his feelings, and beginning to make friends both within and outside the group.

How is therapy understood?

In terms of our understanding of men, psychoanalysis and subsequent psychological theories represent an important strand in the science of masculinity over the last hundred years. In order to understand their influence on our thinking about gender and gender relations and about the theory of therapy and clinical practice, I briefly review the legacy of the principal and different therapeutic traditions and their implications for men and masculinity. Some of the characters in the vignettes are developed in examples of the application of the various approaches.

Freud developed a view of a complex masculinity based not only on the Oedipus complex but also on an inherent bisexuality, a pre-Oedipal femininity, and a parental super-ego. Connell (1995) suggests that Freud thus "provided a method of research, 'psychoanalysis' itself; a guiding concept, the dynamic unconscious; a first map of the development of masculinity; and a warning of the necessary complexity and limits of the idea" (Connell 1995: 10). It was a later, more conservative and orthodox psychoanalytic establishment that subsumed such complexities to a view of "normal", heterosexual masculinity. As regards the clinical application of Freud's ideas, in classical psychoanalysis transference and free association enable the client to access their unconscious conflicts which, when brought to consciousness, can be properly assimilated rather than repressed.

- During the first week of a fortnight's residential therapy intensive, Eamon experimented with free association, telling his female therapist with whom he met for an hour every day whatever came into his mind.

Eamon experienced this process as very liberating. Initially, as he talked about his own "feminine" feelings he experienced himself as very young. Then he worked through negative parental views about sex and attraction, including his attraction to the therapist. Continuing the process in the second week working with a male therapist, Eamon began to feel extremely angry, initially towards the therapist and then, as he worked through this transference onto the therapist, towards his father. During this second week, Eamon projected his bad feelings onto the male therapist and his good feelings onto the female therapist, attempting in the process to split them and play them off against each other. This was confronted through interpretation, which Eamon gradually assimilated and, as a result, he began to own these parts of himself. By the end of the fortnight he was relaxing and enjoying himself more and beginning to view himself as a sexually attractive man.

Like Freud, Jung subscribed to the theory of the inherent bisexuality of human beings and a conviction that femininity is a part of man's character. However, in a number of areas, issues of gender and sexuality were central to the theoretical and personal break between Freud and Jung. Jung believed that childhood problems are caused by parental neuroses and that the libido (life energy) is not primarily sexual but a source of undifferentiated energy. While Freud attempted to understand and overcome the masculine/feminine polarity, Jung accepted and emphasized it (Jung 1989). He developed notions of *persona* – that aspect of the personality which mediates between the ego and the social world – and of *anima* in men (*animus* in women). For men, this is the archetypal "soul image" which stands for our feminine aspect, and which is informed by our images of women that we carry as individual men (e.g. a good mother, a spiteful sister) and as a human species (our Eve, Virgin, wise woman, wicked witch, etc.). In Jungian analytic psychology, the goal of therapy – as of life – is individuation or wholeness of the individual (maturity). However, because Jung essentially accepted the masculine/feminine polarity, change through analysis is, in this respect, limited to changing the balance of this duality – which is the basis for much of the psychological work specifically with men by Jungians such as Moore & Gillette (1990) and the mythopoetic men's work of Bly (1990).

- Early on in therapy David recounted a dream in which he had struggled to get to therapy and, indeed, on a number of occasions he was late for therapy, apologising profusely to the therapist. He began to talk about his various relationships, friendships and commitments both within and outside the shared house in which he lived. After a time, his therapist challenged how much work David was doing in supporting others. He became aware how angry he was with himself for allowing people to impose upon him and, later, with others for making assumptions about his availability. At this time David was having a lot of violent dreams in which he was chased. Gradually, he moved from blaming (himself and others) to having a greater sense of his own responsibility. Through the analysis of his dreams, David (re)discovered his ambivalence about his mother: both wanting her love and wanting to keep her at a distance – which he linked to how he managed his friendships. By this time David had moved out of the shared house and was living on his own. In therapy, he reported a dream in which he had been in a small room with three other figures, David had reached out to these figures and was held by them. David realized how much he wanted to love actively and consciously (as distinct from being loved, passively). At this stage, and with the encouragement of his therapist, David began to attend men's workshops and to develop a more assertive, masculine self.

Although I have represented the application of these approaches to working with men, psychoanalytic theory and therapy has not been without its critics – of its views of sexuality, culture and society. Feminists such as Deutsch (1944, 1945), Horney (1967) and Mitchell (1975) have all challenged and synthesized Freud's ideas in developing a psychology of women and of femininity, and an account of the ideological oppression of women. Others such as Foreman (1977), Moi (1981) and Wilson (1981) have, in turn, challenged any synthesizing project. Jung, too, has been criticised for his racist, national psychology (Dalal 1988; Samuels 1993). Samuels also offers a political critique of the mythopoetic aspect of the (so-called) "men's movement":

... the separation of men from women, the bifurcation around gender, the drawing of a line in the sand, and the compulsory inscription of identity on either side of that line according to anatomy – these actually lie at the heart of oppressive social organisation. (Samuels 1993: 190)

Notwithstanding such serious criticisms, it is easy to forget, a hundred years on, that early psychoanalytical insights were considered radical and even revolutionary in their implications for human sexuality, gender relations and society. Some early figures, notably Adler (a socialist) and Reich (a Marxist), were also explicitly radical in their politics, and in linking the psychoanalytic and the political spheres. Adler, the first therapist to promote an explicitly holistic and social view of the individual, argued that all human problems are essentially social in nature and that generally in society the feminine is devalued. Children (of both sexes), being powerless, in effect inhabit the "feminine" position and thus will develop doubts about their "masculinity". This has a particular impact on the development of masculinity in boys and leads to an exaggerated masculinity – what Adler referred to as the "masculine protest"; indeed, Adler took a critical view of dominating masculinities and excessive manliness (Connell 1995). Adlerian therapy comprises a (re)learning process in which the therapist confronts faulty perceptions and encourages the development of social feelings in the client through four stages: establishing a co-operative relationship, information gathering, interpretation and giving insight, and reorientation (Clifford 1996).

- Iain found his therapist's insistence on setting goals and on his responsibility as challenging. He felt that he was a victim of circumstances and of his depression. However, once Iain and his therapist agreed the goals "To feel and express my feelings, to make friends and to develop a sexual relationship", he felt some relief. He and his therapist then explored his family background, including the significance of Iain's position in the family: he was the youngest of three, having an older brother who was successful and an older sister who was initially "daddy's girl" and later his mother's companion; Iain, who had been unplanned, felt "spare". His assumption or "private logic" was to be quiet and to "get it right" by being a (traditional) man like his father. At this stage in therapy, Iain's generalizations about his life – and lifestyle – were challenged and, through the insights he gained, he began to change his assumptions about men, women and relationships. At the same time, he began a new relationship which, although short-lived, gave Iain confidence in his new learning.

Reich argued that the primary life force is genital sexuality, a force that is repressed in patriarchal–authoritarian systems – hence his interest in and analysis of *The mass psychology of fascism* (Reich 1975). Although, unlike Adler, Reich did not address the issue of masculinity directly, he developed a method of "character analysis", which describes sets of resistances or protective mechanisms that are reflected in distinct armouring of the body and need to be broken down before therapy can begin. Of Reich's character structures, his original phallic–narcissistic character is particularly associated with men, being:

> ... self-assured, sometimes arrogant, elastic, energetic, often impressive in his bearing ... his facial features usually exhibit hard and sharp masculine lines ... behavior ... is usually arrogant, either coldly reserved or contemptuously aggressive ... The aggression in his character is expressed less in what he does and says than in the way he acts ... erective potency, as opposed to orgiastic potency, is very well developed ... this character type ... reveal all the marks of obvious masculinity in their appearance. (Reich 1961: 217–19)

- Gil came to therapy extremely wary of seeking help, particularly from another man whom he saw as less obviously successful. He did not see that he had a problem other than not getting the contract at work; however, he agreed to a short-term therapy contract. In this time, he talked about his drive to succeed in life, doing things "the right way"; obstacles and opposition only made him try and work harder. Gil appeared attractive, athletic and "ready for action"; he was intelligent and quick to learn. He described how these characteristics attracted people, including his wife, but that recently she had become bored with him and he too had moved away from being intimate with her. During this time, Gil had trouble in keeping appointments: he often came late, in a rush and sometimes cancelled them at the last minute. The therapist acknowledged how much pressure Gil was under and how much effort it took to hold things together, and showed his concern for him. The therapist encouraged him to talk about his problems, without necessarily seeking a solution. At this point Gil renegotiated an open-ended contract for therapy. Gradually, he relaxed, opened up and talked more about how vulnerable he felt. Now, working in conjunction with a colleague whom Gil saw for regular massage at the therapist's suggestion, the therapist did some bodywork with him: encouraging him to slow down, to relax, to breathe deeply into his chest and his belly, and to express feelings and needs. Gil began to focus on what was pleasurable in his life and how to do things with minimal effort.

In many ways, Adler and Reich were the forefathers of humanistic psychology. Maslow (1962), who first named humanistic or "third-force" psychology, acknowledged the influence of the first two psychological traditions by describing it as "epi-Freudian" and an "epi-behavioristic" (Gk *epi*, upon). For Maslow, humanistic psychology was not only concerned with disturbance and behaviour, but also with health, human motivation, self-development and "self-actualization", values and aesthetics. The humanistic or humanistic/existential force includes many "schools" of therapy, including psychodrama, the person-centred approach, transactional analysis, gestalt therapy, existential therapy, personal construct therapy, various body oriented therapies and, arguably, feminist, intercultural, gay affirmative and transpersonal therapies – each with their own particular emphases about human nature and the nature of change. Rowan defines humanistic psychotherapy as including all approaches that value authenticity and have a concept of the real self (however this is described) (Frick 1997). In addition, in the last ten years a few books have emerged specifically on the subject of men in therapy (Scher et al. 1987; Meth & Pasick 1990; Rowan 1996) and on the psychology of men (Levant & Pollack 1995). Here I briefly consider some aspects of two humanistic approaches relevant to working with men: transactional analysis and the person-centred approach.

Transactional analysis (TA) has a tradition of translating complex psychological concepts into accessible language for use with clients. Thus Freud's (1984) "repetition compulsion" (an innate tendency to revert to or re-enact earlier conditions, often expressed through behaviour) is explained in terms of "life script", which is "an ongoing program, developed in early childhood under parental influence, which directs the individual's behavior in the most important aspects of his life" (Berne 1975: 418). In the translation, script becomes decisional rather than determined and thus in TA there is a notion – and an aim – of "script cure" or breaking free from the script. Steiner (1966) explains Freud's recognition of pre-Oedipal femininity (see the case of *Eamon* above) as a particular "non-masculinity" script, which is non-verbal, pre-conscious and visceral (gut level), and which is reinforced by *both* parents. Steiner and other colleagues also represent a tradition of radical psychiatry that, over the years, has developed ideas about men and women (Steiner 1974; Roy & Steiner 1988) and about power (Steiner 1981). In the

Box 7.1 Discounting (based on Schiff et al. 1975)

The existence of the stimulus What migraine? I don't get migraines. That's a woman's illness	**The existence of problems** I'm fine, I've always had a little pain there	**The existence of options** Well, men have always expressed themselves that way. My dad hit my mum and he loved her
The significance of the stimulus The pain? No, it's nothing serious	**The significance of problems** Well, it was only a slap	**The significance of options** Even if I changed, it wouldn't do any good. He'd still be the same
The changeability of the stimulus She really winds me up: it just gets to me	**The solvability of problems** I feel stuck, I just don't see a solution	**The viability of options** I do know someone who goes for counselling. It's just that it's not for me: it's not the sort of thing I do
The person's ability to react differently I can't leave him	**The person's ability to solve problems** I'm not very good at taking advice	**The person's ability to act on options** I know what to do, it's just that I find it hard to do it

Introduction to this chapter, I suggested that men's reluctance to seek help represents a level of discounting. In working with clients in general using TA and especially with men, I have found the discount matrix (Schiff et al. 1975) particularly useful in understanding and confronting their different levels of discounting (Box 7.1). The arrows linking boxes represent the fact that one discount (e.g. of the existence of problems) will always entail the other (i.e. the significance of the stimulus) as the different linked examples indicate.

When people discount they do so internally; that is, it is not observable unless they speak (as in the examples) or act in some way which indicates that they are discounting. Transactional analysts have identified four types of behaviour which always indicate that someone is discounting:

- *Doing nothing*: generally being passive, being silent having been asked to speak (rather than saying "I don't want to speak"), saying "My name's Peter, but I don't mind what you call me".

- *Overadaptation*: usually by being helpful, adaptable or accommodating to people and in situations by complying to what the person *believes* other people want him or her to do.
- *Agitation*: for example, drumming fingers, waggling feet, coughing (when the person does not have a cough).
- *Incapacitation or violence*: incapacitation involves being passive or becoming incapable (e.g. some forms of psychosomatic disorders such as "hysterical conversion") (Breuer & Freud 1974).

Incapacitation or violence often follows a period of agitation.

- In therapy, Harold was initially very agitated, moving around a lot in his seat and fidgeting with a handkerchief. The therapist identified this as behaviour which indicated some discounting. Harold then began to talk about his wife's abuse in some detail; as he did so, initially, he became less agitated. As he recounted her story, his therapist identified that, in not believing her ("Perhaps it was only fondling"), Harold was discounting the significance of the problem for his wife – and for himself. The therapist introduced the discount matrix to Harold, and together they identified further beliefs consistent with this level of discounting ("Well, in a way, I understand that he [the abuser] might have been lonely", "She was very attractive"). As he identified these beliefs, Harold grew silent (incapacitation). After a while he talked about how sad and angry and confused he was. This led him to discuss his childhood and family. The therapist drew up a script matrix (Steiner 1966) in which he and Harold identified the parental messages he had internalized (from his mother, disapproval for showing traditional masculine behaviour and thus "Don't be a man" and, from his father, modelling of passivity and compliance/overadaptation). Harold had grown up wanting to please both parents and had done so by being a non-traditional, passive and largely non-sexual man. Learning about his wife's sexual abuse had triggered Harold's resentment about these early messages. In therapy he was now clear of the difference between anger (a feeling) and violence (a behaviour) and redirected and expressed his anger towards his early conditioning (scripting), thus releasing himself from his parents' messages. Returning to his relationship with his wife, Harold came to accept her truth, expressing his anger towards her abuser (rather than towards her).

The person-centred approach, developed from the ideas of Rogers (for a collection of whose writing see Kirschenbaum & Henderson (1990)) has a central hypothesis that, for constructive personality change to take place, the following conditions are necessary:

- That two people (i.e. the therapist and the client) are in psychological contact.

- That the client is in a state of incongruence.
- That the therapist is genuine.
- That the therapist experiences unconditional positive regard for the client.
- That the therapist experiences empathic understanding for the client.
- That the client experiences these last two conditions (Rogers 1959, 1990).

Rogers hypothesized that these six conditions were both *necessary* and *sufficient* in order for people to change.

- Adam came into therapy in a state of shock. Initially, he only appeared interested in getting his partner and his son back. After a couple of meetings in which the therapist had not experienced himself to be in contact with Adam, he confronted him about this. Adam acknowledged that he had come to therapy initially in the hope that it would be seen as a sign of good faith by his partner (rather than *being* good faith on his part). Once he had acknowledged this, Adam began to talk more directly to the therapist about himself, how he saw the world, his feelings, how he experienced himself and others, his problems and how he related to people. In many of these areas he was quite fixed, construing the world in rigid terms ("I'm not that kind of man"). At this stage, Adam came across as being very stuck and several times expressed a desire to end therapy. On reflection in supervision, the therapist realized that he was having some difficulty in experiencing unconditional positive regard and empathic understanding for Adam, wanting instead "to make him understand" (about his need to control and dominate his partner and about the consequences of his violence). His supervisor observed that the therapist wanted "to make Adam understand" (to control and dominate him) rather than to understand him (to be empathic). The therapist experienced this as helpful and as a relief. Subsequently, the therapist worked alongside (rather than opposed to) Adam, as a result of which Adam began to experience this and to loosen up in talking about himself, his thoughts and feelings. At about this time, Adam heard from his partner that she had moved to the other end of the country and that, while she was prepared for him to have contact with their son, she wanted only minimal contact with him to effect this. This was a difficult time for Adam: on the one hand, he wanted to go down and "sort her out" and, on the other, he wanted to "sort things out with her". In those two phrases, he realized just how much conflict he experienced internally and how much he expressed – or wanted to express – externally: he was "that sort of man". He began to have some contact with his son, but found this painful. After six months of regular travelling to see him, Adam decided not to have contact with him. This led him into a period of real despair about his life and how he was. In this phase of his therapy, Adam realized how much his perceptions were distorted (for instance, about men's and women's roles) and how much he denied his own awareness (his sadness, his rage, etc.) until "it burst out". With his therapist, he actively worked through these distortions and denials and became much more genuine or congruent, more fluent emotionally and more fluid in terms of living moment by moment (rather than being stuck in and by the past). At this point, over a year after he had last seen his son, he initiated contact with his son, which was welcomed by both his son and his ex-partner.

Although therapists are influenced by particular traditions or schools of therapy (usually those in which they trained and/or those in which their own therapists were trained), many therapists are interested in and indeed trained in a number of approaches. Over the last ten years, there has been an increasing interest in integrative or integrating therapy, that is therapy which brings together different – and differing – theories of psychology. Clarkson & Gilbert (1990) suggest an integrative perspective on psychological disturbance, which I find helpful in understanding the matter as well as in working therapeutically with men. This identifies and is concerned with, respectively, an interference in functioning (confusion model), internal conflict (conflict model) and developmental deficits (deficit model). Comments that men I have worked with have made coming into therapy reflect these perspectives.

Confusion model
- I can't understand her. She wants me to be gentle and caring, a "new man" and bringing in the money and buying the drinks at the same time.
- I'm not sure how to identify myself sexually: I've only had relationships with women, I'm attracted to men but I'm afraid of that.
- I don't know what's wrong. I have a good life: plenty of sex, but I feel empty.

This last example reflects a common confusion amongst men between love, sex and affection.

Conflict model
- I feel so angry with my father. He was such a tyrant.
- God, I hate it when I'm like this: I just can't seem to do anything right.
- Sometimes I just don't feel here at all.
- I so much want to be close to my partner, but when I do I want to go miles away.

This last example reflects a common "pull–push" dynamic in men's relationships – with women and other men – a longing for, and a fear of, closeness and intimacy (Tudor 1995).

Deficit model
- I just don't know what to do. Tell me what to do.
- My dad was never there. I don't feel I had any role model of how to be a man, let alone of being a father myself.
- I'm afraid of my anger. I would never express it 'cos I'd get out of control.
- I don't think I know what feelings are.

These last two examples reflect a common emotional illiteracy amongst men, in response to which I find Steiner's (1984) work on emotional literacy useful in helping men distinguish between feelings and actions – "I feel angry, when you talk to me like that" (rather than "She made me feel angry") – and in helping men to check out what Steiner refers to as "paranoid fantasies" with the other person concerned (e.g. "I think you're fed up with me").

Other forms of integration involve integrating different traditions from both within and outside psychology and therapy. Rowan (1987, 1996), a humanistic therapist with a keen knowledge of both myth and alchemy, has written extensively about men and therapy. For real change to take place he suggests that three "levels" have to be worked through: the conscious, the unconscious and the transpersonal (Rowan 1987). More recently, he has argued that men need to be initiated into a new way of being, viewing therapy itself as initiation (Rowan 1996). Based on the medieval alchemical process, he outlines eleven phases of therapy/transformation (which may or not take place formally "in therapy") – from the primary, raw material of a person, their psyche and their problems (materia prima) through to integration (rubedo). Rowan's work represents a meeting (encounter) between humanistic and transpersonal psychology in a specific application to therapeutic/ transformational work with men.

Men in group therapy

So far, I have considered men in various crises and how different therapies and therapists understand these in the context of individual therapy. I now consider the relevance of group therapy for men in change. (This section is developed from the author's article on men in groups (Tudor 1994).)

When potential clients are interested in joining a group, following the question "Why psychotherapy?", I ask "Why group therapy?" There are two elements to this: one assesses the predicted therapeutic value of group rather than (or in addition to) individual therapy; and the second focuses on group *therapy* as distinct from other forms of group. Much has been written in the literature on groups about the first element. People are interested in joining therapy groups for learning about interpersonal processes, for a reparative experience of group (family), for various social reasons, etc. (Yallom 1995). The fundamental differences between a therapy group and, say, a men's group are: the amount of emphasis on psychological processes and individual change *in the context of a group*, and the acknowledgement, within the therapeutic relationship, of a certain reliance on an unequal therapist– client relationship. These differences, in turn, reflect two important processes for men in psychotherapy: first, a focus on subjectivity and *intersubjectivity*; and, secondly, the potential to experience a different relationship with a man in authority.

By a focus on subjectivity, I refer to the encouragement of men to focus on their subjective experiences (e.g. their feelings) rather than what is "objective" or "rational". Seidler (1989) argues that it is rationalism itself, as the basis for philosophy and social theory, which is at the root of the problems men face when they come to change. Thus, discovering our subjective sense of ourselves as men as both the content and the process of psychotherapy, also reflects an important theoretical shift. The development of intersubjectivity – in this case, the subjective experience of self and others in group therapy – follows from men's attachment to others and the group. Tiger (1984) distinguishes between bonding and male *aggregation*, "a pattern generally associated with male dominance" (Tiger 1984: 20). Men "aggregate" in groups all the time – in pubs and clubs and on street corners – in ways which relate to their "ascribed status" in society. Men rarely attach and "bond", especially with other men, in ways in which might be described as "achieved status". In therapy, the therapist has power, authority and influence (Embleton Tudor & Tudor 1994), in addition to which the gender of the therapist – male and female – means that there is a gendered quality to these factors and to the therapeutic relationship as expressed and experienced through clients' and therapists' perceptions, transference/countertransference, etc.

As men in therapy experience intersubjectivity and a working through of issues in relation to authority, the final question I ask is "Why group therapy for men?" This focuses the client and me on the differences, benefits and disadvantages of a men's therapy group as distinct from a mixed one – especially when some approaches (e.g. transactional analysis) emphasize the psychotherapeutic advantages of non-selected, heterogeneous groups. The rationale for joining – and establishing – such a therapy group is to focus on gender and to highlight gender-role concerns, in a context in which the focus is on change. As I advertise one of the groups I run as a "psychotherapy group for men", the men who contact me are already making some statement about *how* they want to deal with issues and problems: as Stein (1982: 281) puts it: "*membership in a men's group represents in itself a statement of nontraditional masculine values*". Berne (1966) suggests that one goal of a "special" (i.e. selected) group is "the abandonment of stereotyped relationship patterns" (Berne 1966: 8). Stein (1982) suggests three "types" of men for whom a men's psychotherapy group may be the desired treatment of choice: "those with significant disturbance in interpersonal relationships, those with concerns about gender identity, and those men with specific concerns related to gender-role performance" (Stein 1982: 299).

This distinction – between traditional, social male aggregation on the one hand, and male bonding, initially in the context of a therapeutic relationship on the other – is one of the major and positive reasons for men joining together in non-traditional groups and settings. Following the distinction between aggregation and bonding, attachment – which Bowlby (1981: 241) describes as "seeking and maintaining proximity to another individual" – and particularly the attachment of men with other men in the men's group, in the absence of the (stereo)typical reliance on women, is a particularly important and significant aspect of group therapy with men. Such attachments have a profound impact on the individual men in the group; some individuals develop these attachments outside the group and/or beyond the life of the group, and from this they then generalize to other relationships with both men and women in their lives outside therapy. One of the most important and moving benefits of one men's therapy group was its development as a network of friends which lasted beyond the life of the group.

"The dynamics of men's groups can be viewed in the most general sense as a struggle to achieve the expression of the entire spectrum of human attributes within an all-male setting" (Stein 1982: 289), and herein lies the excitement as well as the fear of facilitating men's therapy groups. In a foreword to Tiger's (1984b) ethnological study on *men in groups*, Morris asserts that: "human males operating in groups – talking, planning strategies, devising traps, improving weapons, sharing the spoils – became the most successful biological phenomenon on Earth. In the process, the male-grouping became an essential evolutionary element in human nature. The urge to form male 'gangs' became deeply ingrained in the human personality" (Morris 1984). This proud assertion scarcely conceals the consequence of implied violence of men operating in groups; indeed Tiger (1984) himself suggests more explicitly and honestly that "a particular characteristic of the male bond is its close interconnection with aggressive and possible violent action" (Tiger 1984: 176). Any therapeutic benefit of men meeting in groups and aim to effect expression and change, therefore, needs to be set against and, indeed, counter the history of male dominance, collusion and violence – and dominance and violence in groups.

Men in relationship and male leadership

The relationship between any client and their therapist is crucial to the process, experience and outcome of therapy. In the context of men in therapy, the relationship between the male client and his male therapist is of particular interest. For group therapists the concept and practice of leadership is vital to their role and to the life of the group (Liff 1975). The male group therapist needs "to establish a balance between leadership, which can provide some consistent direction and facilitation for group exchange, and nonadherence to traditional patterns of leadership, which are often directive, prescriptive, or authoritarian" (Stein 1982: 287). Using Clarkson's (1990, 1995) integrative model of therapeutic relationships, which was developed, in turn, from Gelso & Carter's (1985) model, I briefly summarize particular considerations regarding the significance of the therapeutic relationship and the necessary abilities in male leadership of men.

The working alliance

This forms "the ground" of the therapy: here the focus of therapy is often on establishing and maintaining a way of working together, usually defined initially through some form of agreement or contract about the work and, in an ongoing way, through a (continuous) process of contracting. Bordin (1979) conceptualizes this alliance in terms of three components: goal, task and bond. In my experience male therapists working with male clients may focus more on the goal and task in hand than on the bond, that is on "the personal, affective engagement" (Bordin 1979: 255).

- *Ability to engage with men.* The challenge for the male group therapist, then, is to make this bond with a number of clients at any one time and to encourage such bonding between group members. It involves the establishment of boundaries (group rules) and the negotiation of (group) contracts and modelling and fostering co-operation. It requires an awareness of expectations and feelings men may have of the male therapist: a man in a caring profession and role and in authority. It also requires the therapist to be prepared mentally, emotionally, spiritually and physically for therapeutic work.

The transferential/countertransferential relationship

This relationship, emphasized in some therapeutic schools or approaches more than others, is about working with "the experience of unconscious wishes and fears transferred on to or into the therapeutic partnership" (Clarkson 1995: 62) – this last phrase reflecting the fact that both client and therapist transfer across past experiences onto present relationships. Working in and with the transference, male therapists need to be able to accept and help clients work through both positive and negative projections of men, male, masculinity and authority (Frosh 1994).

- *Ability to deal with men's transference.* Working in this relationship involves a willingness and ability on the part of the therapist to deal with what male clients transfer onto him (transference) as well as his own issues evoked by clients (countertransference). This may be expressed (stereo)typically in competition between male group members and the therapist or between group members themselves. Generally, if the therapist ends up feeling smarter than the client, he has got into some competitive, psychological "game" (Berne 1968). The therapist also needs to be able to deal with men's ambivalence towards both men and women, often expressed, respectively, through fear and anger and in relation to him, and through generalizations about himself, others (men and women) and the world.

The developmentally needed or reparative relationship

This is "the intentional provision by the psychotherapist of a corrective/reparative or replenishing parental relationship (or action) where the original parenting was deficient, abusive or overprotective" (Clarkson 1990: 153). This involves clear contracting and specific understanding of, training in and experience of forms of regression therapy.

- *Ability to accept and work with men's developmental needs.* The therapist needs to be prepared, willing and able to allow and encourage men's developmental needs, from attachment to and even dependence on him, through to their need to individuate, separate and become independent from him. This involves creating a facilitative, "holding" environment both metaphorically and, depending on the therapist's theoretical orientation, practice and ethics, literally (i.e. physically). Experiencing and witnessing such reparative experiences offered by a caring – and safe – man is often evocative both for the client and for other group members.

The person-to-person relationship

This therapeutic relationship emphasizes the realness or genuineness and the mutuality of the relationship between the two people or parties involved. For male therapists working with men within this relationship, issues of personal and professional integrity and of trust and self-disclosure often arise – and, as regards the logic of mutuality – of possible friendship. A therapeutic relationship may be the first in which a male client allows himself to be emotionally and/or physically close to another man.

- *Ability to be congruent, accepting and empathic.* This involves the therapist in being genuine, accepting and empathic: in being himself in an "I–You" relationship. This is particularly important in working with men in groups in two respects.
    (i)   Just as, in working with couples or family relationships, the therapist needs to hold present any absent family member, so here the group therapist needs to be able to be congruent and accepting and to hold empathy present for the absent gender, while also being empathic with the individual man and the group of men. This enables the male therapist to achieve the delicate balance between facilitating open, uncensored communication and collusion with other men on issues of sexism and stereotyping.
    (ii) This is also important in co-facilitation whether with another man or with a woman. Co-facilitation involving two men offers the opportunity to model a non-traditional (i.e. a non-hierarchical, co-operative) relationship and patterns of leadership. (This is similarly important in co-facilitation of a therapy group by a man and

a woman, although such co-facilitation of a men's group is rare, except for some anti-violence psycho-educational programmes and in certain settings such as prisons.)

(Clarkson (1990, 1995) identifies a fifth, transpersonal therapeutic relationship which I regard as a transpersonal moment, rather than relationship, in therapy.)

Conclusion

In concluding, I refer to Clarkson's (1989) summary of the features of change and review their relevance for men changing and changing men.

- Change involves an *intensity of struggle*. A crisis is often acute and intense (rather than chronic), producing intense emotions and upheaval. Traditionally, men have struggled by fighting, in battle. Over many years I have witnessed men struggling intensely and differently in therapy to become more expressive, to change firmly held beliefs and to behave differently.
- Change involves the *surrender* of a previous way of understanding or frame of reference. Many men in therapy present or express a need to be in control, to be powerful and to be strong; we may understand this a cultural script for men (e.g. to be the breadwinner). Surrendering, to give this up, to give up control, power, certainty: all this, is frightening: "because [men] have been socialised away from feeling and toward productivity, the amorphousness of emotions can make all feeling frightening for them" (Erikson 1993: 6).
- Change involves *despair*, a hopelessness, and experience of the *void*. In the gestalt cycle of formation and destruction, there is a fertile void in which (if we spend long enough) we become aware of the next sensation. In many cultures, there are myths about journeys of descent into the (psychological) underworld of despair and hopelessness. Bly (1990) describes this as *katabasis*, or the road of ashes and descent.
- In order to effect change, we need a *sense of mission*. Over the years, I have been influenced by: liberal theology; socialist politics and values about culture, welfare, community, parenting and children; feminism and critiques of patriarchy and gender relations; and humanistic therapy. These influences have shaped my development as a man and given me a sense of mission and vocation. I believe that in order to develop as men we need to know about patriarchy and power, gender issues, women's studies, masculinity, sexuality, etc. Training in therapy is largely apolitical; indeed, raising "political" issues is even pathologized. Male – and female – therapists with a sense of mission thus need to develop a countercourse of studies on, or in addition to, their therapeutic training.

- In order to achieve specific and lasting change we need *archetypal images of transformation* such as provided by literature (poetry), art, music, myth, etc. (Bly et al. 1993). The hero's journey – as represented in stories from ancient to modern, from Ulysses to Luke Skywalker – is a potent symbol of man's transformation from innocence to wisdom.
- In effecting change the *importance of relationship* is central. This refers not only to a specific micro-therapeutic relationship, but also to the wider, macro-relationship between men and women. Genuine, respectful, accepting and understanding relationships and alliances between men and women help overcome oppressive and divisive social organization.
- Change requires *community validation*. Such validation is particularly important for men in deconstructing masculinity and male sexuality. Some men with whom I have worked have felt held back from changing – by other men and by women – who have wanted them to remain in traditional roles and subscribing to supporting beliefs. In these cases, the importance of the group as community in supporting and validating change cannot be underestimated.

Some are sceptical about men's motivation, desire and ability to change. Sustainability of any change is also questioned, especially (as noted in the Introduction) for men who are, or were, violent. However, while (stereo)typically, men have and express power in the external world, many men do not feel powerful or potent in their internal or immediate world. Through change in therapy, this is often reversed: men become more potent psychologically and, *if this change is genuine*, have no need to express their potency in traditional, negative and dangerous ways in the external, social world. Crisis is danger and opportunity; it also provides the opportunity to change and personal change inevitably effects social change in both immediate and wider social spheres.

References

BENNETT, M. (1995) Why don't men come to counselling? Some speculative theories. *Counselling* **6**(4), 310–13.

BERNE, E. (1961) *Transactional analysis psychotherapy*. New York: Grove.

BERNE, E. (1966) *Principles of group treatment*. New York: Grove.

BERNE, E. (1968) *Games people play*. Harmondsworth: Penguin. [Original work published 1964.]

BERNE, E. (1975) *What do you say after you say hello?* London: Corgi. [Original work published 1972.]

BLY, R. (1990) *Iron John*. Reading, MA: Addison-Wesley.

BLY, R., J. HILLMAN, M. MEADE (eds) (1993) *The rag and bone shop of the heart. Poems for men*. New York: Harper Perennial.

BORDIN, E. S. (1979) The generalizability of the psychoanalytic concept of the working alliance. *Psychotherapy: Theory, Research and Practice* **16**(3), 252–60.

BOWLBY, J. (1981) *Attachment and loss*, Vol. 1, *Attachment*. Harmondsworth: Penguin.

BREUER, J. & S. FREUD (1974) Studies on hysteria. In *The Penguin Freud library*, Vol. 3, *Studies on hysteria*, J. STRACHEY, A. STRACHEY, A. RICHARDS (eds), J. STRACHEY, A. STRACHEY (trans.), Harmondsworth: Penguin. [Original work published 1895.]

CHARLTON, P., S. KELLY, K. DUNNELL, B. EVANS, R. JENKINS, R. WALLIS (1993) Suicide deaths in England and Wales: Trends in factors associated with suicide deaths. In Office of Population Census and Surveys, **71**, 34–42. London: HMSO.

CLARKSON, P. (1989) Metanoia: a process of transformation. *Transactional Analysis Journal* **19**(4), 224–34.

CLARKSON, P. (1990) A multiplicity of psychotherapeutic relationships. *British Journal of Psychotherapy*, **7**(2), 148–63.

CLARKSON, P. (1995) *The therapeutic relationship*. London: Whurr.

CLARKSON, P. & M. GILBERT (1990) Transactional analysis. In *Individual therapy in Britain*, W. DRYDEN (ed.), 199–225. London: Harper & Row.

CLIFFORD, J. (1996) Alderian therapy. In *Individual therapy in Britain*, W. DRYDEN (ed.), 103 20. London: Harper & Row.

CONNELL, R. W. (1995) *Masculinities*. Cambridge: Polity.

CORNEY, R. (1990) Sex differences in general practice attendance and help seeking for minor illnesses. *Journal of Psychosomatic Research* **5**, 525–34.

DALAL, F. (1988) The racism of Jung. *Race and Class* **29**(3), 1–22.

DEPARTMENT OF HEALTH (1993) *On the state of the public health: The annual report of the Chief Medical Officer of the Department of Health for the year 1992*. London: HMSO.

DEUTSCH, H. (1944) *The psychology of women*, Vol. 1, *Girlhood*. New York: Grune & Stratton.

DEUTSCH, H. (1945) *The psychology of women*, Vol. 2, *Motherhood*. New York: Grune & Stratton.

EMBLETON TUDOR, E. & K. TUDOR (1994) The personal and the political: power, authority and influence in psychotherapy. In *The handbook of psychotherapy*, P. CLARKSON & M. POKORNEY (eds), 384–402. London: Routledge.

ERIKSON, B. M. (1993) *Helping men change – The role of the female therapist*. London: Sage.

ESTERSON, A. (1970) *The leaves of spring: A study in the dialectics of madness*. London: Tavistock.

FOREMAN, A. (1977) *Femininity as alienation*. London: Pluto.

FREUD, S. (1984) Beyond the pleasure principle. In *The Penguin Freud library*, Vol. 11, *On metapsychology. The theory of psychoanalysis*, A. RICHARDS (ed.), J. STRACHEY (trans.), 269–338. Harmondsworth: Penguin. [Original work published 1920.]

FRICK, W. B. (1997) Interview with John Rowan. *Journal of Humanistic Psychology* **37**(1), 131–56.

FROSH, S. (1994) *Sexual difference: Masculinity and psychoanalysis*. London: Routledge.

GELSO, C. J. & J. A. CARTER (1985) The relationship in counseling and psychotherapy: components, consequences and theoretical antecedents. *The Counseling Psychologist* **41**(3), 296–306.

HABERMAS, J. (1971) *Knowledge and human interest*. Boston, MA: Beacon.

HAY, J. (1992) *Transactional analysis for trainers*. London: McGraw-Hill.

HEPPNER, P. P. & D. S. GONZALES (1987) Men counseling men. In *Handbook of counseling and psychotherapy with men*, M. SCHER, M. STEVENS, G. GOOD, G. A. EICHENFIELD (eds), 30–8. Newbury Park, CA: Sage.

HORNEY, K. (1967) *Feminine psychology*. New York: W. W. Norton.

JUNG, C. J. (1989) *Aspects of the masculine*, R. F. C. HULL (trans.). London: Ark.

KIRSCHENBAUM, H. & V. L. HENDERSON (1990) *The Carl Rogers reader*. London: Constable.

KUPERS, T. A. (1993) *Revisioning men's lives: Gender, intimacy and power*. New York: Guildford.

LEVANT, R. F. & W. S. POLLACK (eds) (1995) *A new psychology of men*. New York: Basic.

LIFF, Z. A. (ed.) (1975) *The leader in the group*. New York: Jason Aronson.

MASLOW, A. H. (1962) *Towards a psychology of being*. New York: Van Nostrand.

METH, R. L. & R. S. PASICK (1990) *Men in therapy: The challenge of change*. New York: Guildford.

MITCHELL, J. (1975) *Psychoanalysis and feminism*. Harmondsworth: Penguin.

MOI, T. (1981) Representations of patriarchy. *Feminist Review* **9**, 60–75.

MOORE, R. & D. GILLETTE (1990) *King, warrior, magician, lover*. San Francisco: HarperCollins.

MORRIS, D. (1984) Foreword. In L. TIGER *Men in Groups*, 2nd edn. New York: Marion Boyars.

NATIONAL AUDIT OF DRUG MISUSE STATISTICS (1990) *Drug misuse in Britain*. London: London Institute for Drug Dependence.

OFFICE FOR POPULATION CENSUSES AND SURVEYS (1991) *General household survey 1989*. London: HMSO.

OFFICE OF HEALTH ECONOMICS (1992) *Compendium of health statistics*, 8th edn. London: HMSO.

PALMER, I. (1996) *Counselling and psychotherapy resources directory 1997*. Rugby: BAC.

PLECK, J. H. (1987) The contemporary man. In *Handbook of counseling and psychotherapy with men*, M. SCHER, M. STEVENS, G. GOOD, G. A. EICHENFIELD (eds), 16–27. Newbury Park, CA: Sage.

PROCHASKA, J. O. & C. C. DICLEMENTE (1992) *The transtheoretical approach: Crossing the traditional boundaries of therapy*. Homewood, IL: Dow Jones-Irwin.

REICH, W. (1961) *Character analysis*, M. HIGGINS & C. M. RAPHAEL (eds), V. R. CARFAGNO (trans.), 3rd edn. New York: Farrar Strauss and Giroux. [Original work published 1933.]

REICH, W. (1975) *The mass psychology of fascism*, V. R. CARFAGNO (trans.), 3rd edn. Harmondsworth: Penguin. [Original work published 1942.]

ROGERS, C. R. (1959) A theory of therapy, personality, and interpersonal relationships, as developed in the client-centered framework. In *Psychology: A study of science*, Vol. 3, *Formulations of the person and the social context*, S. KOCH (ed.), 184–256. New York: McGraw-Hill.

ROGERS, C. R. (1990) The necessary and sufficient conditions of therapeutic personality change. In *The Carl Rogers reader*, H. KIRSCHENBAUM & V. L. HENDERSON (eds), 219–35. London: Constable. [Original work published 1957.]

ROWAN, J. (1987) *The horned god: Feminism and men as wounding and healing*. London: Routledge & Kegan Paul.

ROWAN, J. (1996) *Healing the male psyche: Therapy as initation*. London: Routledge.

ROY, B. & STEINER, C. (1988) *Radical psychiatry: The second decade*. Unpublished.

SAMUELS, A. (1993) *The political psyche*. London: Routledge.

SCHER, M., M. STEVENS, G. GOOD, G. A. EICHENFIELD (eds) (1987) *Handbook of counseling and psychotherapy with men*. Newbury Park, CA: Sage.

SCHIFF, A. W., K. MELLOR, E. SCHIFF, S. SCHIFF, D. RICHMAN, J. FISHMAN, L. WOLZ, C. FISHMAN, D. MOMB (1975) *Cathexis reader: Transactional analysis treatment of psychosis*. New York: Harper & Row.

SEIDLER, V. (1989) *Rediscovering masculinity: Reason, language and sexuality*. London: Routledge.

STEIN, T. S. (1982) Men's groups. In *Men in transition: Theory and therapy*, K. L. SOLOMOM & N. B. LEVY (eds), 275–307. New York: Plenum.

STEINER, C. (1966) Script and counterscript. *Transactional Analysis Bulletin* **5**(18), 136–7.

STEINER, C. (ed.) (1974) *Readings in radical psychiatry*. New York: Grove.

STEINER, C. (1981) *The other side of power*. New York: Grove.

STEINER, C. (1984) Emotional literacy. *Transactional Analysis Journal* **14**, 162–73.

TIGER, L. (1984) *Men in groups*, 2nd edn. New York: Marion Boyars.

TUDOR, K. (1994) Men in groups. *Cahoots* **50**, 31–2.

TUDOR, K. (1995a) Masculinity and violence. Unpublished report, King's College, University of London.

TUDOR, K. (1995b) Power and pleasure: male identity and intimacy in relationships. *Journal of Couples Therapy* **5**(1/2), 69–94.

TUDOR, K. (1997) Social contracts: Contracting for social change. In *Contracts in counselling*, C. SILLS (ed.) 207–15. London: Sage.

WALDRON, I. (1986) What do we know about sex differences in mortality? A review of the literature. *UN Population Bulletin* **18**, 59–76.

WEST, M. (1990) *Lazarus*. London: Methuen.

WILSON, E. (1981) Psychoanalysis: psychic law and order. *Feminist Review* **8**, 63–78.

YALLOM, I. (1995) *The theory and practice of group psychotherapy*, 4th edn. New York: Grove.

Chapter Eight

Talking spaces: a therapeutic groupwork approach to HIV prevention with gay men

Tim Foskett and Alfred Hurst

Dedicated to Stephen Lumley, *who believed*
in the power of the talking space.

Introduction

This chapter sets out the research background and theoretical approach of the Project for Advice, Counselling and Education (PACE) Workshops for Gay Men towards human immunodeficiency virus (HIV) transmission prevention work in London. It provides information about the workshops that took place between October 1995 and February 1996, and details of a summative evaluation of the programme, using follow-up questionnaires to participants. The results of the evaluation indicate that the intended outcomes of the interventions were achieved, and in particular that emotional well-being and interpersonal skills were considerably enhanced by participation in workshops. The chapter concludes with a discussion of the issues raised and recommendations for future work.

PACE

PACE has been established in London for over ten years, providing counselling and other personal development opportunities from a variety of therapeutic approaches to lesbians and gay men, as well as training and consultacy services to a wide range of local and health authorities in the fields of lesbian and gay equality and HIV prevention and care.

PACE has provided HIV prevention services directly to gay men for six years. Since the beginning of 1995 the emphasis of our HIV prevention work has shifted away from information-giving activities, towards longer experiential and therapeutic workshops and groups.

Philosophical approach

Our philosophy as an organization is based upon the principles of the counselling, psychology and psychotherapy movements that have developed over the last 50 years. Counselling is an effective means of self-empowerment, following the principle that an individual who experiences problems or difficulties is best placed to find their own solutions to those problems or difficulties. PACE supports the provision of counselling services from a range of different perspectives, including the psychodynamic, humanistic and existential schools. The role of the counsellor or therapeutic group facilitator is to help create an environment where the individual is able to consider issues or difficulties in their life, experience the reality of their feelings about these issues within a therapeutic relationship, and explore the options available for meeting their needs (Rogers 1961; Egan 1975).

PACE also recognizes the experiences of lesbians and gay men in our society, and particularly the experience of oppression. The impact of heterosexism and homophobia on the emotional well-being of lesbians and gay men has only just begun to be documented (Odets 1995; Davies & Neale 1996; Young 1996), and yet it is clear to us that these experiences have had a considerable impact on the way lesbians and gay men perceive themselves and their place in our society. As a result of heterosexism, many lesbians and gay men may not experience support and affirmation for their sexuality, and ultimately for themselves, until they become part of the wider lesbian and gay communities. Homophobia and heterosexism are also inherent within much mainstream counselling and psychotherapy theory and practise. PACE has a long-standing commitment to developing non-pathologizing models of working with lesbians and gay men.

Choice of methodology

Our choice of methodology for this evaluative study was influenced by factors such as the relatively small number of interventions and participants, the amount of funding made available for evaluation purposes, and a desire for the research method to be congruent with the interventions themselves. To evaluate non-directive, person-centred workshops and groups with some form of objective measure designed by people not involved in the experience of the interventions would, in our view, have militated against gaining a full sense of the impact of the experience.

Many commentators have acknowledged the difficulties in researching experiential and therapeutic processes. Clarkson (in press) has commented that using quantitative research methods to evaluate therapeutic interventions is like trying to catch butterflies with bulldozers. It seems to us that the statements of many of the respondents resemble butterflies in their subtlety, and it is a testimony to qualitative, phenomenological research that we have been successful in catching them.

In his review of the use of outcome measures in HIV prevention, Bonnell (1996) offers support for this view:

> Prout (1992) suggests that an "illuminative" approach is required, whereby qualitative methodology is used to question the participants themselves as to how the intervention affected their knowledge, attitudes or behaviour. Given the profound methodological problems often encountered regarding attribution, it may sometimes be the case that an illuminative approach is actually a more reliable way of attributing an outcome to a process than is the use of quantitative measures.

The present evaluation did not attempt to externally evaluate change in behaviour. We find it hard to imagine a methodology that could do this without taking a prominent position within the intervention itself, and therefore fundamentally changing the nature of the intervention. Indeed, one of the uncomfortable tensions for the facilitators of the workshops and groups was, on the one hand, being committed to a theoretical approach that does not prescribe how participants make use of the workshop or how participants should "change" as a result of the workshop and, on the other hand, agreements with funders to achieve a range of specified outcomes.

Principally, we have chosen to ask participants about their perception of the impact of the workshops and groups, on a general level and with particular reference to the intended outcomes of the workshops programme.

Background and research context

There is a range of issues arising from the research context of HIV prevention which in our view demand attention. We have been hindered to some extent by the lack of psychological research in the field of HIV prevention, where the research agenda is dominated by the medical and sociological disciplines. We believe that psychological and therapeutic models have considerable insight to offer in relation to facilitating human behaviour change, and it is to the detriment of us all that they have been neglected by the HIV prevention field.

In addition, other factors have emerged from our experience of facilitating workshops with gay men, which have shaped our approach considerably and are worthy of acknowledgement. These issues can be grouped into three areas: information provision, psychological and emotional issues, and community issues.

Information provision

There is considerable research indicating that most gay men have a reasonable level of knowledge about how HIV is transmitted, and correspondingly how they can protect themselves and others through the use of safer sex (Thornton 1993; Williams 1996). There is also increasing evidence that, while information provision contributed significantly to condom use in the early stages of the epidemic, recent information provision has had little impact on transmission rates (Thornton 1993; Williams 1996).

In his review of research into HIV prevention with men who have sex with men, Aggleton (1995) states:

> There is no evidence that increasing knowledge levels (beyond the near saturation level already reached) is likely to have any beneficial effects on the behaviour of men who have sex with men. Efforts to assess such knowledge levels are best eschewed in favour of those examining beliefs about HIV and AIDS, and the relationship between these beliefs and sexual practice.

In the context of working with young people, Oakley et al. (1996) have said:

> The most outstanding lesson that emerges from many years of studying young people and sexual risk-taking is that *there is no inevitable connection between knowledge and behaviour.* (Authors' emphasis.)

She goes on to say that the challenge to health education is not primarily to give young people knowledge, but to help them "to *apply* it to their own situations" (authors' emphasis). These principles are equally relevant to work with gay men.

Elsewhere, Oakley et al. (1994) have shown that sexual health is only one of a number of priority needs expressed by young people. Concerns such as money, housing and relationships with family often figure as more important. Oakley has concluded that those interventions that meaningfully address some of the other concerns of young people, as well as sexual health, are more likely to be effective than are singular sexual health interventions.

Psychological and emotional issues

Self-esteem and emotional well-being

Our approach starts from the premise that self-esteem plays a critical role in a person's life and is the foundation for their behaviour in the wider world. If a gay man does not value himself, it is unlikely that he will always act in his own best interests. Many lesbians and gay men may have unconsciously internalized oppress-ive concepts, believing, at an unconscious level at least, the negative assumptions perpetrated about them. One consequence of this is that a person may be more likely to practice behaviour that involves a higher risk of HIV transmission. In a study of drug users Mabel Camacho (1996) found that psychological problems such as anxiety or depression were related to risky drug use and risky sexual practice. The San Francisco Department of Public Health has reported a study by Van Gorder (1995) where 119 men were asked their views on the factors that interfere with their commitment to practise safer sex. The issues cited included: feelings of depression, numbness and denial about the epidemic, grief and loss, low self-esteem from the effects of homophobia and racism, ageism and a fear of growing older, the need for greater intimacy, the need to feel that others cared about them, the need for a greater sense of community, and a poorly defined sense of the future. Kelly (1991) has found that one factor in men "lapsing" into unsafe sex is "the wish to please a partner", which may also be an indicator of low self-esteem.

In their review of research on factors associated with unsafe sex, Thornton & Catalan (1993) state: "a wide range of intrapersonal variables have been implicated in high risk sexual behaviour. Among gay men these include internalized homo-phobia, lack of social skills, denial of risk, low self-esteem, depression, suicidality, lack of coping skills to deal with stress and lack of spiritual or religious resources".

The Department of Health has also highlighted the need to address issues of self-esteem in their recent HIV Health Promotion Strategy (1995), stating:

> Information about HIV will need to be embedded in messages which support effective sustained behavioural change, including developing self-esteem and negotiation skills.

Meaning and value

Self-esteem is also related to a person's sense of the ultimate value and meaning of their life. For many gay men, the existential questions of "Who am I?" and "What is meaningful to me?" are difficult to answer. The traditional heterosexual responses to these questions either do not fit or are not easily attainable, and the alternatives offered by existing gay culture are for many gay men equally unattain-able or unfulfilling. There is a need for gay men to talk with others about meaning and value in their lives, particularly in the realm of sex and relationships, and on-going support to develop a true sense of value in themselves and the lives they lead.

Conflicting beliefs, feelings and desires

Through our work with gay men, it has become clear that many gay men live with considerable levels of internal difference or conflict, between what they *believe* about sex and relationships, what they *feel* about sex and relationships, and what they *want* in terms of sex and relationships. These internal differences may be acknowledged by the person, or equally may be denied or suppressed. When they are denied or suppressed the possibility of unconsidered and therefore risky behaviour is heightened. In his book *Games people play*, Berne (1964) develops the transactional analysis model of the inner parent, adult and child, characterizing beliefs and morals, logic and rationality, feelings and desires, respectively. The therapeutic intervention, according to Berne, is to support the individual to make explicit the dialogues and conflicts between the different levels of their inner self, and seek a way to manage or resolve these conflicts, rather than ignore or avoid them.

The psychotherapist Susie Orbach in her book *What's really going on here?* (1994) has proposed the importance of developing *emotional literacy* as a way of managing the dialogue and conflicts between thoughts, feelings and desires.

It is valuable to offer time, space, structure and models (such as Berne's) for gay men to begin to explore their inner conflicts and find their own means of resolving or managing them. It must be acknowledged that this type of psychotherapeutic work cannot be achieved overnight, since it takes time and commitment to develop emotional literacy. Through this process gay men can gradually be encouraged to recognize their own power and ability to make choices within the context of internal conflict about sex.

Relationships and assertion skills

There is increasing evidence that significant HIV transmission between gay men occurs within existing relationships (Hart 1993; Aggleton 1995). There are many factors involved in this phenomenon, in particular the internal conflicts or differences discussed above, between sexual beliefs, feelings and wants. These are difficult enough to manage in one person, but when two people (both with their own set of internal conflicts) come together to engage in a relationship, the situation is fraught with possibilities.

In addition, Thornton & Catalan (1993) have found that "non-assertive attitudes in negotiating safer sex and poorer sexual communication skills" are predictors for lapses from safer practices and consistent high-risk taking among gay men.

It is beneficial for gay men to have the skills and ability to identify these conflicts and find a way to address them within the relationship openly and honestly, as opposed to an unacknowledged move into unconsidered and unprotected sex.

The impact of sexual abuse

We are aware of sexual abuse being raised and discussed quite frequently during PACE workshops and groups. Martindale et al. (1996) have reported that, of a large cohort of gay men aged between 18 and 30, one-third had been sexually abused during childhood. Hickson et al. (1994) have reported that approximately 25 per cent of a large British sample of gay men have reported sexual abuse. The impact of sexual abuse is both complex and variable; however, it seems plausible that if a person's first experience of sexual activity is non-consensual and involves an abusive power dynamic, there may be significant implications in relation to choosing and asserting safer sex with sexual partners. There is a need for significant numbers of gay men to be able to explore their experiences of sexual abuse in a safe and constructive environment.

Community issues

Community culture

Gold (1995) has suggested that some aspects of current Western gay community culture, particularly disrespectful and judgmental ways of relating, may contribute to the incidence of unprotected sex. Many gay men, while deriving support and pleasure from the gay scene, also experience it as hostile and destructive at times. Not only does this potentially cause emotional harm, it militates against honest and open dialogue between gay men.

   Consequently, it is important to provide opportunities for gay men to explore how community culture might be developed that is respectful and inclusive, and fosters honest and supportive dialogue about sex and relationships.

Living in the epidemic

Gay men are living in the centre of a major epidemic, with disproportionately high death and bereavement rates in the contemporary Western world. Whether or not they are affected directly, gay men cannot escape the community experience of devastation and loss. Odets (1995) has highlighted the implications of living within this context for North American gay men; in particular the sense of inevitability of contracting the virus for some gay men, and the role of grief and denial as contributors to HIV transmission. Although our experience in the UK is different, there are strong parallels between the emotional and psychological experiences of gay men in the UK and North America.

The PACE approach to HIV prevention with gay men

The research and issues discussed above raise innumerable questions about how best to respond to HIV prevention, and suggest a range of possible options. We believe that experiential and therapeutic groups for gay men provide a unique opportunity to address the issues highlighted above, and to effect psychological and behavioural change that will contribute to reducing the transmission of HIV.

Experiential and therapeutic groups

In their review of experiential group research, Bednar & Kaul (1994) report a large body of research demonstrating positive outcomes of experiential and therapeutic group work. The shift in the field of education towards participative and experiential learning also highlights the effectiveness of these approaches. Bednar & Kaul identify a range of factors (originally postulated by Yalom (1985)) that, when experienced in a therapeutic group, have been shown to contribute to positive change. These factors are:

- *Catharsis*: the expression of feelings and emotions.
- *Cohesion*: a sense of belonging and safety.
- *Self-understanding*: insight into who I am and what makes me tick.
- *Interpersonal learning*: about interpersonal dynamics and behavioural skills.
- *Instillation of hope*: for the possibility of change or development.
- *Identification*: using others as role models.
- *Universality*: the realization that other people share my concerns or difficulties.

It should be noted that these factors are non-specific to the *content* of the group, but relate to the *process*, the underlying experience, of participating in the group.

Experiential and therapeutic groups for gay men can:

- Encourage participants to talk openly and fully about their feelings with other gay men.
- Foster a sense of belonging and safety as part of a group of gay men.
- Promote insight into personal identity and what is important to each person as a gay man.
- Provide "live" opportunities to learn about relating to other gay men and develop new skills such as assertion and negotiation within a gay context.
- Provide opportunities to identify with a variety of other gay men.
- Provide opportunities to feel understood when talking about difficult or emotive subjects.

Thornton & Catalan (1993) also acknowledge the role of psychological interventions in HIV prevention:

> ... the evidence indicates that psychological treatment approaches are effective in enabling individuals to make and maintain sexual behaviour change.

Conclusion

We acknowledge that this approach does not offer a simple intervention that will dramatically reduce the incidence of HIV transmission overnight. We do not believe that such an intervention exists. Our approach is an holistic intervention that responds to the complex and multi-layered phenomenon of sexual relationships between men in the 1990s. We believe that by a combination of enhancing gay men's emotional well-being, providing opportunities for gay men to explore their personal difficulties or conflicts in relation to sex and relationships, and developing their interpersonal skills, an important contribution to HIV prevention is made. Not only are men more able to promote their own health in sexual situations, but they also become more skilled in providing support and safety to other gay men.

The workshops

Intended outcomes of the workshops and group

From the background and research context discussed above, and in consultation with funders, the following range of intended outcomes for the workshops was developed. As a result of the workshops/groups, participants would:

- Have a more accurate understanding of safer sex.
- Have gained ideas and motivation for better and safer sex.
- Feel more comfortable and confident about talking about sex with others.
- Have an improved understanding of themselves and their sexuality.
- Have identified changes they wish to make in sexual relationships.
- Have identified strategies for achieving their sexual goals.
- Feel more assertive in relationships in general and in sexual relationships in particular.
- Feel more confident negotiating generally and negotiating about sex in particular.
- Feel closer to having the kinds of relationships they want.
- Feel more confident to deal with sexual situations they haven't handled well in the past.
- Have an enhanced sense of emotional well-being.
- Talk about and recommend the workshops to other gay men.

These intended outcomes were therefore the basis for the design and planning of the workshops and groups and the focus of quality assurance and evaluation.

Description of the workshops

Between 8 November 1995 and 4 February 1996 five workshops and one six-week group were provided to gay men in the London region. The workshops are described in Table 8.1. All events had a general focus of sex and/or relationships, and shared the common factors of a group experience for gay men, with agreements and structure to facilitate experiential learning. The average contact time for the workshops was just over ten hours.

The workshops were advertised in the gay press. Participants were asked to telephone PACE to book a place on a workshop. The longer weekend workshops and group proved most popular, in some cases there being twice as many applicants as places available. In total, sixty-four gay or bisexual men participated in the workshops over the three-month period.

Workshops and groups varied in the type of facilitation and structure provided, depending on the specific theme and format of the group. The facilitators for the workshops were experienced counsellors and therapeutic groupworkers who used a range of theory and skills predominantly from humanistic and existential counselling, group therapy and adult learning approaches. Exercises and activities were designed to help participants explore ideas and feelings, and make sense of them within their life. These included talking to others in pairs or small groups, talking together in the large group, using art or movement activities and guided imagery.

At the first meeting of each workshop participants made agreements about how the group intended to work together in a way that was constructive, supportive and rewarding. Participants had the choice not to participate in something if it did not feel right for them. At the beginning of the workshop or group, participants were invited to identify their own needs and expectations within the general topic or theme of the workshop. A summary of what participants hoped to gain from the workshops is given in Box 8.1. Towards the end of each workshop there was an opportunity for participants to review what they had felt and learned during the workshop, and time to think about what differences this may make to their life.

Attrition rates

The attrition (or dropout) rate for the workshops was quite low, varying between none and three men for each workshop. This indicates that participants found the experiences valuable, given that they attended workshops voluntarily in their own time.

Quality assurance

At the end of each event participants completed a quality assurance form, asking them how personally useful the workshop had been, to what extent the aim of the

Table 8.1 The workshops and groups

Workshop	No. of contact hours	No. of participants	No. of respondents
Let's Talk About Sex A six-week group for young gay men (under 30) to talk about sex, relationships and the rest Wednesdays, 8 November to 13 December, 6.30–8.30 pm Neal's Yard, Covent Garden	12	16	5
Sex Positive A supportive, structured two-evening group for gay men living with HIV to talk about sex and relationships Thursdays, 9 and 23 November, 6.30–9.30 pm Shepherdess Walk, Hackney	6	3	1
It Takes Two to Tangle A (two evenings and one day) workshop to explore gay men's experiences of relationships and a chance to develop negotiation and relationship skills. Individuals and couples welcome. Thursdays, 16 and 30 November 6.30–9.30 pm The Landmark, Lambeth Saturday, 18 November, 10.30–4.30 pm South London Venue	12	15	10
Talking Dirty A workshop to explore the fun and the difficulties of talking about sex, and help you develop skills to talk openly about sex with friends and lovers Saturday, 2 December, 10.30–4.30 pm PACE, Islington	6	7	6
Getting What You Want for Christmas! A (one day & one evening) workshop for gay men to develop assertion skills, to get what you want in relationships, in bed and for Christmas! Saturday, 9 December, 10.30–4.30 pm and Thursday, 14 December, 6.30–9.30 pm River House, Hammersmith	9	14	10
Resolutions! Do you want to make 1996 different? Resolutions is a residential weekend workshop for gay men to take stock of sex and relationships in '95, and turn New Year's resolutions for '96 into reality! Starts Friday, 2 February, 7.00 pm, ends Sunday, 4 Feburary, 4.00 pm Little Grove, Buckinghamshire	17	15	8

Box 8.1 A summary of what participants hoped to gain from the workshops

- Self-awareness
- Confronting negative attitudes
- Open-mindedness
- Help to understand people's motivations
- Be healthy
- Increase confidence
- Sort my head out
- Learn from others
- Discuss relationships
- Clearer attitude towards sex
- To face facts about self
- Be more assertive about self and sexuality
- Be with other gay men
- Discuss monogamy and cruising
- Discuss serious subjects outside pubs/clubs
- Telephone numbers
- Psychological barriers to be broken down
- Ability to *really* enjoy sex
- Understand myself and why I do things
- Learn to help others

- Skills involved in initiating healthy relationships
- Unlearning patterns
- Learn new ways of relating
- Dynamics of open relationships (do they work?)
- Discussion of co-dependent relationships
- Ability to deal effectively with specific situations
- How to keep the honeymoon period
- Learn to integrate sexual relationships with longer friendships
- Separate out emotional needs from practicalities
- To relate to others after bereavement
- Greater honesty within all relationships
- Is it possible for gay relationships – or just give up?
- Understand the feelings of being single or a couple – which is appropriate at present?
- Learn about the development of relationships

---

workshop was met and about their future needs. Participants rated how personally useful the workshop or group was, using the following scale:

1	2	3	4	5
Not at all useful	A little useful	Partly useful	Mostly useful	Very useful

The average rating for the workshops was 4.5.

Participants also rated the success of the workshop or group in achieving its stated objective on the following scale:

1	2	3	4	5
Not at all met	Met a little	Partly met	Mostly met	Fully met

The average rating for meeting the objective of workshops was 4.2.

Both figures indicate a high level of participant satisfaction and workshop effectiveness.

The quality assurance form also asked participants what was most effective about the group or workshop. Participants stated:

- Having time to explore feelings in a safe environment.
- Being offered possibilities not doctrines.
- Meeting new people and feeling a bit less isolated for a while.
- The techniques were very effective in helping me to understand how I felt and behaved – this was new to me.
- Listening and discussing issues with people in the same situation.
- I found the workshop very practical.
- Chance to talk to strangers about a topic which is not generally covered with friends.
- Talking about sex.
- The chance to meet other gay men.
- Useful to consider issues for people who are having problems around changing their risk behaviour – never considered that before.
- By analyzing how change affects people, different approaches for help/support can be devised.
- Opportunity to talk through emotionally complex issues in a supportive environment.

When asked about their dissatisfactions, participants stated:

- I felt that there could have been more on negotiation skills.
- Too short.
- Some of the issues addressed by others felt so enormous and needed more time and effort, and made my issues seem inconsequential by comparison.
- It would have been helpful to consider the differences between minority groups.

One of the lessons for us from this series of workshops was to be realistic with participants about the limitations of workshops or groups. By and large we were able to respond to the majority of issues and concerns that participants bring. However, it is clear that there are few quick fixes for emotional and psychological issues in relation to sex, sexuality, relationships and HIV transmission. It is also clear to us that longer workshops and groups are the preferred format for working effectively with these issues.

Other findings from the workshops

One of the most resounding features of the workshop programme was the frequent feedback from participants that they had *never* had an opportunity to talk with other gay men in this way before – and that gay cultural and social norms often militate against expressing thoughts and feelings about sex and relationships honestly. This lends weight to the need for opportunities for gay men to consider how we might develop a community culture that is conducive to peer support on issues such as sex and relationships.

An enormous task: to talk about sex

From the beginning we chose to focus workshops and groups on the themes of sex and relationships, partly in response to Oakley's suggestion that a more holistic approach to sexual health promotion is likely to be more effective. We have found that groups consistently choose to begin talking about the more general relationship issues from their chosen agenda, and then proceed towards the more intimate and sexual. Throughout this process the group will often refer to the difficulty they experience in discussing sex with others.

It could be said that this is because the group are essentially strangers, and it is not surprising that sexual discussion would be inhibiting. There must be some truth in this proposition. However, it is remarkable how much personal history *is* shared between participants about their lives, histories and personal choices (with the same relative strangers). It seems to us that sexual issues are among the *most* personal of all the possible intimate things to talk about with others, whether they be workshop participants, friends or lovers. Difficulties in talking about sex encountered within the workshops, directly reflect difficulties encountered in sexual relationships, and therefore provide opportunities for considerable insight and personal learning.

These findings illustrate the enormity of the task of enabling people to be able to negotiate sexual activity with their lover, and may also indicate why so few HIV prevention initiatives have attempted to achieve this outcome.

The evaluation

Methodology

A more extensive *summative evaluation* (Bonnell 1996) of the impact of the workshops and groups was designed by using a questionnaire (Appendix 8.1) asking participants to self-identify what has changed for them, if anything, as a result of the workshop. The questionnaire asked 19 questions covering: the workshops; the impact of the workshops; personal information about relationships and sex in the last 12 months; and demographic information.

The questionnaire was sent to 64 individuals who participated in workshops. A total of 32 questionnaires were returned, providing a 50 per cent response rate. This level of response to a postal survey in itself suggests a high degree of value in the workshop programme from respondents. Of the respondents, 28 (87.5 per cent) had attended one workshop and, 4 (12.5 per cent) had attended more than one workshop.

The questionnaire was sent to participants during the week of 19 March 1996. The maximum time period between attending the workshop and completing the questionnaire was 4.5 months, with a minimum time period of 6 weeks for the last workshop. The median time period was 3.5 months.

Demographics: information about the respondents

Statistical relevance

Although we state below that certain quantities and percentages suggest or imply evidence in favour of particular theories or propositions, we would like to emphasize that the small size of our sample means that these findings are rarely significant at a statistical level, and should therefore be read and used with careful consideration.

Age

The ages of respondents ranged from 20 to 70, with an average age of 31–35, reflecting an age distribution consistent with a wide range of other study samples of UK gay men (e.g. Hickson et al. 1996).

Ethnicity

The ethnicity of those participating in the workshops and those responding to the questionnaire is detailed below in Table 8.2. Of the 64 participants, 8 (12 per cent) were from black or other ethnic minorities. This percentage is consistent with census data for the London region.

Table 8.2 Ethnicity of participants and questionnaire respondents

Ethnicity	Participated in workshops	Responded to questionnaire
Asian	4 (6 %)	1 (3 %)
Black African	1 (1.5 %)	
Black Caribbean	2 (3 %)	
Chinese	1 (1.5 %)	
Irish	4 (6 %)	2 (6 %)
White other	11 (17 %)	4 (12 %)
White UK	40 (62 %)	25 (75 %)

Relationship status

Of the respondents, 20 (62 per cent) had been in a relationship with a regular sexual partner in the previous 12 months. Given the size of our sample, this figure is similar to that found by other studies. Hickson et al. (1996) report a slightly higher finding (87 per cent) from their survey at the Lesbian and Gay Pride festival.

Unprotected sex

Of the respondents, 10 (31 per cent) had been involved in unprotected anal intercourse in the last 12 months, 6 of these with a regular partner and 3 with a casual partner, and 1 with both a regular and a casual partner. This level of unprotected sex is consistent with that found in a number of other studies (e.g. Hickson et al. 1996).

HIV status

Of the respondents, 16 (50 per cent) did not know their HIV status, 5 (16 per cent) said they were HIV-antibody positive, and 11 (34 per cent) said they were HIV-antibody negative. This is consistent with the findings of other studies of the London gay male population.

A representative sample?

We were struck from the responses to the questionnaire at how similar participants were to other study samples of gay men. Variables such as age distribution, ethnicity, incidence of unprotected sex, incidence of HIV, and relationship status of our sample were remarkably consistent with data from other samples of gay men. Although the sample is too small to draw hard conclusions from this apparent representativeness, it does confirm that therapeutic workshops are accessible and effective for a wide range of gay men, and that the men who were drawn to the workshops had as high a level of risk of HIV transmission as other gay-identified men.

The experiences of black men

Table 8.2 shows that 12 per cent of workshop participants were black or from an ethnic minority. This percentage is consistent with the ethnic distribution of London.

However, we received very few responses to the questionnaire from black and ethnic minority men. The sample is too small to attribute significant meaning to this. However, the workshops themselves raise a number of issues about the participation of black men. The facilitators for all workshops were white men, and in most cases there were only one or two black participants at each workshop. We believe it would take considerable internal resources and trust for black men to feel safe to express their feelings about sex and relationships in a group that is predominantly white. We believe that some black participants felt able to participate fully, while others may have found the group inhibiting.

Participants were invited to identify issues and topics for future workshops on the quality assurance form. One of the most requested topics for future workshops was inter-racial relationships, and PACE has since developed this area of work.

The effectiveness of the workshops

The effectiveness of the workshops can be appraised by answering two questions.

- Did the participants report, over time, that their expectations were met and that the experience was personally useful to them?
- Did the participants report change, sustained over time, consistent with the intended outcomes of the workshop programme?

The results described below demonstrate that the answer to both these questions is 'yes'.

Of the respondents, 17 (53 per cent) stated that their expectations had been fully met by the workshop or group, a further 12 (38 per cent) said their expectations had been partly met, with 3 (10 per cent) stating that the workshop had not met their expectations. It is inevitable that some people will not find experiential group work helpful to them, and in some cases referrals to other types of intervention were made. Over 90 per cent of respondents reported that their expectations had been fully or partly met, suggesting a high degree of satisfaction with the workshops overall.

As stated above, at the end of each workshop participants were asked to rate how personally useful the experience had been to them. Respondents were asked the same question on the follow-up questionnaire. The average rating at the end of the workshops was 4.5. The average rating from questionnaire respondents, 3.5 months after the workshops, was 4.0. Thus, the respondents' rating of personal usefulness was sustained over the 3.5-month follow-up period, suggesting evidence of integration of learning and development on a longer term basis.

Respondents were also asked whether they had discussed or recommended the workshops to other gay men. 81 per cent of respondents had talked to another person about the workshop and 66 per cent had recommended the workshops to other gay men. Again, indicating a high degree of satisfaction.

Participants' perceptions of the impact of the workshops

In evaluating the impact of the workshops in relation to the intended outcomes of the programme, we used a mixture of open-ended questions and a checklist of possible outcomes. The results of the open-ended questions demonstrate that many of the intended outcomes have been achieved. In particular participants frequently reported:

- Enhanced self-confidence.
- Greater clarity about sex and relationships.
- Increased assertiveness and ability to negotiate in relationships.
- Increased determination and ability to make changes in relationships.
- Greater self-acceptance.
- Resolution of historical sexual and relationship problems or difficulties.

The full set of responses is given below.

Overall, what difference if any has the workshop made to you?
- Better understanding of myself re. sex and how I behave in certain situations.
- It was a staging post in being comfortable with other gay men.
- Helped me change my behaviour, be more direct and open.
- I'm less "afraid" of sex, and don't feel bad or guilty in asking for what I want in relation to sex.
- I have sorted out a lot of issues surrounding past relationships and my reactions to current ones.
- Gave support to our relationship on sexual difficulties.
- It gave me the confidence to ask for what I wanted in bed without being ashamed.
- Made me aware of my gay identity and also made me more comfortable in being with other gays in a residential setting.
- It has helped me start moving forward.
- It gave me the confidence to make significant life-changes. It marked a turning point for me.
- More relaxed re. relationships and demands put on partners.
- Made me more confident in myself and reinforced my sense of gayness.
- It gave me time out to consider the future.
- In part because I found the workshop difficult and frustrating it's actually had a beneficial effect – I've decided to *do* something rather than just talk about it.
- Adopting a "clean, clear and concise" approach to negotiating in many areas.
- Unfortunately, understanding assertiveness has backfired. Now that I'm aware of other people's position I've gone on the defensive.
- It has made me more aware of my rights as an individual, in particular to say no, in work/everyday and in sexual situations.

- Made me ten times more assertive and confident around gay issues and my right to exist. Recently confronted homophobic hassles whereas previously I would not have.
- Stopped me worrying about key sexual questions too afraid to ask friends.
- Dealing better with ageing and loss of sex-drive and motivation.
- I felt very positive at the time, but no other major benefits since.
- It has made me look at myself and consider my actions more – also made me realize that in relationships I have to think of two of us and not just other people around.
- It has made me assert my needs within a relationship.
- Nothing tangible, but helped crystallize certain processes already underway.
- Made me think more about *my* behaviour and way of operating in relationships – particularly the current ones.
- The workshop was probably an important part of the whole jigsaw of changing relationships in my life.
- It has given me more clarity and sense of priority.
- None (two respondents).

What difference has the workshop made to your relationships with other people?
- My lover who attended the group with me found, as I did, it began to make it easier to relate to each other sexually.
- I am calmer, I am looking at relationships more objectively.
- It has just made me aware of how hard and easy it can be to "get on" with people.
- I'm easier in groups, I have more confidence in asserting my needs.
- Made me be more honest with what I feel and that sometimes it's good to feel differently from others and express that.
- I feel calmer and more open.
- I've become slightly more self-accepting and therefore more open to others and ready to listen.
- Made me slightly more confident and assertive.
- It's helped me to start to shift the balance of my life toward more social time and a bit less work!
- Indirectly its contributed to greatly improved relationships.
- More focused, better understood.
- Respecting other gay men, realizing that they have an inner struggle. I use the word "Queen" much less, more informed about the virus and pharmacology.
- I am less intolerant of other people's motivations.
- In some ways easier, more confident, but perhaps more self-reliant as well.
- Have become withdrawn and reclusive.
- Made me scrutinize the other person more.
- I feel more in control of my part of the relationship and more aware of my needs.
- Can't describe – too difficult to pinpoint.

- In particular it formed a part of my coming to terms with life as a single man (after many years in a relationship).
- I have become a bit less secretive, sensitive and defensive especially about sex.
- None (6 (19 per cent) respondents).

What impact has the workshop had on your sexual activity?
- None yet, but it has made me more open to the possibility of a one-to-one relationship.
- Less inhibited at sex – talking about it and doing it.
- Easier for a while. Made me more aware of my sexual needs.
- It has helped to clarify possible reasons for particular sexual activity – cruising.
- Slightly increased confidence.
- As a result I do things I want to do and, not things I don't want to (e.g. unsafe sex), without shame, fear, etc.
- Boosted my confidence!
- I've become almost celibate since the workshop while energies are channelled into other directions.
- I feel I can justify my stance without being offensive.
- It has made me more aware of my conduct and sexual practice, but not necessarily stop me from engaging in unsafe practices.
- Less expectations.
- Ground to a complete halt. Fear has overtaken.
- In itself, not very much, other experiences and influences have probably been more important.
- I have differentiated between relationships and physical sex which with my current partner is good for me.
- I have had very little sexual activity since the workshop, but is that a coincidence?
- None (8 (25 per cent) respondents).

Two respondents stated that the workshop had not had any impact on their lives.

The remaining outcomes

The remaining outcomes were evaluated using a checklist of possible changes that respondents may have identified as result of the workshops or groups. We also included a range of variables relating to general emotional well-being, to evaluate the impact of the workshops on this aspect of participants' lives. These are reproduced below. Respondents were asked to tick one of five boxes (as in the example below) indicating how much change, if any, had taken place, and to leave the boxes blank if they were unsure or did not know whether the workshop had affected them in the way described.

Example

A lot more	A little more	No change	A little less	A lot less	
❏	❏	❏	❏	❏	confident in bars

The checklist of possible changes was mixed between variables where the desired outcome was "more" (for instance, comfortable talking about sex with your lover) and others where it was "less" (for instance, likely to have unsafe sex).

Variables where the desired outcome was "more"
- confident in bars
- confident in bed
- able to negotiate generally
- able to negotiate about sex
- comfortable talking about sex with friend
- comfortable talking about sex with your lover
- motivated to keep sex safe
- comfortable being gay
- self-knowledgeable
- sociable
- secure
- self-assured
- assertive
- optimistic
- happy
- clarity about personal goals in relationships
- clarity about personal sexual goals
- confident to handle difficult sexual situations
- confident in having satisfying relationships
- knowledgeable about HIV and safer sex.

Variables where the desired outcome was "less"
- shy
- anxious
- isolated
- pessimistic
- depressed
- likely to have unsafe sex.

The above list is referred to throughout the remainder of the report as the "checklist variables".

Box 8.2 Summary of responses to the checklist variables

More than half the respondents reported being more:
- self-knowledgeable
- able to negotiate generally
- comfortable being gay
- self-assured
- clear about their goals in relationships

More than a third of the respondents reported being more:
- clear about personal sexual goals
- able to negotiate about sex
- comfortable talking about sex with friends
- comfortable talking about sex with their lover
- motivated to keep sex safe
- confident in bed
- optimistic
- secure
- assertive
- confident to handle difficult sexual situations
- confident in having satisfying relationships

More than a third of respondents reported being less:
- shy
- anxious
- isolated

Just under a third of respondents (31 %) reported being less likely to have unsafe sex

Positive impact

A positive impact is reflected by changes reported by respondents which are consistent with the intended outcomes of the workshops. All but two respondents reported some positive change on the checklist variables. The vast majority of respondents reported positive change on more than five variables, and 20 (62.5 per cent) respondents reported positive change on more than ten variables. A summary of the responses to the checklist variables is given in Box 8.2.

The number of positive changes reported by the sample is shown in Figure 8.1 and a graphical summary of respondents' answers to the checklist variables is given in Appendix 8.2.

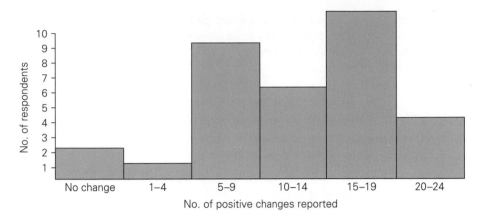

Figure 8.1   The number of positive changes reported by respondents.

Negative impact

"Negative change" refers to changes reported by respondents that contradict the intended outcomes of the workshops. Five respondents reported negative change on one variable on the checklist, and a further three reported 2, 4 and 20 negative changes, respectively. All but two of these respondents reported more positive change than negative change overall. The respondent who reported 20 negative changes seemed to value the workshop experience, stating that he had recommended the workshop to other gay men and had talked about it with others "in a positive way".

In some instances negative change is to be expected. For example, someone who has historically lived by very simple, moral rules about sexual activity may find themselves more confused at the end of a workshop if other participants have questioned the basis of these rules. This state of confusion may be a necessary step to them exploring their sexual belief system, which may also be at the bottom of their reasons for coming on the workshop in the first place. This is an illustration of what Rogers (1961) has called the "paradox of change", which is the experience of regression before progression, or stasis before movement. Alternatively, it is conceivable that someone who knows he and his boyfriend are HIV negative may use the workshop to clarify his ideas about personal risk-management strategies, and may indeed leave the workshop with the intention of having more "unsafe" sex.

In other cases, people may be registering their discontent with the workshop they experienced, or indeed they may have identified negative change in themselves as a result of the workshop. We believe it is not possible to obtain a 100 per cent success rate with any intervention, and particularly an intervention that has a non-directive ethos such as ours. Our concern is to maximize the safety and minimize the destructive possibilities of workshops and groups, which we believe has been achieved to a very high degree. This is an on-going clinical concern for group-workers, and we are aware of the power of this approach for both positive and negative change.

The nature of change

While a few respondents claim that their experience of the workshop has changed their lives enormously, most responses declare small but fundamental changes consistent with the intended outcomes of the interventions. These changes were reported after a median follow-up time of 3.5 months. Lasting changes at the psychological, emotional and behavioural levels are, in our view, more likely to be incremental and cumulative, rather than Earth-shattering.

Relationship skills

We found that respondents who had been in a relationship in the 12 months preceding the workshop reported significantly more change on the checklist variables than did those who had not been in a relationship ($r = 0.168$, $p \leq 0.05$). This does not indicate that the workshops are of no use to single men, but it does suggest that men in relationships gain more from the experience, possibly because they have more of an opportunity to apply their learning within their lives.

Sex and relationships

Our observation (discussed above) that groups consistently choose to begin talking about the more general relationship issues and then proceed towards the more intimate is reflected within the responses to the questionnaire. We received 27 written responses to the general question *"Overall, what difference if any has the workshop made to you?"*, compared with 20 responses to the more specific question *"What difference has the workshop made to your relationships with other people?"* and 15 responses to the last and most personal question *"What impact has the workshop had on your sexual activity?"*

This concept is also reflected in the responses to the checklist variables. Twenty men stated that the workshop had improved their ability to negotiate generally, compared with 14 men who state they are better at negotiating about sex, and 12 who state that they feel more able to talk about sex with their lover.

This indicates the need for on-going provision of opportunities for men to explore their feelings about talking about sex and relationships, since the task is not at all simple. Again, this supports the suggestion that HIV prevention initiatives should engage in a model of on-going cumulative change and development, rather than pursuing a dramatic quick-fix.

Reliability of responses

There is a significant correlation ($r = 0.309$, $p \leq 0.1$) between the personal usefulness rating and the amount of change reported on the checklist variables. The more useful the respondent found the workshop, the more change is attributed to the workshop. Not only does this imply a degree of consistency in responses, but it provides evidence that perception of usefulness actually translates into perceived changes in respondents' lives. This correlation is important since it suggests that, while participants may enjoy the workshops, there is also evidence of integration of learning and development into their lives on a longer term basis.

Conclusions and recommendations

This evaluation demonstrates the effectiveness of a therapeutic group work approach to HIV prevention with gay men. Workshop participants report the following changes, sustained over time.

- enhanced self-confidence
- greater clarity about sex and relationships
- increased assertiveness and ability to negotiate in relationships
- increased motivation and ability to make changes in relationships
- greater self-acceptance
- resolution of historical problems or difficulties with sex and relationships.

Our findings highlight the enormity of the task to enable gay men to negotiate sexual activity with a partner. This supports the need for on-going provision of opportunities for men to explore the wide range of issues involved in sex and relationships.

Psychological and therapeutic models have considerable insight to offer in relation to human behaviour change. Our findings demonstrate that, on the whole, these models have been seriously neglected by the HIV prevention field.

We recommend that:

- HIV prevention initiatives engage in a model of on-going cumulative change and development, at the levels of the individual, their sexual relationships, and the gay male community as a whole, rather than pursuing a dramatic quick-fix.

- The establishment of a larger, long-term experiential group work programme for gay men, offering a variety of workshops and counselling groups on the themes of sex and relationships.
- That such a programme be supported and evaluated by an integrated, rigorous evaluation system.
- That black organizations be funded to provide groups for black men, that black facilitators be employed where possible and that PACE continue to pursue joint working with black HIV prevention organizations to address the issues and dynamics of inter-racial relationships.

Acknowledgements

We would like to thank the following people for their encouragement and contributions to PACE Workshops for Gay Men and to this report. Gregor MacAdam for his support and facilitation of Let's Talk About Sex. The staff of PACE for their comments and support, and particularly Hamid Kamara for his administration of the programme, and Julienne Dickey for her assistance with the report. Ford Hickson from Sigma Research for advice on the design of the questionnaire and assistance with the report. Kristina Bird from the HEA's National HIV Prevention Information Service for her assistance in tracing references and journal articles. Jim Mills for his assistance with statistics. Wendy Clarke and John Foskett for comments on the report. Supervisors Lois Graessle and Alvin Marcetti.

We would like to thank Lambeth, Southwark and Lewisham Health Commissioners for funding this evaluation project. PACE Workshops for Gay Men were funded by the following local and health authorities: London Borough (LB) of Camden, Camden and Islington Health Authority (HA), Ealing, Hammersmith and Hounslow HA, East London and City HA, LB of Hackney, LB of Hounslow, LB of Islington, LB of Kensington and Chelsea, Kensington & Chelsea and Westminster HA, Lambeth, Southwark and Lewisham HA, LB of Newham, LB of Westminster and the North Thames Regional HA.

References

AGGLETON, P. (1995) Men who have sex with men. *Social and behavioural research: implications for needs assessment.* London: Health Education Authority.

BEDNAR, R. & KAUL, T. (1994) Experiential group research: Can the canon fire? In *Handbook for psychotherapy and behaviour change* (1994), eds A. BERGIN and S. GARFIELD. New York: John Wiley & Sons.

BERNE, E. (1964) *Games people play.* London: Penguin.

BONNELL, C. (1995) *Outcomes in HIV prevention*. London: The HIV Project.

CLARKSON, P. *An integration of theory, research and supervised practise. Counselling psychology* (in press). London: Routledge.

DEPARTMENT OF HEALTH (1995) *HIV & AIDS health promotion: An evolving strategy*. London.

DAVIES, D. & NEALE, C. (eds) (1996) *Pink therapy*. Milton Keynes: Open University Press.

EGAN, G. (1975) *The skilled helper*. Pacific Grove, California: Brooks, Cole.

GOLD, R. (1995) Why we need to rethink education for gay men. *AIDS CARE* Vol. 7, Supplement 1, 1995.

HART, G. J. (1993) Risk behaviour, anti-HIV and anti-Hepatitis B. *AIDS* 7(6), 1993.

HICKSON, F. C. I. et al. (1996) No aggregate change in homosexual HIV risk behaviour among gay men. *AIDS* **10**, 1996.

HICKSON, F. C. I. et al. (1994) Gay men as victims of non-consensual sex. *Archives of sexual behaviour* **23**(3), 281–94.

KELLY, J. A. et al. (1991) Situational factors associated with AIDS risk behaviour. *American Journal of Public Health* **81**(10), 1991.

MABEL CAMACHO, L. (1996) Psychological dysfunction and HIV/AIDS risk behaviour. *Journal of AIDS and Human Retrovirology* **11**, 1996.

MARTINDALE, S. L. et al. (1996) Risk behaviour and HIV seroprevalence among a cohort of young men. Paper presented at 11th International Conference on AIDS, Vancouver 1996.

OAKLEY, A. et al. (1996) *Review of effectiveness of sexual health promotion interventions for young people*. EPI Centre, London University Institute of Education.

OAKLEY, A. et al. (1994) *Young people, health and family life*. Milton Keynes: Open University Press.

ODETS, W. (1995) *In the shadow of the epidemic*. Durham, North Carolina: Onke University Press.

ORBACH, S. (1994) *What's really going on here?* London: Virago.

PROUT, A. (1992) Illumination, collaboration, facilitation, negotiation – evaluating the MESMAC Project. In AGGLETON P. et al. *Does it work? Perspectives on the evaluation of HIV/AIDS health promotion*. London: Health Education Authority.

ROGERS, C. (1961) *On Becoming a Person*. London: Constable.

THORNTON, S. & CATALAN, J. (1993) Preventing the sexual spread of HIV infection: What have we learned? *International Journal of STD & AIDS* **4**, 1993.

VAN GORDER, D. (1995) Building Community and Culture. *AIDS and Public Policy Journal* **10**(2), 1995.

WILLIAMS, D. I. et al. (1996) A case study of seroconversion in gay men. *Genitourinary Medicine* Vol. 72, 1996.

YALOM, I. (1985) *Theory and practice of group psychotherapy*. New York: Basic Books.

YOUNG, V. (1996) *The equality complex*. London: Cassell.

Appendix I

The Questionnaire

Pace Workshops for Gay Men Feedback Questionnaire

This questionnaire asks you questions about yourself and your experience of PACE Workshops for Gay Men. The questionnaire is anonymous, and we will keep all information you provide confidential.

Please try to be as honest as possible when answering the questions, tell us what you did like as well as what you did not like. Where we ask for more details please try to give as full an answer as possible. If you attended more than one workshop and have different answers to some questions, please put both answers down.

Please complete the questionnaire as soon as possible and return it to PACE in the envelope provided by **Tues 2nd April 1996.**

The Workshops

1. Which of the workshops below did you attend?

    ❏ *KY Babies*   (Oct 95 – iCare – Listening Skills and Change)
    ❏ *Basic Delights*   (2 Nov 95 – Red Admiral Project – Condoms
                               and Safer Sex)
    ❏ *A Night of Fireworks!* (3 Nov 95 – Route 15 – Fireworks)
    ❏ *Let's Talk About Sex*   (Nov/Dec 95 – Covent Garden – Young Gay
                               Men's Group)
    ❏ *Sex Positive*   (Nov 95 – Shepherdess Walk – For HIV
                               Positive Men)
    ❏ *It Takes Two to Tangle* (Nov 95 – The Landmark – Relationships)
    ❏ *Talking Dirty*   (Dec 95 – PACE – Talking About Sex)
    ❏ *Getting What You*   (Dec 95 – River House – Assertion Skills)
      Want for Xmas
    ❏ *Resolutions!*   (Feb 96 – Little Grove – Making Changes)

2. Did you attend all the meetings of the workshop or group?

   ❏ Yes   ❏ No   If no, what were your reasons for not attending?

   _____

   _____

3. What were you hoping to get from the workshop?

   _____

   _____

4. Were your expectations met by the workshop?

   ❏ Yes   ❏ Partly   ❏ No   ❏ Don't Know

   Please give details _____

5. How personally useful was the workshop for you?

   ❏ not at all useful
   ❏ a little useful
   ❏ partly useful
   ❏ mostly useful
   ❏ very useful

6. Are you likely to attend another PACE workshop or group in the future?

   ❏ Yes   ❏ No

The Impact of the Workshops

7. Overall, what difference, if any, has the workshop made to you?

   _____

   _____

8. What difference has the workshop made to your relationships with other people?

   _____

   _____

9. What impact has the workshop had on your sexual activity?

   _____

   _____

10. Below is a list of possible changes as a result of the workshop(s). For each possible change please tick the relevant box indicating how the workshop has affected you, if at all, in the way described. If you are unsure or don't know whether the workshop has affected you in the way described, do not tick a box.

a lot more	a little more	no change	a little less	a lot less	
❑	❑	❑	❑	❑	confident in bars
❑	❑	❑	❑	❑	confident in bed
❑	❑	❑	❑	❑	able to negotiate generally
❑	❑	❑	❑	❑	able to negotiate about sex
❑	❑	❑	❑	❑	comfortable talking about sex with friends
❑	❑	❑	❑	❑	comfortable talking about sex with your lover
❑	❑	❑	❑	❑	motivated to keep sex safe
❑	❑	❑	❑	❑	comfortable being gay
❑	❑	❑	❑	❑	shy
❑	❑	❑	❑	❑	sociable
❑	❑	❑	❑	❑	anxious
❑	❑	❑	❑	❑	self-knowledgeable
❑	❑	❑	❑	❑	secure
❑	❑	❑	❑	❑	isolated
❑	❑	❑	❑	❑	self-assured
❑	❑	❑	❑	❑	assertive
❑	❑	❑	❑	❑	optimistic
❑	❑	❑	❑	❑	pessimistic
❑	❑	❑	❑	❑	happy
❑	❑	❑	❑	❑	depressed
❑	❑	❑	❑	❑	clarity about personal goals in relationships
❑	❑	❑	❑	❑	clarity about personal sexual goals
❑	❑	❑	❑	❑	confident to handle difficult sexual situations
❑	❑	❑	❑	❑	confident in having satisfying relationships
❑	❑	❑	❑	❑	likely to have unsafe sex
❑	❑	❑	❑	❑	knowledgeable about HIV and safer sex

11. Have you talked with other people about the workshop?

❑ Yes   ❑ No   If yes, what did you talk about? _____

12. Have you recommended the workshops to other gay men?

❏ Yes   ❏ No

Relationships and Sex

13. In the last 12 months have you had a regular sexual partner?

❏ Yes   ❏ No   If No go to Question 15

14. In the last 12 months have you fucked without a condom or been fucked without a condom, with a **regular partner**?

❏ Yes   ❏ No

15. In the last 12 months have you fucked without a condom or been fucked without a condom, with a **casual partner**?

❏ Yes   ❏ No

About You

16. How old are you? _____

17. How would you describe your ethnic origin?

Ethnicity	Asian	Black-Other	White-UK
	Black-African	Chinese	White-Other
	Black-Caribbean	Irish	Any Other

18. In which London Boroughs do you:

In which London Boroughs do you . . .	Live	
	Work	
	Study	

19. Please tick the box that applies to you.

    ❑ I do not know my HIV status
    ❑ I am HIV positive
    ❑ I am HIV negative

Reproduced courtesy of The Project for Advice Counselling and Education.

Appendix II

Participants' perceptions of the impact of workshops.

Key – each box represents 2 responses (6 per cent or sample).

a lot more	a little more	no change	a little less	a lot less	no answer

Variables where the desired outcome is "a lot more" or "a little more".

Successful outcomes are indicated by significantly more shading on the left hand side of the table, compared to right hand side.

	confident in bars	
	confident in bed	
	able to negotiate generally	
	able to negotiate about sex	
	comfortable talking about sex with friends	
	comfortable talking about sex with your lover	
	motivated to keep sex safe	
	comfortable being gay	
	self-knowledgeable	
	sociable	
	secure	

a lot more	a little more	no change	a little less	a lot less	no answer

Variables where the desired outcome is "a lot more" or "a little more".

Successful outcomes are indicated by significantly more shading on the left hand side of the table, compared to right hand side.

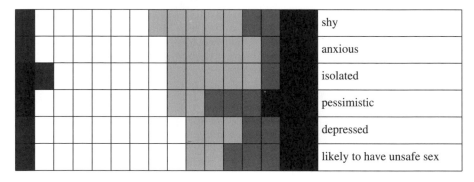

															self-assured
															assertive
															optimistic
															happy
															clarity about personal goals in relationships
															clarity about personal sexual goals
															confident to handle difficult sexual situations
															confident in having satisfying relationships
															knowledgeable about HIV and safer sex

a lot more	a little more	no change	a little less	a lot less	no answer

Variables where the desired outcome is "a lot less" or "a little less".

Successful outcomes are indicated by significantly more shading on the right hand side of the table, compared to left hand side.

													shy
													anxious
													isolated
													pessimistic
													depressed
													likely to have unsafe sex

Reproduced courtesy of The Project for Advice Counselling and Education.

Chapter Nine

Men, violence and love

Paul Wolf-Light

Introduction

Violence and abuse do not exist in a vacuum but are nourished and encouraged by the values and beliefs of both individuals and societies. The wish to dominate and possess others, the seeing of others as objects rather than human beings, self-importance and greed, the fear of intimacy, the need to be tough and hard alongside the avoidance of vulnerability. These are just some of the conditions in which violence and abuse thrive. They are also strongly associated with male identity and would appear to be inimical to love.

However, the single largest category of assaults uncovered by the latest British Crime Survey was domestic violence, and the vast majority of these assaults were by men against women. Yet, unlike other violent crime, domestic violence takes place within the framework of a close relationship that in theory has love as its foundation. Furthermore, it is not uncommon for men to say that their violence occurs because they love their partners so much. Despite the obvious contradiction, they seem to believe not only in the importance of love but that they themselves are acting under its influence.

This raises a number of questions, in particular what do such men mean by love, what else do we mean by love, and what, if any, is the connection between these different meanings. For if love can be seen as the very antithesis of violence, then it would seem to be a crucial part of any attempt to change violent behaviour. Yet if love can also be seen as a cause of violence, then caution and a clear understanding of what is meant by love is called for.

Two types of love

In this regard there are two particular meanings of love that seem to form the basis of these opposing tendencies. The first can be described as self-centred love. It is that which we find attractive in another that makes us feel good inside, that nourishes our well-being and satisfies in some measure our wish for relationship. In drawing us to another, it is a source of pleasure, inspiration and desire.

Even if connected with experiences of joy and beauty, such feelings of love are invariably bound up with our needs, particularly those of affection, nurture and security. This perception of the loved one as a source of personal gratification creates strong feelings of bonding and attachment. However, such attachment can soon invoke equally strong feelings of dependency, where the loved one is perceived as being the only one who can provide for us. If coupled with a fear of dependency alongside emotional immaturity, overwhelming feelings of insecurity and a terror of abandonment by the loved one are likely to be present.

It is not difficult to see how this can lead to possessive and tyrannical behaviour. Control in the form of domination then becomes the basis of relationship, and abuse and violence invariably follow. The object of such love becomes reduced to just that: an object, valued as a commodity rather than a human being. The relationship becomes one of consumption rather than consummation, where the loved one is consumed and drained of love by the possessive lover.

The other type of love, which is the antithesis of violence and abuse, can be described as compassionate love. This is the loving of another for themselves, valuing someone for who they are rather than for what they may give us. It evokes feelings of support and care and is grounded in the recognition that we are already connected, that the other is, like ourselves, part of something greater. Whether described in terms of the divine, nature, community, or some other greater ground of being, it acknowledges connection and relationship that transcends mere personal needs and desires and therefore is not limited to them.

Such love flows from a benevolence of heart and the pleasure of giving, a generosity rooted in the enjoyment of the other's well-being. It can inspire a wish to offer ourselves in service to the loved one, grounded in affection and a profound gratitude for their existence. The connection between loved ones here is empathic and intimate, and such love can indeed be seen as antithetical not merely to violence but to any form of abuse or domination.

What seems central for the compassion at the heart of such love to be experienced is that an individual has the capacity to empathize fully with others. Empathy in this full sense can be described as the ability of an individual to be touched inside by another in a way that gives them a sense of that other person's interior being, that which enables him or her to recognize the human quality of another. While a basic requirement of empathy is the ability to resonate consciously with another person's emotions and feelings, to be fully empathic requires one to be in tune with the whole person. Without such empathy others can only be perceived as objects rather than persons, which inevitably reduces relationships to struggles for power and control. Whereas compassionate love sees relationships as being founded upon intimacy and trust.

But, despite what may seem at first glance different and opposing perspectives and consequences, these two types of love are neither contradictory nor disconnected. On the contrary, there is a clear link between the two and it is possible to experience both types of love simultaneously. The pleasure and desire felt in the presence of another does not preclude us from feelings of appreciation and generosity or the wish to serve their happiness. Self-centred love need not remain selfish and does not inevitably become possessive and dominating.

Our very desire for and attraction to the other is what can allow us to be touched by them and invoke feelings of affection and warmth. Our perception of another as a source of our fulfilment can ignite our longing for intimacy and inspire the first stirring of compassionate love. In such a context, personal desire, whether for intimacy, support, nourishment, sex or just plain recognition, becomes an offering that may be accepted or refused, rather than a possessive longing that has to be gratified whatever the cost.

The problem then is not the experience of self-centred love, but that such love remains self-centred and gratification oriented. It is the lack of compassionate love that creates the problem. So the questions that arise are not simply why are so many men violent and abusive in relationships with women and how can we stop such violence continuing? But also, why do so many men find it difficult to love compassionately, what are the conditions that discourage their developing a genuine compassionate love? And how can they be encouraged to connect their self-centred love to a compassionate love, what conditions do we need to create for such men that will lead and support them into becoming fully loving?

Aggression and assertion

Before attempting to give some answers to these questions it seems equally important to examine the nature of aggression. It is also a term that covers a wide range of behaviours and meanings. It is not only the source of violence, but at its most basic aggression is synonymous with all active behaviour, including acts of generosity and caring. For any activity must have an impact on its environment, and even acts of benevolence and kindness can be experienced by the recipient(s) as disturbing and threatening. So it is necessary to unpack and differentiate different forms of aggression.

In this respect, I have found it helpful to split aggression into two distinct types, which have certain similarities with the two types of love described above. In particular, the qualities associated with being self-centred in approach as opposed to being compassionate. For clarity, I wish to use the term "aggression" specifically for self-centred aggression, but use the term "assertion" for what would otherwise be termed "compassionate aggression".

One of the defining qualities of aggression is that it objectifies those at whom it is directed. When acting aggressively individuals tend to perceive themselves as detached and separate from those others rather than being connected. Others are seen as having no particular value in themselves, being reduced to mere objects of amusement, gratification, or annoyance. In this respect aggression can be said to be self-centred and lacking compassion.

An assertive individual, on the other hand, has an empathic relationship with others, recognizing not only their value but also their connection with himself or herself. The relationship between them is important and each individual's needs and desires sit within the larger framework of all their needs and desires. There is recognition and valuing of the other's autonomy, seeing it as important as his or her own. In this way assertion can be said to be compassionate rather than self-centred.

To help clarify further the particular qualities of aggression and assertion and the differences between them, I will introduce four distinct categories of behaviour, namely exploration, gratification, protest, and remedy. While not mutually exclusive in any absolute sense, they offer distinct descriptions of particular motivations initiating behaviour.

Exploration

By exploration I mean activity that is motivated by curiosity. Its purpose is discovery and its consequence is an increased awareness of environment and self. Such behaviour is not driven by the wish to manipulate the environment, including others, for the purpose of control and dominance. Rather, although active and so manipulative in effect, it is essentially receptive and concerned with understanding, taking place in a spirit of inquiry and play.

The aggressive quality of an individual's exploring is revealed by the lack of concern for the object of exploration. Detached and distant in attitude, everything is seen from a mechanistic viewpoint. In the context of relationship, there is a general indifference to the effect his or her conduct might have, with no concern for the physical or emotional health of others. Whether playful or thoughtful in intent, such activity can easily slip into destructive and wounding behaviour.

An assertive individual is engaged with what has excited his or her curiosity, the environment is not seen as something completely separate. Empathic and connected in attitude, everything is seen from an ecological perspective. Within relationship there is not merely concern for the well-being of others, but genuine interest in them. Curiosity is directed inside as well as out, and whether playful or reflective, activity is primarily motivated by a wish to participate with others rather than use them for amusement.

Gratification

By gratification I mean activity that is motivated by the wish to satisfy desire and hunger, and which attempts to influence the environment, including others, towards that end. This may be for the satisfaction of personal needs, whether physical or emotional, or an attempt to manifest some vision or ideal, which may be perceived as collective or individual. Its purpose is satisfaction and its consequence is modification of the environment and others. It is manipulative behaviour, attempting to change what is around one (or have things remain the same) so as to satisfy one's appetites, whether nutritional or ideological.

The aggressive quality of behaviour motivated by gratification is revealed by the attempt to impose one's personal will upon the environment, with a lack of concern for and detachment from that which is being controlled. Others are perceived as resources to exploit, their needs and desires being of little consequence. Relationships are based on exploitation and domination, communication being reduced to demands and ultimatums. Gratification is achieved by coercion, with violence and the use of force considered as just another resource to use towards that end.

An assertive individual's attempts to achieve gratification are based upon negotiation and co-operation. The relationship with the environment is seen as a reciprocal one, based upon exchange rather than exploitation. Such exchange is seen as a creative possibility in which something new may emerge, that satisfaction can be achieved outside of one's original desires. Others are seen as being sources of support and inspiration, whose needs and ideas are equally as important as one's own. Relationships are based on collaboration and compromise, and communication is empathic and flexible. Gratification is achieved only to the degree that mutual agreement can be found. There is a willingness to put oneself on the line in terms of stating what one wants, yet also to accept the disappointment of potential rejection. In this way assertive behaviour always contains an inherent sense of vulnerability, in its willingness to accept failure, not from a position of fear but from a recognition of mutual need and genuine affection.

Protest

By protest I mean activity that is motivated by the wish to register a complaint and put a stop to what is perceived as threatening. The threat may be to oneself, to others or to one's environment, but the purpose of protest is to protect and its consequence is the creation of boundaries between the recipient and that which is threatening. It is a response to perceived external activity rather than an internal initiative towards one's own ends. It is controlling, but its purpose is limitation not expansion or gratification.

The aggressive quality of an individual's protesting behaviour is revealed by the hostility directed towards that which is perceived as threatening. The source of the threat is demonized, seen as something separate and disconnected from oneself, which has to be threatened in turn. Others are seen as sources of intimidation who need to be kept at bay by further threats. Relationships in this context are based upon fear, and communication is hostile and threatening. Protest is achieved by intimidation, with violence and the use of force always an option. The vulnerability that the threat must have touched upon for it to be effective is defended against, either by complete denial of any weakness or by using it against the other, blaming them in an attempt to make them feel bad rather than to have them understand how one feels.

An assertive individual's protest is grounded in communication and protection, seeing the threat as needing to be challenged and defused. It is about taking responsibility for setting things right again rather than compensating for feeling threatened by becoming confrontational and intimidating. Others are seen as being similar to oneself and therefore as receptive and capable of understanding. Their behaviour is perceived as being likely to be rooted in their own fears and insecurities, eliciting in oneself compassion alongside a firm rejection of their threats. Relationships are based on clear boundaries and communication is direct but respectful. Protest is achieved by communicating not only terms and conditions but also the feelings of vulnerability and hurt that the threat has elicited in oneself, not from a wish to blame the other but to have them understand and empathize. For such protest is empathic in nature and has as its basis the wish for relationship to continue.

Remedy

By remedy I mean activity that arises from the experience of being damaged and wounded and is motivated by the wish to counteract the conditions that are perceived to have caused the damage and restore to health that which has been injured. The injury may be to oneself, to others or to one's environment, but the purpose of remedy is to rectify the damage, and its consequence is the convalescence and improved health of that which is injured. It can be directed as much against what is seen as causing the damage as towards healing and restoration, the intention being to restore balance and gain relief from what is painful.

An aggressive individual's remedy is grounded in the wish to inflict injury upon that which is perceived as having created the damage. Satisfaction is gained by the destruction, or at least wounding, of the source of the damage, said source being seen as cruel and malignant, something completely other than and hostile to oneself. Other people are perceived as dangerous and abusive enemies who must be controlled by fear and punishment. Protection is achieved by the destruction of the other's power and relief is offered in the form of sadistic pleasure. Relationships are based upon retribution, while communication is vindictive and wounding. Remedy is accomplished by punishment and abuse. Revenge rather than healing is the goal, a restoration of balance by inflicting damage on that which has been experienced as injuring and causing pain to oneself.

Such aggression has a strong connection to sadism, the pleasure felt in inflicting pain on others. For sadism functions through what could be termed fragmentary empathy. This is the ability to identify and resonate with the feelings of pain inflicted on the other without seeing them as a whole human being, instead reducing them to the status of an object containing emotions and sensations. These then become selective fragments of arousal for the sadist, who empathizes with these "bits" of another so as to enjoy vicariously the emotions and sensations evoked. The pleasure experienced in this way can clearly have a sexual dimension and thus become entangled with the individual's sexual behaviour. In this context sadism is motivated by gratification rather than remedy, but the initial wish to cause pain seems to be rooted in remedy.

The remedial action of an assertive individual is grounded in restoration and healing, the wish to restore health to what has been damaged, and rehabilitate and change the destructive source. It attempts to see the connection between perpetrator and victim and takes responsibility for changing the whole rather than just the wounded parts. Others are perceived as being more than just their destructive behaviour, as potential allies who are also damaged rather than evil enemies. So, while destructive behaviour is challenged and condemned, the perpetrators are neither demonized nor sadistically punished. Sanctions are based upon containment and rehabilitation rather than revenge and suffering.

Relationships are based on compassion and transformation, while communication is rooted in honesty and oriented towards mutual understanding. Remedy is accomplished by restoring balance in a way that integrates the needs of all parties. Vulnerability is acknowledged as being implicit and inevitable, being a source of healing and change.

Assertive qualities

There are four particular qualities that emerge as being present in assertion and are lacking in aggression. The first of these is *responsibility*, the willingness not only to take responsibility for oneself but also for the environment and those around one. Aggression is indifferent to the well-being of what is outside oneself, and is therefore likely to deny responsibility for the consequences of any actions taken. The second quality is *vulnerability*, the acceptance not only of one's susceptibility to injury but the inevitability of loss and disappointment alongside joy and achievement. Aggression on the other hand attempts to maintain the illusion of being powerful and always in control, considering weakness as unacceptable and to be defended against at all costs.

Following on from vulnerability, the third quality is *empathy*, the capacity to be touched by another, to resonate with their humanity and so to be intimate and feel compassion. Aggression does not empathize in this fully human sense, instead seeing others as objects to be used and discarded for one's own purposes. The fourth quality is *creativity*, the ability to be flexible and open to new and different possibilities. Aggression tends to be destructive and rigid, attempting to impose its own views and break whatever conflicts with these.

Social construction of masculinity

On the basis of the above, it seems appropriate to look at what it is about men that seems to predispose so many of them towards both self-centred love and aggression. The most useful starting point seems to be to examine masculinity as a social construct as, despite what appears to be a disposition of men in general to behave aggressively, by no means all men manifest such behaviour and attitudes. This suggests that they are not inherent to men biologically, but are an attribute of masculinity.

Masculinity as understood here stands for the qualities socially attributable to men. These are not necessarily exclusive to men but are generally expected of men. They are reflections of gender rather than sex, an aggregation of social expectations rather than biological imperatives. Being therefore effected by differences in cultural and social values, there can be no single definition of masculinity. However, there is what can be called an hegemonic masculinity, which reflects the dominant and therefore most influential definition of masculinity in our culture today. (Many of these qualities also seem present with relatively minor variations in most other cultures, east and west, north and south.) It is this hegemonic masculinity that I wish to explore here.

Control

The particular quality that pervades this masculinity can be defined in one word: control. There is an expectation of men that they should be in control at all times. This message is supported by two further demands, that men should not be vulnerable and that they should be rational. These qualities can clearly be seen to reinforce each other. The demand not to be vulnerable includes the demand not to allow emotions such as fear and grief, which are associated with vulnerability, as well as not to allow feelings of dependency and intimacy. The demand to be rational supports this movement away from emotion and feeling, creating a hierarchy of mental "attitude" and ideology over feeling and emotion.

The relative ease of controlling thoughts as opposed to feelings reinforces this process. We can control what we do with our feelings and emotions, but we cannot control their emergence. Therefore the desensitizing of awareness of feeling and emotion becomes a way to overcome their spontaneous emergence, at least as far as consciousness is concerned. The fact that they do not disappear, but simply become repressed and get expressed unconsciously does not effect this process because the very unconscious nature of their expression means they can be denied or projected onto others.

The consequences of such a process are manifold. There is a tendency for awareness of all feeling and emotion to be diminished. Furthermore, those emotions such as anger and rage, which are not identified with vulnerability and are therefore considered acceptable, tend to be the conduit of expression for all emotion. Because of the general desensitizing of awareness, the more subtle levels of emotion and feeling are simply not recognized. One consequence of this can be a build up of unexpressed emotion that eventually erupts in an explosive and intense outburst. Such a pattern clearly lends itself to violence.

Fear of dependency and intimacy

The wish to avoid vulnerability creates a fear of dependency and intimacy. This has a major impact on close relationships, which are based upon an interdependency and shared intimacy. The need to control the other person in a relationship becomes paramount as a way of denying dependency and avoiding intimacy. However, being human, feelings of dependency on the one hand and a longing for intimacy on the other are always going to be present and to emerge at times. This is likely to reinforce and increase the need for control as a defence against feeling vulnerable in this way. In addition, the avoidance of intimacy will tend to reduce the other person to the status of object, and the fear of intimacy is likely to create feelings of hostility towards the same person, who is seen as invoking such vulnerability. The use of violence as a means of maintaining control and punishing the other for causing the threatening feelings becomes then not merely a possibility but a probability.

A further consequence of the processes above is that the ability to empathize fully is severely reduced. However, although underdeveloped, a limited empathy will invariably be present. Unfortunately, this is unlikely to promote a healthier relationship. Instead the resonance is likely to be with a part of the other person rather than the whole of them. The emotions empathized with consciously are generally going to be those of anger and rage, because these are the emotions a man knows. He is therefore likely to feel hostile in response and express his hostility through further anger and rage.

On the unconscious level, feelings of fear and pain in the other are likely to be empathized with as a form of sadistic pleasure, as in the process of fragmentary empathy described previously. In this way the other person is not seen as a fully human other but as a source of emotional arousal. The construction of masculinity as described encourages these conditions and, therefore, abusive behaviour.

Following on from the process described above, the difficulty men have in accepting vulnerability and intimacy tends to create an emphasis on excitement as the dominant experience of pleasure. This becomes most obvious in men's sexual relationships, where sexual partners, whether male or female, can easily become primarily identified as objects to arouse and then satisfy sexual desire. In this case sexuality itself tends to become both genitally oriented and ejaculation focused. The more sensual range of pleasures on the one hand, and the surrender to the more intimate and emotional experiences that sex invokes on the other, are both denied, in the latter case often actively defended against. This splitting of sexual partners into objects of arousal apart from reducing a partner to the level of an object can also easily become sadistic. This can be seen most clearly on a broader social level in the pornography industry. Whereas soft porn essentially functions as a producer of images of sexual arousal, such images in hard porn become explicitly sadistic and often violent.

Expectations of women

In addition to the above, there are two quite explicit social messages that reinforce the propensity towards violence and away from compassion in men. The first of these affects men's relationships with women. There is a fairly explicit social expectation of women that, on the one hand, they should be the source of nourishment and support for men, particularly in the area of emotions and physical gratification, and on the other that they should acknowledge men's dominance and superiority over them in terms of status. This can often create a split in a man's perception of women in general, which becomes intensified within any relationship he has with a particular woman. She then becomes seen as either an idealized princess/good mother figure who will satisfy all his needs, or a witch/bad mother figure who is denying and threatening him. When she fails to live up to his idealized expectations she becomes the demonized witch, who then has to be punished and "put in her place".

This wish to punish invariably leads to abusive and violent behaviour, serving the purpose of ensuring his control and dominance on the one hand and warding off the emotional terrors and dependency on the other. Genuine intimacy in such a relationship is not possible at an adult level, although the regression to an infantile symbiotic state on occasions while the woman is in the idealized position can create the illusion of closeness and mutuality. However, it is likely to be constantly punctuated by periods of violence and abuse.

Expectations of men

The second fairly explicit social message is that men should be able both to give and to take a certain degree of violence. This begins in childhood where boys are expected to be able to fight and not to cry, and continues in adulthood. The expressions "a man's man" and "a man's game" invariably refer to the willingness of such men to accept violence without complaint or judgement. This value, whereby men are only considered "real" men if they are capable of such violence, is reinforced further in the fictional stories prevalent in our culture. Whether in films, television or books, one of the dominant themes is of the heroic "good" man overcoming evil "bad" men by the use of violence. The underlying message is that to be heroic it is essential to be a better exponent of violence than the perceived villains. Often the message appears to be that all other human values owe their existence to such heroic violence. Yet in virtually all these fictional depictions it is men who are the heroic perpetrators of violence. Women are generally represented only as victims or grateful beneficiaries of male violence.

Finally, following on from this, men tend to be valued socially for their status but not as human beings. Their willingness to give and take "acceptable" levels of violence is an important factor in this, being part of the price to be paid for such status. On a human level, men are generally regarded as being expendable unless they have a suitable degree of status. In times of war this becomes heightened so that the vast majority of men are expected to risk losing their lives as a matter of course. As well as sanctions such as imprisonment, their masculinity is also brought into question should they refuse.

This process results in them becoming objectified and dehumanized, relying for their sense of value on an external image based upon recognition of status and position. Of course such status as can be obtained is generally reserved exclusively for men, including the underlying assumption that a man will have a woman to respond to and satisfy his needs whatever his status. But the point here is that this valuing of a man by his external status and not by his basic humanity colludes with the general thrust of masculinity towards violence and away from compassion.

Summary

It seems clear that the hegemonic masculinity so described encourages aggression and potential abuse, including violence, in men, while discouraging compassion and intimacy. Reducing others to the status of objects and therefore being indifferent to their needs, attempting to control and dominate others while destroying any opposition, all these qualities of aggression are promoted by this form of masculinity. This offers some answers to the question of why so many men behave in such a way.

Changing violent men

Clues to the answers to the more important question of how such behaviour can be changed are revealed by the qualities of assertion and compassionate love, in particular those of responsibility, vulnerability, empathy and creativity. How can these be developed in practice in a therapeutic programme for changing men? Taking these four qualities as basic principles, the following is a description of a particular approach towards working with men who are violent that has been developed at the Everyman Centre, originally in London and now in Plymouth.

Responsibility

Being responsible means recognizing that our behaviour, although influenced by a range of factors, is always a matter of our choice. We do what we do because we have decided to, nobody makes us and no-one else is responsible for our actions. It means recognizing that we have an impact upon others and that there are consequences to our actions. That we do not exist in isolation but are part of an environment, social and physical, that supports and nourishes us, and that we participate in a shared responsibility for its well-being and development. It means having values and standards based upon integrity, which we demonstrate by example in both our behaviour and attitude. To be aware of and be honest about our mistakes and being willing to be accountable, to make reparation and to change. It is having the courage to ask for help rather than to demand or expect it, and being willing to take care of ourselves when help is refused or is unavailable.

In practice, the principle of responsibility focuses upon three particular areas. The man's ownership of his behaviour, the immediate containment of his violence and abuse, and his changing from a self-centred and aggressive personality to one identified with compassion and assertion.

In the first instance, the acknowledgement of his violence as emanating from him and him alone has several consequences. By recognizing that the violence has been a matter of choice, it becomes possible to choose not to be violent. It may invoke guilt and shame, but it also gives hope and encouragement. It also engages immediately with the man's adult self, so that the basis of the counselling relationship is that of one adult to another rather than a parent to a child. This supports him adopting a responsible attitude as an adult towards his violence rather than a regressive one as a child, for as a child he is likely to see himself as the helpless victim of provocation rather than the powerful agent of abuse. In addition it sets clear boundaries around expectation and offers him a model of appropriate authority to begin to internalize, based on agreed terms and commitment. As violence is a violation of boundaries and an expression of abusive authority, the setting of such examples is imperative.

Having acknowledged that the violence is his problem, a man is required to take responsibility for ceasing such behaviour immediately. He is therefore requested to make a commitment in the presence of the counsellor to stop his violence and abuse as of now: not to try to stop or want to stop, but to stop. It is pointed out to him that the foundation of the counselling work is his decision to stop his violence: without that decision little can be achieved. A man needs to make this commitment for himself, but it is important that it is witnessed. Furthermore, it must be stressed that the decision to cease violent behaviour needs to be remade each and every day, that there is no cure as such, only this internal and constant decision, and he alone is responsible for making and maintaining this decision.

If subsequently the man should disclose further violence or expresses an abusive attitude, he can be challenged within the framework of his own commitment (e.g. How do you feel about your behaviour in the context of your commitment to stop being violent?) and his own stated purpose of attending counselling. While this will not stop a man attempting to justify his violence or taking a defensive response, it undermines his justification and defensive attitudes and gives more weight to the challenge. Because it is not merely the counsellor challenging him. His own stated purpose and commitment is used to challenge him and support his taking responsibility both in terms of examining the incident in detail and in renewing his commitment.

Having got the man's commitment to stop his violence, he needs to have appropriate strategies and techniques to ensure he can carry out his commitment. In the short term these will be behavioural techniques that rely upon him recognizing when he is becoming potentially violent, and either calming down or removing himself in a non-abusive way from the situation. These will vary from simple strategies such as "time out", "the six foot rule" and breathing exercises, to his moving out of the house. If he is in a relationship with a partner, he needs to share these procedures with his partner so that she (or he) understands them in terms of both purpose and practice.

If a man has his own methods already, they need to be looked at to ensure that they are not abusive and are practical. For example, leaving a situation by shouting abuse, slamming doors and giving no indication of when he might return is abusive in itself, although he might well avoid inflicting physical violence directly on his partner. It is therefore important to make clear the difference between this and an appropriate use of "time out"; for example, where he states clearly that he is going to leave the situation because he does not wish to be violent and recognizes his own danger signals, leaves quietly and returns after an agreed and clearly stated period of time.

All this serves to place the safety of those who he has abused and that of others he might abuse at the forefront of the counselling work. The aim is to ensure he is as safe in his behaviour as possible now and to have the maintenance of that safety as an overt priority, acknowledged by both himself and the counsellor from the beginning.

The third area of responsibility is that of personal change, transforming attitudes and behavioural patterns that support and underly his violent behaviour. The starting point for this is to have him recognize not only the cognitive decisions he is making but what he feels and how this affects his behaviour and attitudes. The starting point for this is to ask him to describe a violent incident in detail, a procedure he is likely to go through several times during his attendance. This will involve taking him back to the point when there was no conflict and then looking at how the build up towards violence developed. During this description, points where he escalated the conflict rather than defused it are brought to his attention and examined, with the intention of having him recognize for himself the choices he made in this escalation. The feelings and motives behind his choices can then also be examined. The purpose of all this is to enhance his awareness so as to increase his capacity for responsibility and change.

Once a man has demonstrated his commitment and responsibility in the ways described above, he is asked in some detail about his history. This focuses on his childhood in terms of family relationships and school life, and his adult life in terms of work experience and significant sexual relationships, particularly those in which he and a partner were living together, whether married or not. This can enable connections to be made between both his current behavioural patterns and attitudes and relevant past events in childhood. In this way he develops a greater understanding of himself and his behaviour and begins to recognize the origin of abusive attitudes he now holds. But, equally importantly, its purpose is to enable him to realize that, while as a child he may have had limited options, as an adult he has many more available and he is now responsible for finding non-abusive alternatives.

Although all the principles seem equally important in terms of long-term change, responsibility is the framework in which the other principles must function, it is the container that puts safety at the forefront. It is therefore essential to challenge any statements that deny, justify or show acceptance of violence or abuse. In practice this needs to be done immediately, holding the session right there and looking at the statement made. This not only avoids collusion but also reinforces both boundaries and authority. The feelings and emotions that may emerge from this holding are likely to be more implicitly connected to the violence than whatever material would otherwise have been followed. This can enable the man to explore his underlying motives and feelings more directly, bringing the here and now of the session into play.

Vulnerability

Being vulnerable means accepting our limitations, our weaknesses, our feelings of hurt. It means accepting that we can never be in total control of our environment, that life will always bring both surprises and disappointments. It is recognizing that others are not there to serve us, that they are of equal value to ourselves, and that if they happen to be different from us in a way that disappoints us, that our disappointment is simply a reflection of our humanity. As a human being our lives will always contain sorrow as well as joy, pain as well as pleasure, death as well as life. It is therefore not only acceptable to feel vulnerable at times, it is inevitable. When we feel powerless and afraid, we feel vulnerable. Violence is not an antidote to vulnerability, it is love that can make vulnerability bearable.

The principle of vulnerability in terms of relationship is founded upon the acceptance of relative powerlessness and dependency. So that not only is it impossible to constantly be in control either of others or the environment, but that one is also always going to be dependent upon others at some times in some ways. In practice this means helping a man to tolerate and express those feelings and emotions that are associated with vulnerability, in particular grief, fear and shame, alongside a recognition that an interdependency based upon mutual affection and care is not only healthy but also the foundation of adult relationships.

There are two particular procedures that arise early in the programme that tend to elicit acknowledgement of vulnerability in a man. The first of these is the afore-mentioned examination of violent incidents in detail. In the vast majority of cases, what emerges is that during the build up there was an increasing feeling of being powerless and of losing control of the situation. This in turn seems often to heighten feelings of dependency as well as disappointment, anxiety and anger. The point at which violence erupts is when these feelings are experienced as intolerable. The purpose of getting the man in touch with this is to encourage him to sit with the feelings, to help him contain, accept and tolerate them. Often the experience of being powerless is accompanied by considerable anxiety, which is intensified by a belief system that as a man he ought not to feel vulnerable. He needs to be sup-ported in the recognition and acceptance of the fact that sometimes we are less powerful than another and that this is neither good nor bad but simply part of being human.

The second procedure that facilitates vulnerability is when the man reveals his history. It is often the first time he has talked about his childhood experiences to anyone, which in itself will elicit a range of emotions. In addition, his past experi-ences of both dependency and powerlessness in childhood begin to surface and become more conscious. Sharing this with another person is itself an exercise in trust, which is usually reinforced by the experience of someone really listening and being with him.

A particular focus of the history session is brought to bear on the man's own experiences of being treated violently. It seems to be a common trait of many men that they have experienced violence during their childhood, whether directly or indirectly. As a dominant expectation of masculinity is to be able to give and take a certain amount of violence, this is hardly surprising. A significant, but in the framework of masculinity, a comprehensible factor is the non-acknowledgement that such ill-treatment was damaging and hurtful. In many cases the initial state-ment made by men is that there was no violence at all during their childhood. When they subsequently describe incidents containing violence the response is generally that such behaviour by parents or others was simply normal discipline rather than violent, and as such was no more than they deserved. In this there is usually little connection with how it felt to be on the receiving end of violence. The pain, humiliation, resentment, shame, etc., having been repressed and replaced by a rationalization of their experiences as "normal" and acceptable, and as having been necessary to keep them as boys under control.

Getting them in touch with their own experiences of being treated violently does not merely render them vulnerable. It also enables them, often for the first time, to realize the full consequences of what they are doing to others when they behave violently. The rationalizations they have applied to their own experiences have equally been applied to the experiences of their victims. The recognition of the interior experience of being on the receiving end of violence forces them to face fully the damage they have caused to others. This is often the most painful part of all, but it is from this experience that genuine remorse can emerge.

Empathy

Being empathic means being emotionally in tune with another person, allowing ourselves to be touched inside by others and recognizing that they also are like us. That others feel sadness, anger, joy, fear, emptiness, despair, pain and pleasure, and have their own needs and desires which are as important to them as ours are to us. It is recognizing the connection between ourselves and others, that we share a common humanity, a mutual need for relationship and affection. That what we do and how we are has an effect upon others, not only on their external bodies, but also on their internal thoughts and attitudes, feelings and emotions. It is the ability to put ourselves in someone else's shoes, to imagine not only what they might be thinking but also how they might be feeling. It is the basis of intimacy, compassion and genuine relationship.

The principle of empathy is rooted in the recognition of mutual relationship and interdependency alongside the capacity to perceive others as autonomous human beings rather than as objects to manipulate and control. It is not merely an intellectual process, for the ability to resonate with another's feelings and emotions consciously is the very essence of empathy. This requires not merely an awareness of one's own feelings and emotions, but also the ability to be touched inside by another.

However, our model of hegemonic masculinity discourages men from expressing or even acknowledging the existence of feelings and emotions that are categorized as vulnerable. As a consequence their feeling capacity and emotional awareness tends to be impoverished, resulting in difficulty articulating and expressing such feeling and emotion even to themselves. This severely limits their ability to empathize with others. It is therefore necessary for the men to become re-sensitized and develop their emotional vocabulary and interior world in terms of experience and articulation.

Many men attach a great deal of embarrassment and shame to emotions such as grief and fear because of their association with vulnerability. The one emotion that they consider acceptable to express as men is anger; yet, because the other feelings are denied, this emerges not as assertive anger but as aggressive and even violent rage. There is a need for this rage to be contained and unpacked so to speak, so that the pain and disappointment underlying rage is allowed to be expressed in grief. Equally the anxiety and fear that are often present need to be recognized and acknowledged.

The purpose in all this is to allow the emotions and feelings to be expressed in a non-explosive cathartic way, for the violence itself is effectively an explosive catharsis. It is not a release as such that is being looked for but a softening and a healing process that can be ongoing and maintained. Similarly, there is a need to manage regression so that the man's adult self is always present and able to take responsibility for his experiences. The intention is to get the man to recognize and express what he is feeling before it becomes intense and extreme, to deepen and make more subtle his feeling capacity and emotional awareness.

It is maintaining a focus on empathy throughout this exploration and development of the man's feeling and emotional world that supports the recognition and contained expression of what is often a very painful and frightening experience. The empathic connection to another opens up a channel for the intense feelings that can emerge. This functions both as a conduit and healthy release, as well as offering a general expansion of the space in which they exist. Without this channel there is the danger that the man will become too self-centred and self-pitying, with the feelings and emotions building up inside as if in a pressure cooker that then explodes. The recognition not merely of others who also suffer, but of others whose suffering he has caused, functions as an "earthing" process. It is through this that he can develop remorse for his behaviour, so that a genuine and deep-seated wish arises to heal himself and those around him who he has damaged. This is what will sustain his decision to change his behaviour and render it something other than a mere rational exercise.

An important factor in the development of empathy during the counselling is the recognition of different forms of social oppression. For this to be effective it has to be educational in more than the cognitive sense. To facilitate this, alongside the dissemination of information on oppression, the man's own personal experiences are used as guides to understanding how it must be for others who are the victims of social prejudice in areas such as class, race, sexuality, culture or religion. But, in particular, the counselling focuses on an awareness of sexism and the oppression of women, as the man himself has participated in the perpetration of this by his own behaviour. The purpose is not only for him to develop empathy for those that he has oppressed and change his behaviour and attitudes towards them, but also to engage in challenging all forms of oppression, to become an activist for social change.

Creativity

Being creative means becoming an agent of change, offering ourselves in service to beauty and love rather than to destruction and power. It means stepping into the unknown and trusting, exploring and discovering new meanings in our past histories and our present situations. It is being willing to experiment, to allow ourselves and others to be different, to let go of habit and surrender to spontaneity and change. Accepting our playfulness and not taking ourselves too seriously, letting our imaginations offer alternative ways of responding to things. It is seeing difficult and painful experiences as invitations to change and grow, recognizing that rejection and disappointment offer opportunities for further learning just as much as acceptance and satisfaction do. It is being open to the wonder of life and participating in its constant renewal.

The principle of creativity is founded upon flexibility and change. Its essence is the allowing of space for something new to emerge, which demands a willingness to let go of habits and expectations and become receptive and open to what is not yet known. In terms of relationship, it means recognizing that different people will create together conditions and situations that are at variance with any one individual's vision. It means trusting one's heart to find an appropriate alignment with new circumstances, seeing conflict as an opportunity for change and renewal rather than oppression and rigidity.

In practice there are specific areas where creativity is called for. The primary one is a man's need to change his patterns of behaviour, to experiment with different and more constructive responses to situations rather than relying on old habits that lead to abuse. He needs to become flexible in both attitude and conduct, to move beyond rigid expectation and open up to the wider possibilities inherent in any situation. His imagination needs to be both stimulated and given expression so that he not merely accepts change but also participates in its inception and unfolding. During the counselling this capacity will be explored by direct example in the sessions and through his descriptions of how he is dealing with situations outside.

The second area that engages a man's creativity is in his relationship to his own history. He is encouraged over time to create the story of his life, one that incorporates the facts of his history but transforms their meaning by finding potential redemption and healing in the present and future. Often the meaning he gave in the past to his life story was negative, fuelled with resentment and resignation or grandiosity and contempt. He is encouraged to find a meaning and purpose in his history that is constructive and leads to healing, one that will give direction and value to his future life. Taking into account his past abuse, this needs to incorporate reparation and humility towards others, as well as healing of his own wounds. It creates a soil within which compassionate love can take root and blossom and flower.

Structure of the counselling programme

The programme that is founded upon these four principles uses a combination of time-limited individual counselling (usually twelve one-to-one sessions of one-hour duration on a weekly basis) and a longer period of groupwork (usually thirty-six two and a half hour sessions on a weekly basis). The individual work enables the client to look at his violence in depth by connecting it more clearly with his personal history, as well as enabling him to develop an emotional vocabulary. This short-term approach was adapted from cognitive analytical therapy (CAT), which was developed in the British National Health Service and unites object relations psycho-analysis with cognitive behavioural therapy. It aims to limit regression while allowing expression of feeling and expanding the client's capacity for self-observation and self-control. Apart from the maximizing of resources, the short-term approach ensures firm boundaries and a clear focus.

The groupwork that follows functions as a transitional experience between the private and closed world of the individual counselling session and the public world outside. Because of the social dimension to his violence as reflected in the expectations of masculinity, it is considered essential that much of this work takes place in a group setting with other men. Here men can both challenge and support each other, as well as open up and allow intimacy and empathy. Both the individual counselling and groupwork incorporate the cognitive and educational approaches recognized as necessary for challenging and changing abusive behaviour and attitudes, within a more psychodynamic approach that acknowledges and works with the emotional damage that invariably underlies such abusiveness.

The changes expected of the men in this programme are not simply self-oriented and self-healing. Rather they demand engaging with and participating in the maintenance and healing of all the systems that the men are not only part of but are sustained by. In this respect it could be said that the therapeutic model is ecocentric, rather than egocentric, in principle, seeing the men as participants in not only their own stories, but also in those of their family, society and the world as a whole.

Chapter Ten

Safety issues for women co-facilitating groups for violent men

Susan Cayouette

Introduction

Although leadership of batterer groups creates many challenges and dangers to both men and women, this chapter seeks to address those issues that are problematic for women in particular. Many batterer intervention programmes now use male/female teams, or in some case even female/female teams, creating a large group of potential female group leaders who may experience abusive and controlling behavior from group members.

At Emerge, our approach assumes that violence against women is fuelled by sexism, which is the unfair and hurtful treatment of women based on their gender. We also believe that oppression other than sexism fuels violence against women, so that racism, homophobia and classism (and other oppressions) fuel the violence that is particularly directed towards women in our society.

Given these assumptions that these "power over" relationships create an atmosphere in which domestic violence can occur without much obstruction, we assume that the forces that endanger women in abusive relationships are also going to come to bear down on the women who are leading the batterers' groups trying to address those very issues on a relationship by relationship basis.

How women began running batterer groups

Emerge was started in 1977 by a group of men in Boston, MA, USA, who were friends with women working in battered-women's shelters. They were asked to create an organization in which men would be asked to help other men take responsibility for their violence against women. Because of this challenge from women, a collective of men formed to work on the problem of male violence, thus creating the first batterers' programme in the USA. They initially considered both confrontive and supportive approaches to working with batterers. After many years of trial and error they settled on an approach that attempts to hold men responsible for abuse, while modelling respectful behaviour between group leaders and members.

Ten years ago, Emerge decided that women should be a part of the organization, and hired several women to work as supervisors. As one of those supervisors, I have experienced several stages of Emerge's integration of women as staff members. Initially, women were only supervisors, offering clinical input into groups, with no authority to demand accountability of group leaders. This stage lasted several years, during which time women supervisors discussed the gender politics of their situation and decided that they wanted more *real* power in the organization, particularly around group practices and their effects on the safety of partners and the accountability of male group leaders.

In the second stage of women's integration into the staff more women were hired, and I started running a batterers' group with a male staff member to see whether male/female teams were a workable premise. There was some confusion at this stage as to whether this female presence in groups was more to increase the male leader's accountability, or to model respectful male/female relationships. Initially, it seemed the former was expected, so that women were expected to somehow provide "on the spot" monitoring of leaders and the programme. Eventually, the impossibility of that task became clear, as the myriad of power dynamics between the male/female leader became more demanding, as well as the need for a female leader to be even more aware of her own safety needs than her male counterpart.

The third stage that I have observed has occurred in the last five years, during which time women have been integrated into the staff in a much more substantial fashion. Women are supervisors, part of the management, on the board of directors, and a part of almost every counselling team. Women are no longer seen as the monitors of groups and the programme, with no real power on an organizational level to effect change or demand accountability.

Many women who are survivors of domestic violence seem particularly drawn to working with batterers. This may be because this work demands accountability from abusers in a clear and direct way, unlike many other institutions, such as the courts or the church. While running a batterers' group, female leaders are in the unusual position of hearing batterers admit to their abuse and helping them develop long-term accountability plans. This level of accountability is often unheard of in our everyday life.

The motivation for doing this work is often complex. Some female leaders believe they can help create an environment where a batterer will admit his abuse and work on changing his behaviour. Other leaders believe that batterers' groups offer women the opportunity to get information from the programme, monitor their partner's behaviour, make long-term safety plans, or give her input into her batterer's goal-setting process. Other leaders feel less positive, and see the groups as an extension of the court, a sort of necessary evil, which has no real impact on the batterers' ultimate behaviour.

I believe the most successful leaders have a combination of healthy skepticism about the batterers' truthfulness and willingness to make necessary changes, show respect in their behavior in group, and believe in the possibility of change within group members, tempered by a demand for complete honesty and ongoing and consistent accountability.

The structure of Emerge's batterer groups

There are three main components of these groups as they currently exist: educational presentations by group leaders, in which members participate; "check-ins", in which group members describe abuse; and "turns", in which one group member is given time to describe abuse, and the group analyzes the underlying negative thinking and effects of the abuse.

We follow an Emerge-designed curriculum for batterers' groups, which features educational units about abuse related topics: the effects of violence on women, the effects on children, positive and negative self-talk, respectful and disrespectful communication, the continuum of abuse and control, as well as later stage educational units on jealousy, lying, and topics tailored to each batterer's particular pattern of abuse.

In check-ins, group members are asked to report what they did and said to their partner that was abusive and controlling. They are not allowed to drag her into the story, blame her, or characterize her in negative ways. They are asked to take responsibility for what they did without side-tracking onto what she was doing or saying, or onto other issues such as whether or not the police were biased, or why the batterer's bad childhood or tragic life circumstances were responsible for making him respond abusively.

They are asked to imagine responding non-abusively in circumstances where they may not have been treated fairly. We want to remind them that at various times in their lives they will encounter abuse, unfairness or cruelty. The question becomes one of whether they can still respond non-abusively, without retaliating or seeking revenge. We do this because we want batterers to have a more realistic sense of what they encounter, since it is easy to be non-abusive when things are going their way.

Groups also ask batterers to give feedback to other batterers and to offer constructive criticism of each other's statements. We expect them to not bond around negative remarks about each other's partners, to adopt a norm of respect for others, and to work on recognizing and changing the negative thinking (negative self-talk) in their head, which both fuels their rage and gives them permission to escalate the abuse of others. This self-perpetuating hate talk can and must be stopped by them – otherwise they are likely to continue to abuse in the future.

With positive and negative self-talk, the group member may be asked to explain their negative thinking and offer non-abusive alternatives to the behaviour.

They may be asked to describe the effects of the abuse and to re-enact the incident in a role play, then to re-do the role play so that respectful behaviour is modelled.

After going over basic concepts with each group member, the goal is to then work on outlining their particular relationship history with different women, highlighting abusive behaviours with each prior partner, and trying to recognize a pattern over time. We then ask the batterer and group members to develop a set of goals based on his history, prior group participation and the expressed desires of the partner. These goals should help the member work toward a cessation of violence and controlling behaviour and work on developing respectful behaviour towards his partner (or expartner) and others. For instance, a goal might be that John (the batterer) does not attempt to contact Jill by phone or letter unless first contacted by Jill. Or, if they are living together, that John allow Jill to initiate discipline of their children, and that John not do any physical reprimanding of the children. On a more positive note, a goal might be that the group member develop self-care habits, such as keep a regular job, take responsibility for his emotional health, or if he is depressed, take action in some positive way, without burdening his partner with his negative moods.

Common problems for female group leaders

There are three levels of problem, and these are addressed in this section. The first are the problems that exist between a female group leader and the men in her group. The second level comprises the problems that exist between the male and female co-leadership team. The third level comprises the organizational power imbalances which adversely affect female group leaders.

Problems with the men in the group

Tokenism

One way of distorting the relationship between group members and the female leader is to see her as representing all women. Instead of viewing her contributions to the group on their own merit, she instead comes to represent the feelings, beliefs and reactions of all women. This, of course, devalues her personal experience, since her personal viewpoint is no longer seen as one piece of a larger tapestry of women's experiences. It also makes her more vulnerable to criticism, since her viewpoints cannot represent those viewpoints of all women.

Helpful suggestions. It is important for both group leaders to address this problem head on each time it arises in the group. Both leaders need to plan who is going to address comments that tokenize the female leader. It is probably a good idea for both to share in the initiating of responses, as well as providing support to the person who brings it up. Group leaders need to address how tokenism devalues the individual experiences shared in group by the leaders, and how it attributes responsibility to a general class of people (women) for ideas and perceptions that belong to one person. Group leaders could try to make connections between token-ism and the objectification that women experience on a daily basis. An example of a particular interaction might go as follows:

Batterer: I shouldn't have to see my daughter at a visitation centre.

Female leader: You see your children there because you tried to strangle your wife in front of your five-year-old.

Batterer: You women are always against fathers seeing their children. I'm a better parent than she is.

Female leader: We're talking about your relationship with your children, not all men's ability to parent, or all women's opinion about men having visitation. I am giving you my opinion, not that of all women, and it's based on what I know about what you did with your partner.

Male leader: Your comment to Susan is just another way to sidetrack away from looking at your own behaviour. Social services actually made the decision – your partner has no control of it.

Obviously, it's not always this easy, but taking the approach that tokenism is both devaluing and a sidetrack away from the man's real issues is one approach that makes the points *and* tries to return quickly to the issue at hand.

Invisibility

Many women who have led batterers' groups talk about feeling invisible. They are describing the experience of being in the room yet feeling that their words, feelings, and leadership in general are being denied by the group members. For instance, a woman may throw out information to the group about why a particular man was abusive in a specific situation. The group response may be to proceed as if she had said nothing, by ignoring her or by changing the subject to another topic. It is likely that if another group member or the male co-leader makes similar remarks they will not be ignored, whether or not the batterer agrees with them.

Another way men make the female leader feel invisible is by addressing the majority of their remarks to the male leader. In fact, batterers often go so far as to turn in their chairs and respond to the male co-leader after the female leader asks a question. Men sometimes congratulate the male co-leader for the wisdom of his comment, despite the fact that the comment was made earlier by the female co-leader.

Helpful suggestions. With this problem it is particularly important that the male co-leader is working with his co-leader in terms of strategies to attack the problem. It is likely that this problem will occur in all groups, whether or not both leaders are careful to share group responsibilities, feedback and confrontations. If it is the case that the dynamics are positive, the solutions are easier to institute than if group-leader dynamics have not been given prior attention, or if they are out of balance.

Some strategies could include the following interventions. The group leaders can decide who is going to respond and when, and what the other person should do to be supportive. The male co-leader needs to not accept the attention and bonding offered by men who address him while ignoring his co-leader. It may be appropriate to do an education piece focusing on respectful communication and looking at the differences between responses to men and women.

There are specific things that the male leader can take responsibility for. Concretely, the male leader needs to give eye contact to the female leader both when she speaks and at other times. He needs to convey to the men that he respects his co-leader, and do so by listening to her statements, occasionally following up or supporting her work in the group, and by pointing out that the female co-leader actually made the admired response or statement attributed to the male. It needs to be clear to the men that the leaders function together with a team approach, and strong disagreements between group leaders should not occur in front of the men. The male leader should not function like a renegade cowboy, making decisions without the input of the female leader, going off on unpredictable tangents, and leaving the impression to group members that the female leader is not a part of decisions about which directions the group should go.

Overprotectiveness

Batterers sometimes decide that the female group leader needs protection while doing her job, and will give her that (whether she wants it or not) in various ways. A man may support her by intervening when she is criticized by other men in the group who don't like what she is saying. They may back her up and support her positions with other batterers, despite their true beliefs. They may hang around after the group and try to spend more time with her and walk out with her to her car. They may try to be extra helpful towards her, both in and out of the group, by giving, or at least offering, her special treatment. Obviously, all these protective (and preferential) strategies are patronizing, because she cannot accept protection from group members, and because it is being offered without regard to whether she in fact wants protection.

Helpful suggestions. Female leaders need to set limits with men in a firm, yet respectful, way. For instance, if someone in the group were to offer you his business card for preferred treatment on some service, the leader should make it clear that they could not take advantage of this offer because of the need to have clear boundaries with the group member. If the leader were to use the service, for instance, it would place that group member in a preferred status, it might compromise the real or perceived objectivity of the group leader, and it might give a message to the partner that her husband was doing so well that the group leader trusted him to provide her with cut-rate services. The key is setting a firm limit, while explaining to the client the problems with the dynamic he is trying to establish.

In terms of offering protection, that issue should be handled by both leaders and the supervisor. If indeed the female leader does need protection, that needs to be taken very seriously and addressed by the leaders, the supervisors and possibly the organization. Steps may need to be taken such as not leaving one counsellor in the room alone, walking together to cars, purchasing safety alarms, cellular phones for inaccessible group rooms or, more generally, working on total building safety. Safety issues which have come up at Emerge include issues such as town parking or dump stickers on cars may need to be covered, cars may need to be cleared of identifying papers, books or family photographs. Group leaders may need to be instructed about using caller ID blocking codes when calling group members or partners, and they may need to have unlisted phone numbers.

Overcompensating by the female leader

Women leaders sometimes feel that they must present a gentle and supportive image so that they're not seen as the "bitch" or "man-hating lesbian". Women are often placed in a double bind while running a batterers' group: if they come on too strong they are seen as a controlling bitch, but if they hold back and don't express themselves they are seen as ineffectual and weak. It is a treacherous pathway to tread. It is a little like Indiana Jones avoiding the crushing stone, poisonous snakes, and sudden thrusts of knives. The female co-leader must navigate her way through disrespectful men, hostile confrontations and disbelieving stares. She must present useful information that does not alienate the group members while still being willing to ask the tough questions that may elicit hate-filled responses.

Helpful suggestions. Obviously, it helps if the female group leader is somewhat thick-skinned so that the disrespect and abuse directed at her doesn't throw her off balance. I can't stress how important it is to stay in balance, so that attacks by members do not deflect your natural instincts. If the female group leader can base her self-esteem on both group response and self-assessment gained from talking with the co-leader and supervisor it is much more likely that she will remain empowered. One of the most destructive tendencies I have observed with women co-leaders is the urge to overthink responses, so that their timing is sufficiently off that they are a little too late, or not assertively phrasing their responses. Experience logged doing groups helps moderate negative self-assessments, when you realize that some of the self-doubt is being fuelled by the weekly abuse or indifference of the batterers.

Susan Cayouette

Safety issues: individual and group

Having done groups for the last eight years, the safety issues sometimes seem endless. However, for the purposes of this chapter, I will artificially divide them into a number of categories: individual attacks, group attacks and post-group attacks.

Individual attacks

Attacks by one batterer at a time are often more manageable for the female co-leader. A man may attack around a specific piece of feedback which he considers undesired or offensive. Alternatively, an attack may issue because of his anger at his partner or other women, and is not based on any one thing the female leader said or did. Attacks also occur as a diversionary tactic, as a way of side-tracking from the work at hand, particularly if that work is related to the batterer who is the aggressor.

Helpful responses. Here the rule to follow is that you should proceed in a way which feels comfortable for you. I suggest that all group leaders decide how they plan to respond to an attack way before they walk in the room, and create a safety plan for themselves that they have shared with their male co-leader. Some women feel totally comfortable going ahead and dealing with individual attacks head-on. Other women prefer to have their co-leader step in and take either a strong or an equal response. Either approach will work if both leaders are on board with the plan, and have a safety valve if the plan does not work. For instance, I may decide that I want to work personally with an individual attacker, then have my co-leader jump in a little later down the road as a support person. However, the scene goes unexpectedly out of control and several other men start attacking me. At that point, my group leader and I have created the final piece of our safety plan. We tell the group we're going to take a brief break outside the room and ask them to remain inside. Outside of the group room, we decide how to continue the group. We could possibly suspend the group for the evening. We could ask the original aggressor to leave for the evening, with the understanding he return next week. We could also return and try to directly address the aggressive exchange, under more controlled conditions.

Group attacks

Group attacks are dangerous and frightening for the group leader and often signal ongoing problems with the group process. They may start off as an individual attack, then escalate into a multi-pronged attack by several members at once. Often group members may pig-pile issues onto the female group leader: "You've always hated me", "You hate all men", "You were unfair to me several months ago", "You always interrupt us", "the other group leader is always fairer to us". Obviously the laundry list of criticisms is endless, while the individual complaints are determined by the experience of each man with that group leader and with his particular brand of sexism and misogyny.

One manipulative strategy is to split the leaders during the group attack, praising the male co-leader while viciously criticizing the female co-leader.

Helpful responses. The velocity of the attacks can be stunning, and the importance of intervening as quickly as possible cannot be overstressed. It is vital that both group leaders be well prepared for a group attack on the female co-leader. A unified response is almost essential in order to stabilize the situation quickly. All the points outlined about individual attack responses remain true, with an added caveat that this attack may be even more debilitating to the woman, and she may have less ability to respond and even less credibility within the group immediately after the attack. If the group's process is relatively healthy, it will probably be possible to have a group discussion of what has happened, either that week or the next. If the group process has deteriorated seriously over a period of time it is more likely that ongoing work on the group will occur both in supervision meetings and in the group itself. It is possible that drastic measures may be necessary in the long run, including transferring men to different groups to break up cliques that have formed over a period of time.

Post-group Attacks

Attacks on the group leader may occur in or out of the group. After the group is over, batterers will frequently try to get a "private audience" with one or both of the group leaders, to continue their defense of abusive behaviours or to convey negative information about their partner. The group leaders should not give private time to the batterers unless there is a need to assess their potential for suicide or homicide. Otherwise, the leader is supporting the batterer's attempt to carry special favour with the group leader. Saying "no" to attempts at post-group attention may result in a hostile outburst then, or it may result in an attack later in the group.

There are many dangers to allowing post-group conversations, such as taking discussion of issues out of the appropriate group milieu, splitting of group leaders into one who allows post-group discussion and one who doesn't, and starting a conversation which may turn threatening or violent.

Sometimes the group members continue discussion outside the group. It is important that group leaders try to avoid leaving at the exact same time as group members so that their cars may not be identified, or that they cannot be stopped or pressured into discussion outside the relative safety of the office.

Helpful responses. The group leader needs to be clear that they do not speak to group members about group issues outside the group. If necessary, you should explain that a suicide/homicide assessment is the one exception to the rule. It is easier to enforce this stance if group leaders do not engage in casual chatting with members before and after group, since this encourages the perception that the leader/member boundaries are somewhat loose.

If the batterer becomes hostile because of your enforcement of these boundaries, you need to be willing to refer them to the next group and then discuss the incident in front of the group. If he refuses to leave, it may be necessary to threaten to, or actually, call the police.

Power issues of the male co-leader

A male/female team is first and foremost a model to the group members of how people work together, much as a healthy couple would. However, it can also be a model of an unhealthy relationship, so that both counsellors need to be vigilant about their treatment of each other both in and out of the group.

There are a number of power issues that surface while doing batterers' groups which need to be recognized and addressed so that they don't endanger the female group leader or subvert the group process. Some common ones include not sharing confrontation or other aspects of group leadership, and taking up too much space either physically, verbally or emotionally. Others include overprotectiveness or ignoring, abandonment during attacks, or devaluing of the female leader by not responding to her approach during group, not looking at her, or bringing too much of their own stuff into the group in a male bonding type way.

Not sharing leadership or other things

In our experience at Emerge, one common leadership problem is that men either do dominate the leadership team, or they are perceived as dominating by the men. Both phenomena present a challenge to the team.

If your male co-leader is dominating, he's reinforcing the image of men as more powerful and women as subservient. He is also undermining the credibility of his counselling partner, and discrediting the whole idea behind batterers' groups, namely that we believe that it's possible to have a healthy, balanced and respectful relationship, both in and out of work. In this case work needs to be done by the male co-leader on his own, and the problem also needs to be addressed by the team.

In the best-case scenario, the male group leader will recognize his behaviour and its effects, bring it to supervision, and work with his co-leader to change it. Although he may be dominating or controlling, he may seriously want to change his behaviour, and take the initiative to begin steps without forcing the female co-leader to take the lead. Remedial steps might include doing more pre-group planning so that workloads are shared and ideas are agreed upon before coming up in the group. He may become more attuned to his body posture, and to his physical and verbal acknowledgements of his female co-leader.

In the worst-case scenario, the male co-leader will either not be aware of or refuse to acknowledge his dominating behaviour, and the female co-leader will have to take the initiative to bring it to him, either privately or within the supervision. This puts most of the responsibility and pressure on the female co-leader. It also assumes that the supervisor will be open to hearing the concerns of the female co-leader, and willing to intervene in an active way.

It is more likely the response will be some moderation of the two extremes, which will involve an acknowledgement of the behaviour by the male co-leader, a willingness to work through feelings and residual group damage by the female leader, and help from the supervisor in addressing the denial, minimization and side-tracking that threaten to derail the process.

If the male co-leader is *perceived* as dominating this presents a different problem, since his behaviour is not creating the perception, yet it still exists in the minds of the group members. It is important that the team come to some agreement about just what is going on, as this is a necessary precursor to making an action plan.

Taking up too much space physically

There are several ways to take up space in the group. For instance, body posture, the way you sit in your chair, impacts on how others perceive you. If your male co-leader is expansive, with arms extending out, legs apart, or feet stuck out in front of him, he is in fact laying claim to more space than the group leader who is sitting upright in her chair writing on her pad. This conveys a sense of added power, which may skew the leadership dynamics so that the female leader appears smaller, less dynamic or less powerful.

Helpful suggestions. The male co-leader needs to be particularly careful about how he sits in the room, whether he extends his hands and legs in a casual way that gives the message, "I'm in charge", or worse "I'm taking your side" (group members) rather than "I'm listening, working in a team, and not trying to bond with group members".

Taking up too much space verbally

It is not uncommon in this world that men speak more than women, as they are often perceived as being in charge and to have more knowledge. I believe the taken-for-granted perception that abusers have upon entering groups is that the man is the senior member of the leadership team, and that the woman will or should defer to him. This perception may change with time, but it is up to the group leaders to not reinforce that image by having the female co-leader speak less frequently, or not take the lead in confrontation or education pieces, or defer to the wishes of the male co-leader in terms of group direction.

Helpful suggestions. Plan. Plan. Plan. The best way to avoid imbalance in the team is to do your homework before the group starts. Spending time choreographing what is going to happen in the group is the best way to avoid one person dominating. Whether you choose to do an education piece, use a video, confront a particular man, or do goal sheets, planning can balance the leadership. This may mean that a more aggressive man needs to tone down his style. Or that a quieter female leader needs to raise the volume and frequency of her comments.

There is no advantage to having a two-person team that functions as one superstar and one silent partner. It only emphasizes power imbalances that are so destructive in the batterer's own relationship.

Taking up too much space emotionally

If your co-leader is getting personal needs met through the group process, then he may be taking up group space with his emotional needs. Some examples of this include leaders who bond with group members as a male in order to shore up their own sense of inadequacy, abandoning the female group leaders to get positive attention from the members, or bringing details of their home life into group in order to get either feedback or support from group members.

Helpful suggestions. It would be easier if the group supervisor addresses the issue first in supervision, discussing appropriate conduct for male group leaders in heterosexual groups. There are many ways to bond with group members that leaders are often unaware of, such as chatting casually before group, making references to male sports events such as football or boxing, or referring to their own experiences of being abusive (in a way that is gratuitous rather than educational).

Abandoning the female leader

This can occur when the male co-leader simply ignores the path she's taking, while then proceeding along a different path. It is important to follow through with your co-leader's line of thinking, and work out differences either before or after the group in supervision.

Organizational safety

It is important to examine both the mission of the organization and the structure that enforces that mission. Batterers' groups are run in many different ways, with very different philosophies. For instance, Emerge has an expressed mission of working with battered women and children to help with safety issues either directly or indirectly. That means we will contact women and offer them information, work with them in developing a safety plan, direct them to shelters or other resources, and generally try to advocate for their well-being.

Other programmes do not necessarily share the same approach and may feel it is inappropriate to have contact with the women. Some will do so for reasons related to women's safety, while others will do so in deference to men's rights of confidentiality.

The expressed mission of the organization will ultimately determine the acceptability of the counselling approaches used there. For instance, an approach that advocates encouraging the batterer to pursue the relationship, even after his partner had expressly stated she wanted no contact with him, could not exist within the mission statement of Emerge.

It is in the best interest of female group leaders to look at the organization, to see whether its politics are in line with their thinking. Questions that might be posed include: Is it being monitored by a shelter? Does the programme look to battered/formerly battered women for direction? Are women on the board? Do women have power to veto male decisions? Are there more than one or two female group supervisors? Is there structural support for women workers (what does this look like)? Is there diversity in terms of race, class, and sexual preference? Do male staff enact the angel/whore syndrome in their perception and treatment of female staff? Is there an understanding that the abuse is the batterer's responsibility, that the victims should not be blamed for the violence? Is there an understanding that batterers' groups often provide a limited and often ineffective way to monitor further abuse, to help women have time to get away or make safety plans? Is there a social analysis of male violence, that sees it as part of a larger problem of male dominance and abuse in a sexist, misogynistic society? Is there a connection made here between the violence and control of racism, homophobia and classism, which fuel the abusive mentality, or is battering attributed solely to patriarchal, women-hating attitudes and practices? What happens when there are race/sex/class/sexual preference issues that occur in the group and within the organization? Is there an ongoing structure to address these problems, or are they reactively addressed?

For lesbian group leaders, is there a plan to deal with group and organizational homophobia, as well as the isolation caused when heterosexual staff bond together? Is there ongoing education about diversity that includes education to heterosexual staff about gay, lesbian, bisexual and transgendered communities? Are the viewpoints of lesbian and gay staff isolated or incorporated into the general dialogue that exists around counselling and staff issues?

Many organizations are either just beginning or currently struggling to deal with power and control and diversity issues. The question that women might ultimately ask is: Does the organization attempt to grapple with these issues because of its desire to create a safe and respectful workplace, or is this happening because the organization feels it has to? Ultimately, the answer to that question will set the tone for both the specific safety issues that occur with batterers and group leaders, and with the organization as a whole.

Chapter Eleven

One man's struggle for transformation

Luke Daniels

Editor's introduction

As part of this publication I wanted to include a "personal testimony" from a man who has gone through a process of change. Luke Daniels' chapter does not fit into either "theory" or "practice" because of its unique autobiographical character. It provides an honest and moving account of Luke's struggle to move away from the violence of his past, and of his courage in facing responsibility and moving towards change. Luke now works to educate practitioners who help violent men, and he travels around the world acting as a consultant to social care workers. (Jim Wild)

Hitting my wife of ten years was one of the saddest days of my life, but also one of the most important turning points. Our relationship had been difficult for some time when, after one incident, I hit her. I think she was as shocked as I was. We had argued many times but I had never threatened violence. As a matter of fact I looked down on men who hit women, so when I did this thing that I detested I tried to make sense of my actions. I could not face my friends, and when I heard that women activist friends of ours were planning to beat me up I almost wished they would. Not that I could live with that either.

Eventually, I had to seek some counselling support and was introduced to a co-counsellor. Later, my counsellor began to teach me counselling skills, and later still I enrolled for a fundamentals class. In trying to understand my behaviour I had to examine my past experiences. Now, after years of counselling, the life I lived then seems so far removed in many respects from the life I live now.

Childhood

I was born in Guyana, a former British colony, and most of my boyhood years were spent on the East Bank of the Demerara River in one of the roughest villages in the country. There were many bad men there; men with nicknames like "Weapon" or "Razor", whose reputations spread far and wide. We had to learn to fight to survive.

My brothers, friends and I were always practicing how to fight. My memory of school days is one of at least a fight a week at one stage. I had become very skilled at fighting and developed a reputation for being a fierce fighter. I soon had a gang around me. We had strict rules about fighting, and fair play was important; fighting with girls was definitely not on. Only "sissies" fought with girls – not that the girls couldn't fight, they just fought differently from us. I remember being very careful not to get into an argument with any of the girls at school who had a reputation for fighting: nothing terrified me more than to find myself in a situation where I would have to fight with a girl. That would be too demeaning. "Real men don't hit women" was one of the codes I probably learnt from my dad.

I learnt early on that as a man you had to be able to protect your family. Once, when the shopkeeper refused to take back the stale bread, my father, in a rage, took me with him to the shop where I had bought it and demanded he change it. When he refused on a "matter of policy" my dad grabbed him by the collar yanked him over the counter and beat him up. It was the first time I had seen him in a fight, but he told us of his many adventures in the interior of Guyana where the only law was hundreds of miles away. You had to fight for your right, and often might was right. Whenever my dad was in town I was that much braver and bolder; maybe the fight I had avoided weeks ago I was ready for now. My dad would coach us about where to hit and in different kinds of strangle holds I had two older brothers to practice with and they were both good fighters. I was constantly fighting with my brother who was slightly older than myself. I hated losing a fight. Looking back on it, I can see why I got into so many fights, usually with boys bigger and older than me. If I felt that I was about to be humiliated or attacked I would strike the first blow to try and gain the psychological advantage. I won nearly all my fights, and if anyone boasted of beating me I would challenge them again and again if necessary. I probably ran out of boys to fight because I remember a long period without any fights at school, where the staff were trying their best to stop the fights by whipping us with a cane if we were caught.

To escape this we used to arrange fights away from school after hours. These fights hardly ever involved serious ingury, as only fists were permitted, strictly no biting and scratching – that was girls' stuff. There were no organized play areas for children, so we never discovered the joy of swings, sea-saws and slides. We had to make and create our own means of entertainment. My big brother was really good at this. He made all the usual stuff, go-carts, scooters, pea-shooters, bows and arrows, kites, sling shots and blow pipes. But he was an inventor too, always trying to make new things, such as the boat out of a saltfish box or the saddle. Now the saddle was real fun. We would capture any donkey or cow, throw the saddle on and away we went. That no one was ever seriously hurt must have been due to sheer luck. The things we enjoyed the most were the most risky ones, like "raiding" the sugar cane fields. There was always the chance of being chased by the "ranger", mostly on foot but sometimes on bicycle or, the greatest challenge, on horseback. Farmers too would chase us out of their fruit trees.

We caught fish, crabs and birds, mostly for the table, but occasionally we cooked outside. I enjoyed swimming a lot. I was thrown in at the deep end a couple of times before I got the hang of it. The swimming "instructors" were ruthless – you either sank or swam. I was nearly drowned a few times; once, before I had learnt to swim, when wading across a trench to the sugar cane fields and falling into deep water. Cries for help were always taken seriously and my big cousin was quickly to the rescue. There were no swimming pools; we learnt to swim in the canals surrounding the sugar cane fields and then graduated to the Demerara River. Now this river was where the real fun was. Once I had learnt to swim well, almost every day we were in the river. There was only one problem – my mom was terrified we would drown, and she had reason to be frightened. If we got into difficulty here we had to rely on each other, and this was a dangerous river – one and a quarter miles wide at the point where we swam, with strong currents that occassionaly swept us away. We knew not to fight it for too long and to save our energy and look for an opportunity further along the river where we could get out and walk back.

Disclipine

Mom did all she could to keep us from that river, but it is the beatings I remember the most. It was while waiting for my turn to be beaten, as she usually started with the eldest, that I made a decision that I would never beat my children. The beatings stopped when my eldest brother was about fifteen – he stood his ground, not moving an inch or making a sound, as the lashes rained in. Mom then threw away the strap and started hitting him with her fist in frustation, when he still didn't move she stood defeated, "It's up to your father now". I was overjoyed, no more beatings. My dad was hardly around as he was in the interior prospecting for gold and diamonds for most of the year except the rainy season. He did not beat us much, although mom occasionally would threaten us with getting dad to do the beating. I still bear the scars on my body, from one such beating. I can't imagine what my offence could have been. Mostly I have good memories of my dad, he was a very skilled man and taught me how to use tools. He was a carpenter, cabinet-maker, shoe-maker, mechanic, excellent cook and gold and diamond prospector. When he had had a few drinks he played the guitar and sang. He always had many friends, he lived life to the fullest, and I shall always be grateful to him for his modelling that for me. I guess like most of my friends I had a love–hate relationship with my parents; they did their best to care for us under the circumstances they found them selves in. I think almost all adults agreed that "children were to be seen but not heard".

Under the Colonial system we had caning in schools as standard. Every school had at least one teacher with a reputation with the cane. Some students failed themselves rather than be promoted to their class. Our hated teacher was Mr Best, who was also the PE teacher. I can never forget the beating he gave me and my best friend for talking during registration. I took my six lashes with the cane in front of the school, determined not to show any feelings. I just about managed it and walked back to my seat. I hated him for what he did to my best friend. Mike squirmed with each lash that was delivered from great height and with considerable force. He could not walk back to his seat upright and clutched his bottom as he stooped low to the ground and barely made it back. This humiliation affected Mike badly, and a few years after we had left school Mike beat up Mr Best, who had been reduced by alcohol from a strapping six footer to just a shell of a man. Mike became mentally distressed soon after, and still suffers from mental health problems. We all got beatings; I later found out that even the friends who I felt had an easy time with their parents were getting the same treatment. Once when I complained to the old woman who lived next door, she said we were lucky. When she was a child she was made to kneel down in the hot sun on a grater. She was the daughter of a slave. The legacy of slavery and colonialism has a lot to do with the violent societies we now have in the Caribbean. Almost every parent I know would defend their right to hit their child. But, if smacking children was good for them, we would have some of the best societies in the world by now.

Boys to men

The worst thing we could do as boys was to do anything that girls did. We did not hang out with them. The worst thing to be called was "sissy". As we became teenagers the emphasis changed; we could now "tackle" girls for sex. The pressure to "score" was enormous, so much so that most boys lied about their encounters. If they got close enough for a kiss they would claim they had had sex. The challenging and teasing was relentless. It was not about forming relationships but about sex. If you held hands and showed caring you were "soft". Having more than one girlfriend was proof of how good you were at "hustling", and that was OK providing you did not let them find out about each other. It was all a game, and we would stop at no dirty trick to "score", as "all is fair in love and war".

The pressure to be real men also involved learning how to drink. Here again there was great competition to show who could "hold" the most drinks and still walk straight. For us a great session would have been an all-night one, when we would have averaged at least a bottle of rum a man – and these were just drinking sessions. What we talked about is anybody's guess, but we talked a lot as the alcohol loosened tongues that were sometimes shy. My first part-time job before I left secondary school was on a truck delivering rum to all the rum shops on the East Bank Demerara. I resisted all offers to take a sip for about three months. I was really sick after my first few drinks, and swore never to drink again. When another three months had passed I tried drinking again. I handled it a bit better this time, and soon I started to enjoy it. By the age of seventeen all my friends were drinking and sometimes we drank at each other's parents houses. I had the feeling our moms preferred we drank at home as then at least they knew where we were. They usually cooked for us and we were generally well behaved, except on one occasion when one of us got drunk. He was practising for the next day's football match by running on the spot naked on a bed. He soon sobered up when he received a couple of slippers on his bare backside from the hostess. He stayed away from that house for a very long time.

I was the first of my friends to move away from home. After school I signed up for an apprenticeship and moved away from all my friends and immediate family to work in the bauxite industry in the mining town where I was born. My parents had just split up and I was glad to have my own place; and it was lucky that I did so, for my brothers had to stay with me for a while. I was bitter at my parents separating and started drinking heavily. I drank almost every night. I was angry at women, because I held my mom responsible for the break up. I was determined that I would never get married, and any relationships I had with women were with women who were not looking for marriage.

The transition from boy to man had been at breakneck speed: one minute I was living with my parents and at school, next thing I was living away from home without my closest friends and working. I remember sitting drinking on my own sometimes – even seasoned drinkers found that hard to do. But at times I just wanted to be on my own to think. Also I was in a rough mining town, and I wanted to send out a message that I was a hard man. As a boy I had spent a lot of my time fighting for my pride, and we had always sworn that if anyone should shed our blood they would be dead. The one time someone shed my blood I had been drinking and did not expect an attack. I was at a public fair and had passed between a man and woman on either side of the top of a stairway. The man attempted to stop me and said that I should say "excuse me". I told him that was no place to hold a conversation and walked on. Next thing I knew I was hit on the head with a bottle from behind. As I put my hand to my head and felt the blood I went berserk. I picked the man up by the neck and crutch, lifted him above my head and slammed him to the floor. I then quickly sat on his chest, grabbed him by both ears and was about to smash his head on the concrete when I was grabbed by two police officers. I don't think I would have stopped hitting his head. Those days I was an angry young man; sometimes I hoped that someone would give me an excuse to fight. I just hated seeing people happy because I was so unhappy. The police took me to the station and made me promise to end it there or they would press charges.

About a year later another guy, Frank, pulled a knife on me at a party. Some months before, Frank had been looking for a place to live and had pestered me for weeks to let him stay at my flat where I had a spare bed. I reluctantly gave in, but reserved the right to kick him out if we did not get along by not charging him to stay. Three weeks after he had moved in, my girlfriend Fauzia wanted a fag but I didn't have one. I noticed a pack of Frank's. He was out, so I took the liberty of offering a couple to Fauzia. When Frank returned he was furious that I had taken his cigarettes. I was being embarrassed in front of my girlfriend in my own home! This loss of face made me react strongly by asking him to take his belongings and leave immediately. He never forgave me for that, and when he had the opportunity he picked a fight with me.

After Frank had pulled the knife, I broke the glass I was drinking from and attacked him. I barely scratched him, as the glass had broken badly. People separated us quickly. Frank then threatened to "chop" me anytime he saw me. Now this guy was older and bigger than me and I thought of going to the police for protection, but decided not to as it would be admitting that I was scared. I wished my close friends were around to give me support, and for one moment I thought of sending for them. Next day I went to work and made a dagger that was at least twice as long as the knife he had pulled on me. Then I decided to go look for Frank. He had threatened me and I had every right to defend myself. I was usually out all hours and walking home alone on some very dark streets. I was not prepared to go around being scared of every shadow or continually watching my back. I would walk proud and tall, like a man or not at all – this was a fight for my manhood. As I prepared for battle I remembered my brother's friend who was serving time for murder. He had made a shield with his mother's breadboard, armed himself with a cutlass and gone after a young man who had humiliated him at a dance by stubbing his cigarette out on his face. I remember people talking about the way the guy who got killed ran trying to hold in his gut before he collapsed and died. I thought of making some protection for my gut, but decided against that as it would give away that I was afraid and it would restrict my fighting.

Next day I armed myself and walked to the hospital to visit my grandmother. I planned to visit her and then go look for Frank to settle things. Well, I didn't have to search, as from her room I could see Frank and a friend approaching the hospital. They must have seen me go by as I walked to the hospital. I thought "What a bastard, he would fight me at my grandmother's bedside". It made me more resolute that no quarters would be given; I was also reassured a little that medical attention would be at hand if I was wounded. Fauzia was with me, and I warned her of the coming danger and told her to get out of the way as soon as she saw trouble starting. She said she would step in between us. I told her not to, as Frank was spiteful and would hurt her.

As they approached the hospital I left my Gran's bedside to meet them in the reception area. I stood chatting with Fauzia, my left forearm concealing my dagger in a brown paper bag as I leaned against a railing. My right hand was hanging loose in readiness to grab the handle of the dagger. Frank walked towards me with his friend, stopped about three yards in front of me, pulled his pen knife from his pocket and opened it, saying "let's finish it now". I saved my breath, swinging my right arm to unsheath my dagger and in the same motion I took one step towards Frank, plunging the dagger straight at his chest. He was really surprised. His eyes nearly popped when he saw my weapon. He had not been prepared for a fight, probably expecting me to beg or something. He snatched his head and body back and to the side, barely missing my thrust. I was surprised at how quickly he moved. The adrenalin was now pumping like mad. I was prepared to take him before he had a chance to do me any damage. I quickly recoiled, shifting my feet, prepared to strike again, no longer fearing being stabbed. I had been prepared to be cut, but I was convinced I would fatally wound him. Frank did not wait for my second thrust. He turned on his heel and high-tailed it out of the hospital. I gave chase for about thirty yards but his burst of acceleration was so fast I could never catch him. I ran back to Fauzia, adrenalin still pumping. A crowd had gathered. We slipped away and, as soon as we were in a safe spot, I started shaking, and was really glad I had Fauzia there to calm me.

Next day, as I approached the town centre with a friend, I saw Frank with his friends. I had to pass within yards of him. I was unarmed, but not fearful – I had seen the whites of his eyes and knew that I had really scared him. I now walked as if I was carrying a weapon concealed under my armpit to "grandcharge" Frank. As I drew close I pretended to grab at something at my waist. Frank jumped the gutter and landed in the street. I pressed home the advantage: "Don't jump. I'll kill you if you fuck by me". I stared at him for a minute and then walked on. That night he approached me and apologized. I accepted as, "I don't want trouble but don't fuck with me". He always hailed me after that, but I didn't trust him for a long time. He became a policeman after I left Guyana, and when I returned there years' later we talked and laughed.

I recount this story because as a counsellor for violent men I think my own experience of violence gives me the confidence to challenge men with violent patterns in a way that no amount of theoretical training can give. I can listen to their violent stories without becoming scared, and can challenge their behaviour. I never lose sight of the fact I have changed, and I know that they can change too.

The power of love to transform

For a couple of years after my parents split up I hated people, especially if they seemed to be happy, and often wished anyone I didn't like would give me a excuse to fight them. This hate was eating me up and I had to make a conscious decision to stop, as I felt it would destroy me in the end. I hadn't spoken to my mom in at least a year, as we boys had decided that she was responsible for the break up of the family. I was about seventeen at the time and it hurt me deeply, as everything I had done was to make my parents proud of me. Now I was drinking every night after trade school and stayed clear of women. McKenzie was a boom town, with people coming from all over the country and from the Caribbean islands to make a living. There was a lot of hustling going on and I made friends with lots of prostitutes and hustlers as I liked their company when I was drinking. They liked me because I was a happy spender. I kept away from girls my age and only had "big women" as friends and sometimes as lovers. I wasn't looking for commitment, nor were they. I wanted them for company and sex, and they wanted me for whatever reason. I learnt a lot from them, and had it not been for one of these "big women" the route back to my mom would have been longer, as she made me fully understand my mother's situation. After about two years I sat and wrote my mom a letter from my heart which I understand made her cry volumes. We have always been very close, as she is a truly wonderful mom. Throughout my life women have played a crucial part in my development; without them my life would be that much poorer.

Shortly after making peace with my mom, when I was still drinking heavily and carrying on, I luckily met a young woman and fell in love instantly. I had gate-crashed a party. And there she was. I couldn't keep my eyes off her; she noticed me too. We were soon dancing, but she was with her boyfriend. Well he was not my friend, so I had no problem taking her home after the party. Her mom knew my mom, as they had been at school together. She was really pleased with our relationship and encouraged it. Her dad? Well he probably knew of my reputation – on many a night or early morning I had gone by his window drunk and maybe with a woman. He did all he could to make things difficult for me. I decided it was because my girlfriend was still at high school, and I had never been. So, although still doing my apprenticeship, to prove to him that I was no fool and was good enough for his daughter I enrolled privately for five GCE O level subjects. I bought a syllabus and stopped drinking, womanizing and partying for six months. I passed four of the five subjects, failing chemistry (which is not surprising as I had never seen a lab.). This was no mean feat as, because I was still doing my apprenticship, I sometimes had to work very hard. But I had the support of my workmates, who would cover for me if I had to sleep during working hours because I had studied all night long. The relationship carried on long enough for me to reclaim bits of my caring self. Sadly she left the country and we lost touch.

Working men

When I started a five-year apprenticship in the bauxite industry it was a much sought after position, as the pay in that industry was the highest in the country. Part of the deal was one year as office boy. I was one of the most qualified in my intake so I got one of the best postings – in the accounts department where the controller of the company worked. I soon made many friends and, as a result, I wanted to stay on and work in that department. I was worried about the cut in pay I would take when I moved to the trade school, but staying in the accounts department would mean having to break my apprenticeship. I shall always remember the man who said to me "Take a look around, all you can see is men pushing pens for the rest of their lives". He was right, and some of them were quite old too. So I decided to start my apprenticeship even though four years seemed then like a lifetime. My heart was not really in it. I would have preferred to work in agriculture, but I would have to pay to learn that somewhere else. Here I was getting paid to study, so there was not much choice really. I did just enough to get through the first year and then started my fieldwork as a pipe-fitter. This choice of trade was forced upon me. I wanted to be a draughtsman, which was better paid and carried more prestige, but the principal did not like me. We had a few problems, he had made a racist remark, and I had the right response to it. So, reluctantly, I went to the pipe-fitting department, determined to be difficult so that I would be moved to another department quickly.

However, I soon realized that the pipe-fitting I would be doing had nothing to do with fixing toilets and the men were great. I learnt fast and was very competitive (I had to prove myself) and there were great expectations on me coming from trade school.

I soon realized that this was a highly skilled trade and it really challenged me. But most of all I loved the men. All my experiences with risk taking and having many close friends seemed to prepare me for just such a situation. I was a hard worker most of the time and liked working in challenging situations. I soon gained the respect and liking of the men – it helped that I could hold my drink. I was not always happy, but everyone was understanding. At times I could get away with almost anything. I worked as hard as everyone else and harder than some, and had more skills than many, but as an apprentice I was paid a lot less. The pay increased each year, but I learnt to subsidize my earnings by making jewellery out of stainless steel. I also made all kinds of household things, and had a reputation for being able to make anything. I usually tried to finish my offical jobs quickly so that I had time to do my private work. Sometimes there was a clash of interests between my work deadlines and my need for extra cash. Nevertheless, when I finished my apprenticeship I was sought after by most departments as I was highly skilled, could work hard and was willing to tackle dangerous jobs.

I decided to join the department that had the most exciting jobs and overtime. I was soon earning a lot of money, and had no responsibilites apart from helping out my mom and siblings from time to time. I worked hard and played hard. When a gang of trouble-shooters was formed in the bauxite plant I was a natural canditate. Michael the "devil" was to lead it. I did not know him but had heard of his reputation for hard work (many men avoided working with him as he was seen as a "slave driver"). I liked him straight away. I had never seen anyone work so hard. I often felt he would collapse at any time as his pace was relentless. I tried to keep up with him, and we became close friends. What people hadn't told me was how skilled he was, and I learnt a lot from him. His approach to work was that anything was possible. We soon had a close-knit and powerful gang able to negotiate the price for any job we were called to, depending on how dangerous the working conditions were. Often, to make working conditions safe whole sections of production would have to be shut down, which no general foreman wanted to do. So we would set our price by getting them to agree to pay us the hours we demanded for the job. We would then finish it in about a half the time, enduring the harsh conditions. The gang was small but highly effective. "Workie" was the labourer. He didn't have many skills, but he was strong and willing to learn, and no task requiring courage and strength was too difficult for him. "Singerman" was highly skilled and dependable. He was also the vocalist in a popular string band. Reagan and "Master Fang" were semi-skilled, with their own strengths, and always willing. It wasn't unusual for us to work twelve-hour days, sometimes for months on end. Occassionally we worked sixteen hours, and once or twice in a real emergency twenty-four hours. I was the youngest in the gang and was sometimes treated like a little brother. The men often shared with me the food their wives or girlfriends had brought to the bauxite plant gate at lunch time. I would sometimes get teased for not having someone to bring me food. We looked after each other. Although we were all hard drinkers we hardly ever drank on the job as it was too dangerous. I remember one job – hanging precariously at great height, on looking down I could see the anxiety in the general foreman's face. I was lucky, as sometimes people had limbs broken, and there was the occasional loss of life. I had a finger smashed with a sledgehammer once when Master Fang lost his balance, and once I sprained my ankle when I lost concentration and a falling pipe bounced and hit me. I was eventually seconded to the construction of the largest kiln for baking the bauxite ore, where I worked for twelve hours a day, seven days a week, for about seven months. After this I left Guyana, with my wife and son, for London.

Politics

Guyana had a long struggle for independence from Britain, and as a result the population became highly politicized. The elected government had its constitution suspended when British troops arrived. This was the first popularly elected Marxist government anywhere, and the British and US secret services intervened to prevent them taking power. To destabilize the country, race was used as a weapon. Guyanese had united across class lines to give overwhelming support to the People's Progressive Party (PPP) under the leadership of Dr Cheddie Jagan. With the help of the CIA, a wave of anti-communist propaganda was unleashed in Guyana, followed by bombings of Indo- and Afro-Guyanese families, thus stirring up racial hatred and insecurity. Proportional representation was introduced by the British, but when the PPP won the largest amount of seats the colonial power called on the other two parties to unite, giving them a narrow majority. The British asked the coalition to form the government. The largest party in the coalition, the People's National Congress led by the late Forbes Burnham, soon jettisoned their coalition partner and proceeded to rig several elections to stay in power. This was the dictatorial government responsible for the murder of Dr Walter Rodney, leader of the Working People's Alliance, the opposition party which I had joined. This corruption of power has led to Guyana now being one of the most indebted countries in the world.

During the 1960s the anti-communist literature flooding Guyana also attacked the emerging Black Power movement, characterizing their leaders as evil racists. In Guyana we were against any kind of militancy based on race, as a result of the racial insecurity being stirred up in Guyana, and so the propaganda fell on very fertile ground. When Stokley Carmicheal tried to speak at a meeting it was broken up. When they published a picture of Angela Davis as the most dangerous woman in the USA I could not believe this of the beautiful woman that I had before me. So I started looking for information on the Black Panthers and was able to learn a lot about racism in the USA. More importantly, I discovered Angela Davis and the world of feminist politics as a result.

Helping men to change

As a supporter of the Working People's Alliance of Guyana I came into contact with most of the leaders in London. One of the leaders, Andaiye, was the first woman to challenge my sexisim in a way that made me do something about it. I had believed in the equality of the sexes and had learnt to cook, clean house, wash dishes and was good at hand-washing clothes, was expert at caring for my babies and could do, and often did, any "woman's job" in the home. I felt that this alone was sufficient proof that I was not sexist. When I was challenged by Andaiye for the third time I knew I had to do something. I started reading everything on feminism I could put my hands on. It helped that the woman I was in a relationship with was a feminist. I had access to her books and sometimes knowledge, but she didn't see it as her responsibility to educate me about sexism. Bell Hooks had a different approach to men and sexism, which continues to influence me greatly. It was a pleasure to prepare the food for a gathering of black women to meet with Bell when she visited London to publicise her book *Feminist theory from margin to centre*.

As one who was already involved in fighting injustice and working for change, I eagerly embraced feminism. All of this after I had hit my wife – it was as if a whole new world had opened up for me. I thank all the women who have contributed in some way to my reclaiming of my life. Accepting counselling made me realize that real change comes about not only through education, especially when tackling issues such as sexism and racism, but through a great deal of critical self-examination. Much of this I am able to do in the men's support groups that I engage with.

Soon after starting my counselling sessions I made a commitment to always intervene and stop men from hitting women, if it was happening around me. Two weeks after making this decision I was to be tested. Driving home with a friend after leaving the pub one Saturday night I got him to pull up sharply as I noticed a woman lying on the pavement with a man standing over her, a small crowd gathered nearby. I got out of the car and quickly got over to the woman, bending my knees so that I could hold her head up to ask where she had been hurt. I could see the terror in her eyes as she pleaded with me not to let him take her home. By then the man was enquiring "Who the fuck are you, doctor or something". I raised my hand to silence him and reassured the woman that she was safe. Meanwhile the man was having a row with the crowd that had gathered. I then stood up to face him and tell him that the woman was hurt, I was going to see that she got help, and that she did not want to go with him. He went mad, shouting that I was trying to take his woman and he would be taking her home. I could smell the alcohol as we stood eye ball to eye ball shouting at each other. He knew he had a fight on his hands if he tried to take her away and he backed down when he realized that I was not going to be frightened by him. The police arrived a short while after and he was taken into custody. I then learnt from the crowd that they had tried to intervene on behalf of the woman, but he had pulled a knife on them. I have intervened many more times since, but one has to be very careful in doing this. I guess I'm always prepared for an attack when I do so, but I am now skilful at defusing situations and only once have I had to hit a man as a result of intervening. It is important that we as men intervene, as most men who hit women feel that it is OK to do so and that other men agree with this. Sometimes men are really grateful for the intervention. That intervention could be a simple "Stop it" in as loud a voice as you can from a safe distance. Sometimes women have attacked me verbally for not minding my "own buisness". I reckon this is because they are embarrassed that anyone would notice and want to help, or because they are so scared of the man that they make a show of representing "their man".

In time I became a counsellor for men who have been violent to women and want to change. As a feminist I see my contribution to putting an end to the oppression of women as challenging men to change. I do this not for women but for men, as we can never really claim our full humanity if we continue to oppress women. Of the hundreds of men that I have worked with I have noticed a few things that they all have in common. One is they have all been mistreated as children, either witnessing domestic violence and being hit as children. Often the degree of violence these men are prepared to use is in some way related to on the amount of violence they experienced as boys. Secondly, they all have sexist attitudes.

I firmly believe that no one would hurt another person unless they were hurt in the first place. Nevertheless, men must take full responsibility for their actions if they are to change their behaviour. Understanding why men on the whole behave more violently is key to helping men overcome their violence. The argument between *nature and nurture* has been raging for some time with no conclusive evidence on either side. It may be impossible to ever have conclusive evidence because we are so different as humans. The observation that some men who have been hit or have seen violence and grow up to be non-violent is a classic example. In my experience of working with violent men only once have I seen a man who had never been hit as a child. He was harming himself whenever he was upset and angry with his partner.

My programme for working with men who want to overcome violent behaviour has been published elsewhere, so I won't go into detail here. However, my approach is based in re-evaluation co-counselling. We assume that we all come into this world completely good and that none of us would harm anyone unless we were hurt in some way in the first instance, usually from a very early age. That everyone can recover from the effects of mistreatment with the help of another person, providing there has been no damage to the forebrain. We argue that tears are one of the ways that we as humans are able to heal ourselves when hurting.

The oppression of men

We in re-evaluation co-counselling argue that we live in oppressive societies in which almost everyone is oppressed and in turn acts as oppressor. By oppression we mean the systematic one-way mistreatment of individuals or a group of people by intitutions, politics, economics, individuals or another group. The most common oppression is of younger people, in what we describe as "adultism". Everyone will have been mistreated in some way, whether aware of it or not, by the oppression of adultism. Usually there is another easily identifiable group doing the oppressing; for example, in anti-semitism it is Gentiles doing the oppressing. In Western societies black people are oppressed by white people through racism. The oppression of men is different in that there is no one group doing the oppressing, but rather it is society as a whole. It must be stressed here that women as a group do not oppress men. We live in a patriarchial society in which men play the role of oppressors to women through sexism. It is not that men are inherently sexist, but we live in a society that is saturated with sexism and none of us escape its influence.

The oppression of men can be recognized by the facts that, on average, we die some six years younger than women. That we suffer from more diseases caused by stress than do women. That we often find it hard to take care of our bodies and to seek help when needed. Prostate cancer kills far more men than breast cancer kills women, yet few men are aware of this disease because far less is spent on publicising it than is done for breast cancer. There is no national screening programme, despite the high risk to men aged over forty. However, men are oppressed mainly by the two narrow stereotypical roles that we are expected to play: that of providers and that of killers.

Providers

Historically men are seen as the ones who will provide for the family. The present economic climate is creating more "women's jobs", these being characterized by being jobs of the "caring", part-time, low-paid and poor-conditions type. However, men are still expected to be the ones to provide, as reinforced by the Child Support Agency, which was created to track down errant fathers. Often our manhood will be judged by how well we provide. Sometimes we can only relate our lives to the work we do, and when we have no jobs to go to this creates a great deal of stress. The Samaritans have researched into the four times higher suicide rate for young men as for young women in an impoverished area of Glasgow in 1994. They found that unemployment was one of the major factors in this prevalence of suicide. Society may be changing, but men's perception of their role is not. Yet again it is just expected that men will make the adjustments without any support whatsover. Work in the home has always been devalued because it is unpaid and "women's work". The inclusion of housework in calculations of gross national domestic earnings would go a long way to changing attitudes. The Campaign for Wages for Housework has long been fighting for the implementation of this resolution of the United Nations in Britain. When housework is given the value it deserves men may not feel less valued if a role reversal is required in their familes.

Killers

The history of the world is a history of wars. Men have died in their tens of millions killing each other. Universally, as boys we are prepared for this role from the time we are born. Research has shown that we are handled less as babies and more roughly when we are. The process to make us into tough little men can hardly wait to begin. Before we can walk we will have the tools of our trade: toys of violence, guns, knives, grenades, swords, war planes and at least one of the millions of action men (which now boast an arsenal of over twenty weapons) that are sold each year. Everywhere we will see images of violent men celebrated. The boxing champions, the mega movie stars, the cartoon characters. The socialization for violence is so overwhelming that it is a wonder that any of us reject this stereotype. We will be encouraged to be strong: if we cannot or will not fight we will be ridiculed; if we can fight we will be celebrated.

We will be encouraged to be "cool" and not show emotions. And it his here lies the root of our difficulties: "Come on, big boys don't cry". Many of us will be beaten for crying, and then when we are older we will be attacked for not being able to show feelings. In my programme we argue that crying is one of the most important ways in which we are able to heal and recover from hurtful experiences. When this means of healing and recovery is interrupted on a systematic basis, we store up a great deal of stress – and it is not surprising that most men lead unhappy lives and often hurt the ones closest to them. Through no choice of ours we will be conditioned by society to view women as sex objects and learn to think that women are less important than men. In the interests of patriarchial society we become the agents of oppression of women. All men benefit in some way from the oppression of women, but some men benefit more – low pay for women means huge profits for some men.

Apart from the general socialization of men to be violent, we will be hit as children. There is a great deal of research to suggest that hitting children creates violent adults, although violence to children may in the short term produce conforminity, in the long term it will increase the "probability of deviance, including deviance in adolesence and violence inside and outside the family". If we are to create a society free from violence we have to start by treating our children with the love and respect they deserve.

Chapter Twelve

Men, power, control and violence

Victor Jeleniewski Seidler

For Gabriella Fiori

Men and masculinities

How are we to think about men? We are learning to think about men in relation to diverse masculinities. We have also learnt that there is a dominant masculinity – white, heterosexual, Christian, able-bodied and middle class – and within a Eurocentric vision this dominant masculinity has very much set the terms for modernity. Expressed briefly this means that modernity as we inherit it within an Enlightenment vision is set largely within men's terms, within the terms of this dominant masculinity.

So it is that modernity can be described as a man's world. This means that women and children are largely marginalized in relation to it. They are supposedly there to serve men's needs, and within the institution of heterosexual marriage women are to find their fulfilment and happiness largely through making men happy. So, for instance, if a relationship or a marriage breaks down it becomes easy for her to blame herself, to feel that the break-up is somehow her fault and that she has somehow proved herself incapable of keeping "her" man. Women are traditionally brought up to internalize guilt and responsibility, and to take in on themselves the anger that they might otherwise express.

Within an Enlightenment vision of modernity it was crucial to recognize that it was men alone who lived for themselves. Their lives were to have meaning in their own terms. As I have argued in *Unreasonable men* (Seidler 1994), they alone were able to take their reason for granted and so able to live their lives according to the dictates of reason alone. Aspiring to live up to the ideals set by a dominant masculinity, men were to be independent and self-sufficient. Many men still feel that they should be able to handle their "problems" on their own. To be independent means that men learn that they should be able to cope on their own, and so to have connections with others can be experienced as threatening.

So it is that men often learn to take pride in also being self-sufficient. But often this means they are disconnected in their relationships with others. They can find it difficult to sustain a sense of connection when they are not physically with others. Out of sight can easily mean out of mind. At some level this has been experienced as a sign of male "strength", which has allowed men to leave their emotional problems behind when they close the door to go off to work. It has sustained a sharp demarcation between home as a site of emotional relationships and work as a place of instrumental reason and impersonal contacts. Within modernity this shows the genderization of the split between private and public spheres. Traditionally it meant that the home and family was very much regarded as a feminine space. Men could often experience themselves as on the margins of this domestic world, contributing income as breadwinners, but not really being a "part of" family life.

At some level men can live their lives as a series of discrete and independent actions, events and experiences. Since within modernity men can never take their masculinity for granted, it is something that has to be constantly proved. Men can prove that they are "man enough" by showing that when the chips are down they can survive on their own. Often when men feel upset or depressed they withdraw into themselves and withhold what is going on for them. At some level they often do not want to know themselves, for emotions are interpreted as a sign of weakness and so as a threat to sustaining male identities. This can be difficult within relationships for it is easy for partners to feel redundant.

Some men can only allow themselves to feel vulnerable when they are on their own. They need time to be on their own to discover what they are feeling, but can find it difficult to communicate this need to their partners who can feel rejected. This is partly because they feel that when they are with their partners they cannot really be themselves. This might be because they constantly feel that something is expected of them, even when it is not. There can be an inner pressure "to be strong" so that it can be difficult to explore what they are feeling when others are with them.

But this can be difficult for some men to express because they feel it will be heard as a rejection and they do not want it to be. So it is that men find spaces in which they can be alone, while in the relationship. It can work as a form of inner withdrawal. But often partners in heterosexual relationships recognize that something is going on, even if they cannot name it. They feel lonely as women within the relationship and feel at some level that they are getting very little from the relationship. Men might find this difficult to understand because they think of themselves as available. It is often more difficult for men to recognize when they are not emotionally available within a relationship because they grow up to identify themselves as self-sufficient.

Often it is difficult for men to explore their relationship with their masculinities, because they feel so identified with their male identities. Often men grow up to take their competitive relationships with other men so much for granted that they have a great deal invested in thinking of themselves as individuals. They can feel trapped in seeing themselves as "different" from other men. It is difficult to explore the complexities of men's diverse relationships with their masculinities, when they feel they have to constantly prove themselves to other men. As men learn that to express emotional needs is a sign of weakness, men learn to protect themselves for they know that any sign of vulnerability can be used against them. This can make it difficult for men to listen to advice or to ask for help, for at some level they can be convinced that they "know best" about themselves. In difficult times this becomes a conviction men hold tightly too.

This can make it difficult working with men, for men often assume that they do not need any help and that they are coping on their own. So often it is difficult for men to recognize that they need help for often this is experienced as if it were a sign of defeat or failure. This only confirms what many men fear most, that it is somehow proof that "You cannot even look after yourself . . . so what bloody use are you? . . . so what kind of man are you?" Men often want to foreclose the possibilities opened up by these questions. It seems preferable to cope on your own, for at least then you do not show yet further weakness in needing the help of others. Often it is when men most need the help of others that they refuse it. A sharp rift opens up between the ways they feel in their inner lives, which they are struggling to control, and what they are prepared to show to others. It becomes even more important to "put a good face on things" in public.

Often there is a link between male identities and a fear of rejection. When you are down you can feel that you do not want to give friends yet further reasons for rejecting you. This can make it harder for men to reach out when they feel down, sad or depressed. It seems as if men can reach out, say through the phone, when they feel up and that they close up when they feel down. It is as if they assume that friends will not be there to support them and that, in Kantian terms, it is somehow "better", more morally worthy, if they can get "through it" on their own. At least they would have proved themselves in their own eyes and not sunk any deeper in their self-esteem. These processes can also be at work within heterosexual relationships, when partners can be left feeling useless and resentful, because they sense that something is wrong, but there is a refusal to emotionally share what is going on.

This makes it difficult to work with men unless we understand their complex relationships with their diverse masculinities. Often there are difficulties of communication when men feel little relationship with their emotional lives. It is as if they can be reaching for an emotional language that just was not there for them as boys in their growing up. Rather there is a deeply embedded cultural notion that "boys are animals", which works to separate boys from their inner emotional lives. It is as if they have learnt not to connect with their emotions, for this will only confirm that they are "bad". There is an ethics in relation to emotional life that needs to be carefully explored. At some level, within a Protestant moral culture, as I explored in *Recreating sexual politics* (Seidler 1991), there is a fear that men carry in relation to the revelations of their natures.

As dominant masculinities are identified with self-control, so men can feel that they prove their male identities through proving they have control over their emotions, feelings and desires. But this is to estrange men from their emotional lives, as men learn to harden themselves against their feelings. This is to harden men's hearts and often to make men very hard on themselves. There is a fear that if they let go some of their emotions, then they will be overcome by them. This is why it is felt they have to hold such tight form of control over them. But this does not give men the self-knowledge they need to negotiate in more equal gender relations. It becomes difficult for men to recognize what they emotionally need for themselves, so they can end up feeling resentful at how little they get for themselves.

Power and dominance

Within an Enlightenment vision of modernity in which masculinity can never be taken for granted but always has to be proved, the hidden question that is never far from the surface of consciousness is "Am I man enough?" Often this means that at some level men are often taken up with themselves, with proving themselves in the eyes of other men. It is partly because male identities are proved and sustained within the public realm of work that this is the space that matters to men, regardless of what lip service they might pay to family and relationships. This can make it seem as if men do not care or connect with others, for when the chips are down, they seem to "look after themselves".

But at another level, as Foucault was beginning to explore in *Care of the self* (Foucault 1990), men are often not prepared to look after themselves emotionally. This is partly because so many men have been looked after by their mothers and so grew up expecting to be emotionally and materially served by their mothers. Often they grow up to rely upon women to interpret their emotional experience for them, while at the same time taking this emotional labour, as Miller introduces it, for granted and devaluing it (Miller 1976). But men's dependence upon women's for their emotional labour is often rendered invisible, as men pride themselves (as has already been explained) in their independence and self-sufficiency. But this means that men are often not very skilled in looking after themselves or caring for themselves emotionally. Rather they often deny the needs they have, as a way of affirming or proving their male identities. Often they have learnt that to be a man means "not to need" emotionally.

Within modernity men have been traditionally identified as providers and breadwinners. This meant that they could feel that all their work in the public sphere was being done for their partners and children. So they could expect them to be grateful and show deference. This also encouraged men to feel pride, not only in denying themselves emotionally within a Protestant ethic, but also in the provisions they made for others. This was part of the traditional gender contract in which women took responsibility for childcare and domestic work and men were to act as breadwinners for the family. The division of labour was firmly established, as were the duties and responsibilities that could be expected.

But with feminism the realities of male dominance were revealed and the supposedly equal contract was shown to be a relationship of subordination. As women spoke against their oppression within the domestic sphere, so they argued that they should have equal right to participate in the public sphere. The self-sacrifices that male identities were so often identified with were challenged as men were thought to be selfish, narcissistic and egoistic. It was argued that men were so identified with their egos, with proving themselves in relation to other men, with proving that they are "man enough". In terms of white, middle-class, heterosexual masculinities this was linked to the identification of a dominant masculinity with the mental sphere.

It was a dominant masculinity that could alone take its reason for granted. Life was to be controlled through the mind and it was through their inner relationship to reason, as Kant has it, that men were to be able to legislate "what is best" both for themselves and for others (Kant 1948). Men had appropriated a notion of reason, radically split from nature, as their own. This meant that reason was gendered and that men were supposedly able to take their rationality for granted. But this identification with the mental is often an emotional attachment for men. It is linked to a particular form of male superiority and dominance within modernity.

So it is that a disembodied conception of reason becomes a form of male power within modernity. Men "have to be superior" in order to prove themselves "as men". This involves recognizing the ways boys are brought up to feel that "to be a man" is to be "superior to women". Boys learn at an early age to trivialize and demean the experience of girls as "silly", "emotional" and "soft". This is important because masculinity is so often defined negatively, as a matter of "not being feminine", "not being weak", "not being soft". So where girls are deemed to be soft, boys have to be hard. Since masculinity can never be taken for granted, these feelings are intensified whenever boys feel threatened in relation to their male identities. If they want to repair a damaged ego, it will often be at the cost of the girls.

Often within the public world of where were male identities are sustained, men can feel haunted by feelings of inadequacy and insecurity. Often these emotions are not spoken, for there is a sense that to speak them is to make them real. Men learn to control their emotions through suppression, and this gives then a notion that they are in control of their lives. It is important for men to feel that "life" can be controlled and that it can be organized according to reason. At work men can feel insecure and unsure of themselves, fearing that "they are not good enough", or at least that "others are better than they are". They can feel plagued by feelings that they could always do more, succeed more, achieve more.

It is partly because, traditionally, the public world of work has mattered for men that they are prepared to give up some control within the private realm of family and personal life. But it was expected that their superiority as men, at least in public, would be sustained and legitimated. They expected their partners to show deference and they expected that they would be listened to and allowed, in middle class families, "to blow off steam" if they had too. They expected their wives to be there for them and to know that they would have priority and precedence in the organization of family life. Since it was assumed that their work sustained the whole family, it was understood that the family would be largely organized around their needs.

With the challenges of feminism and the far greater commitment to gender equality these patterns have shifted. There are such significant differences between different countries, even in Europe, that we have to be careful not to generalize or not to assume that linear processes of modernization are at work. There are deeply entrenched cultural and historical traditions that need to be engaged with carefully. But the traditional gender contract has had to be renegotiated. Some empirical work, especially in Germany, shows that when it is a matter of moving work, it might be important to feel that both partners have had an "equal say", but often the move is made because of the employment opportunities it offers to the father. Women might feel that they are benefiting, but often this will be because of the greater space and facilities the move offers to the family and children. Women will more easily identify their own personal interests with the interests of the family.

Even though fathers might no longer expect their word to be law, and although they might be willing to negotiate "as equals", at least in relation to their partners, they also know at some level that reason/rationality is a capacity that they alone can take for granted. They still expect women to be more influenced by their emotions and feelings because they are supposedly "closer to nature". This means that men alone can be expected to be impartial and impersonal in their deliberations. So, at some level, it is men alone who can take the "interests of the whole family" to heart. Others cannot supposedly be expected to exercise their judgement in such neutral terms.

In Kant's terms it is a dominant masculinity that has an inner relationship to reason, while it is only the institution of marriage that allows women to establish a more secure relationship with reason, through their relationship with their husband. But at some level this means that men do not have to listen to what their partners have to say, for they "already know what is best" for the family. Men are often so identified with their minds that it is difficult for them to listen to what others have to say. This was why feminism was so threatening as a psychic level, as well as a political level to men. At a fundamental level it threatened men's power over women's minds, bodies and sexualities, as well as ways that men had culturally learnt to demean and devalue emotions, feelings and intuitions as "irrational".

Feminism and men's power

Feminism not only challenged men's power in relation to women but it also threatened men's relationships to their masculinities. It questioned the terms in which men were to know themselves and experience themselves as men. Feminism encouraged women to recognize that they could live independent and autonomous lives. In this way feminism challenged quite fundamentally an Enlightenment vision of modernity, which was largely constructed in its vision of gender relation through Kant's notion that women needed men in a way that men supposedly did not need women (Seidler 1986). It was through their relationships with men and so through accepting their subordination in marriage that women supposedly became free and autonomous.

So feminism challenged the terms of male superiority which had been written into modernity and its dominant modes of philosophy and social theory. It also challenged the terms of a male identity that was cast in ethical terms in relation of independence and self-sufficiency. Rather, as Gilligan has argued in *In a different voice*, notions of connection and relationship could provide an ethical vision of its own (Gilligan 1982). But, rather than simply create space for women's moral experience, which had been traditionally rendered invisible and demeaned through its being evaluated as lacking when judged exclusively in the universal, impersonal and impartial terms of Kantian ethics, it also served to reveal some silences and gaps in the Kantian tradition that could be more easily related to a dominant, white, heterosexual masculinity.

Rather than accept as unproblematic masculine definitions of independence and self-sufficiency as signs of a morally elevated and principled form of moral consciousness, we could begin to identify the loneliness, isolation and disconnections. Rather than simply accept the terms of a dominant masculinity as establishing the terms to which men should aspire or else to judge themselves as lacking, we needed to revise masculinities and open up a space to investigate complex and ambiguous relationships that men had with diverse masculinities. This also threatened men's power within familial relations for it suggested that men did not automatically "know best".

Many men felt threatened by the challenges of feminism. Men felt exposed for, as I have argued, they had always relied upon women to interpret their experience for them. But now they could feel under attack, as if their ways of "knowing best" had been exposed as a cover for their own male interests and concerns. Women's autonomy and independence and their sense that they could live well enough on their own without men worked to expose the different ways in which men were, in reality, dependent on women. This made men defensive, and they could act violently in order to sustain their threatened position. Often men did not like being questioned and asked to account for themselves. Sometimes they got angry as a way of silencing women and regaining their power within the relationship.

Men could also feel threatened by the knowledge that women have of them. They used to depend upon this emotional knowledge without validating it publicly, but with the new uncertainties in the gender contract exposed they can feel endangered by it. Often the response of middle-class white men was to withdraw into a sullen silence, or respond with anger and violence, attacking and invalidating what their partners have to say about them and reasserting their control over their own lives. They legitimate their violence through saying their partners "lack sense" or are "being irrational" so that force is the only language which they supposedly understand. But this was to fall back on traditional ways of shoring up male superiority.

Traditionally men had been the sources of authority within the family, while women and children were defined the reason they supposedly lacked. It was part of a man's duty and part of his own responsibility to his own manhood to expect his voice to be respected "as law" within the family. There could only be one source of authority and this had to be him, if there was not to be anarchy and disorder. As the representative of God's authority within the family, fathers expected to be obeyed. To be questioned by children was already to have your authority challenged, and they had to pay the price for their disobedience. Fathers had to make sure there was no insubordination. Women and children had to be punished, if necessary, for it was a father's duty to teach them to know their place.

Often men have grown to unconsciously expect the kind of deference their fathers could take for granted. At one level they might be committed to notions of gender equality and to the importance of negotiating a new form of gender contract, but at another level they might feel silently resentful at the relative loss of power they experience. It is threatening for men to recognize that they are not needed in traditional ways, especially when male identities are so tied to notions of "being needed". Being a source of authority was yet another way of being needed within the family. This helped to define what men are for in the family.

As men recognize they are no longer needed for these kind of functions, this throws traditional masculinities into crisis. For men are not used to being needed for who they are personally. This is a challenging notion, as women demand that men be more "present" in relationships and give more of themselves. Women are less likely in the 1990s to stay in a relationship that is giving very little to them. They might as well be on their own, at least this way they will not be responsible for looking after someone else. But it is difficult for men to negotiate a more equal gender contract unless they have begun to work on themselves and engaged in a process of revisioning masculinities. This is to appreciate that gender politics is not something that can be left for women to get on with, but centrally concerns reworking men's relationships with their masculinities.

Men, control and experience

Men often grow up within an Enlightenment vision of modernity to assume that life is to be controlled, not lived. It is to be ordered and regulated, as masculinity is identified with self-control, control over oneself and one's experience. Within modernity experience exists as part of a disenchanted nature that exists to be controlled. In this sense it is often difficult for men to learn from their experience, for any emotions and desires that somehow do "not fit" the ideal that is being lived out is more or less automatically suppressed. This shows itself at an early age in the ways that boys learn to deal with their emotions; for instance, fear "does not exist" for they refuse to acknowledge and name it as such. Rather, as soon as it begins to surface, it is suppressed.

So it is that we begin to understand how young boys learn to grow up into violent men. In different ways they learn to be hard on themselves as they live up to images of their masculinities, suppressing any emotions that might compromise or bring into question these ideals. Boys' relationships with their fathers is often distant and idealized, especially when men are not involved in the everyday care, so their notions of masculinity become idealized. Boys are constantly struggling to live up to these ideals they have accepted for themselves, often quite unaware of the emotional hurt and damage they do to themselves on the way.

Boys have to be hard, or at least show themselves to be hard and unyielding with their peers, for to be soft or vulnerable is to be "feminine". So it is that all signs of tenderness or vulnerability have to be radically eliminated and banished. Often those aspects of our emotional lives we cannot recognize in ourselves, as Freud knew, we project onto others. So it is that the paki-bashing that was a feature of the racist landscape in the inner cities in the 1970s had strong connections to masculinities. Asian boys were seen to be "soft" and "effeminate" by their white peers, and so they were to be punished. They were made to carry the emotions that young white working-class boys could not accept in themselves. But there is also fear in this projection, a fear of the feminine, not just in oneself but also in women. This is why the feminine has to be controlled, because boys often feel uneasy and threatened by it, especially within the new terrains of sexual politics.

This is what it often means for boys to have self-control. It means that your freedom lies, in Weberian terms, in being able to control your life supposedly through being able to control the meanings that your experience carries. This is the link between a dominant masculinity and rationalism. It is in the idea that experi ence is to be controlled and that it is "male" reason that is the source of meaning. This allows first boys and then men to feel that if their sadness, fear or vulnerability is not named, then it "does not exist". Often men learn to automatically transmute emerging feelings of sadness into anger or rage, before the incipient emotions are even acknowledged. The anger is "acceptable" because it affirms, rather than threatens, heterosexual male identities.

This rationalism can sometimes be served, rather than questioned, in the feminist idea that masculinity is exclusively a relationship of power. So it is that it is acknowledged at least that men are not "naturally" violent and aggressive. But it is the institutionalized power that men inherit within a patriarchal society and the control this offers men in their personal and intimate relations that they need to defend. This form of "power analysis", although helpful in some ways, is reductive. It threatens unwittingly to lock men into an unchanging situation, and it makes it impossible to envision ways in which men *can* change.

It might well be that men in general benefit from their power in relation to women and children within a patriarchal society. But it is also important to recognize that not all men are violent and some men are a lot more violent than others. Nor is it enough to say, as a radical feminist argument has it, that at least with violent men you know "who you are dealing with", for all men are "potentially violent". There is an essentialism here that needs to be carefully questioned. It is no less questionable because it applies to men. In threatening to fix men through their identification with power, we lose a sense of the complexities of men's lives and we accept a form of reductivism that we would otherwise keenly challenge.

At the same time it is important to identify the diverse strategies that men might use to sustain their threatened superiority in relation to women and children. There are different ways of putting people down, of not listening to what they have to say, of not respecting who they are, while giving the appearance of the opposite. We also have to fully recognize that the relationships of power and control that operate in a personal and intimate relationship do not operate independently of the larger gender relations of power and control.

But the sources of power that women can also invoke within relationships need to be fully acknowledged so that we move away from too simplistic notions of victim and oppressor. Differences need to be recognized within contemporary gender relationships and changes that women and men have made need to be validated and appreciated. While not underestimating the power that men have at their disposal within a patriarchal society, we need to recognize changes that have taken place. We need to recognize the complexities of personal relationships and the different sources of power that are at work in sustaining long-term heterosexual relationships.

Ethics and violence

Within patriarchal relationships men were often brought up to think that it was their duty to keep women in their place. This was something that was owed to women and men would be failing in their responsibilities if they did not exercise the discipline that was expected of them. Within an Enlightenment vision of modernity, patriarchal relations were refigured as the source of male superiority was legitimated in terms of the reason that men could alone take for granted. Since with Kant there was an identification between reason and morality, this also served to morally legitimate men's power in relation to women. This was an ambivalence that was close to the centre of liberal moral and political theory, which otherwise claimed freedom and equality for all human beings. But the reality was that some people were deemed to be "more human" than others.

Feminism served to challenge an Enlightenment modernity and it recognized the ease with which men were brought up to treat women as sexual objects. Men seemed to be able to feel entitled to their control over women's bodies. Since women lacked a secure inner relation with reason, they could not legislate what they wanted or needed for themselves. This allowed men to feel that their relation with reason allowed them to "know" what women wanted better than women could know themselves. In this way women came to be demeaned in their own eyes and lost their own voices.

The ease with which boys grow up to regard women as sexual objects, to feel somehow entitled to pass judgement on women, is deeply embedded within patriarchal relations. This might offer ways in which boys learn to sustain their own uneasiness in relation to their diverse masculinities, but this shows the importance of revisioning masculinities if we are to work with men. The objectification of women as sexual objects shows the ease with which women can be regarded as "less than human" within modernity. It helps to prepare the ground for men's violence in relation to women.

There is a terrible scene in the movie *Thelma and Louise* when a man, having got one of the women drunk takes her outside to rape her. He will not listen to what she says and he gets angry when she resists him. Somehow he feels entitled to having sex with her, and she is crying desperately. He only stops when a gun is put to his head. But even then he says that he thought she was enjoying it. He is firmly reminded that if a woman is crying in that way, she is not enjoying anything. He gets abusive and says that she can suck his cock, so that you only feel that in some way he has got what he deserves, when he is shot.

When you confront the realities of male violence to women, the intense sufferings of rape and sexual harassment, the horrors and brutalities of physical and sexual violence, you recognize the urgency of working with boys before they become violent men. It becomes tempting to think of masculinity as exclusively a relationship of power, for you recognize that this sex is an assertion of male power. You want there to be zero tolerance for these forms of behaviour, but you also recognize that it is not an issue of individual will alone, but is deeply implicated in the organization of contemporary masculinities. As traditional gender contracts have been challenged, the domestic sphere has become contested and men have often resorted to violence in order to silence the challenges of their partners. Even if they regret their behaviour and feel remorse afterwards, often it is the only way that men know how to behave without threatening their male identities.

We have to question the legitimations of male violence and the ethics that sustain a sense of male superiority. It is crucial to explore the diverse forms of male violence, but it also important to acknowledge that women are also capable of violence. It is misleading to think that whenever a woman is violent in her relationship or with her children, this can adequately be explained as a consequence of the ways she has been violently treated by men. While engaging with the overwhelming realities of male violence, it is important also to recognize, in the context of intimate relationships, that it is not always that "women are right and men are wrong".

Feminism has helped to articulate its own gendered ethics, but it is not that women are always right, anymore than in Marxist theory it was helpful to assume that the proletariat had an exclusive relationship to morality and justice. The issues about the relation of ethics to oppression are complex, as Weil recognizes (Blum & Seidler 1989). At the same time it is crucial to appreciate that traditional forms of philosophy and social theory often served to at least implicitly legitimate male violence. Often these traditions were silent when it came to the injustice done to women through rape, violence and sexual harassment. It was too easy to assume that these were private matters to do with personal life and that injustice and oppression were only "real" when they took place within the public sphere. These were not concerns of civil society. The pain was too readily diminished as "subjective" and "personal".

In her seminal essay "Human Personality", Weil prepared the ground for a refusal to think of rape in terms of an infringement of rights. She thought that this language was inadequate to the "moral reality" of the situation (Blum & Seidler 1989). She recognized it as a limit to liberal moral and political theory. She insisted that the rape, imagined in her example as a young girl being dragged into the brothel against her will, was a "violation" of the person. But she refused to understand this "damage" in psychological terms alone. She refuses to separate ethics from power, and in this context we also have to come to terms with the realities of rape and sexual violence. We have to recognize the depths of the hurt and the years it can take to recover, if you ever do.

But this also involves exploring men's relationships with their own bodies and questioning the instrumentality in relation to an ethics of embodiment. As boys learn to trivialize their own experience of their bodies, so they also diminish what women are made to suffer. Some engagement with the realities of male rape could help here. Within a Cartesian tradition men and women, in different ways, tends to separate from their bodies which become the objects of medical knowledge. The women's health movement served a fundamental challenge in its notion that "our bodies, ourselves". At some level this questions a Christian assumption which too readily identifies the body with the "sins of the flesh".

We need to differentiate between different forms of male violence towards women. We must refuse a single scale of measurement, but we must learn to listen to the voices of the women themselves. Within discourse theory it is too easy to lose touch with the pain of experience, with the notion that experience is articulated through available discourses. This is part of Weil's challenge when she talks of the "inadequacy" and "inappropriateness" of a discourse of rights to illuminate the young girl's suffering. For her it is more than an injury to the person, it is a violation of the soul. She invokes a spiritual language partly to escape a prevailing psychologism that would assume that counselling, however helpful, would heal the wounds.

Often men are insensitive to the sufferings they have caused, and it is important for men to learn to take responsibility for their actions. But if this is to be helpful it is not enough to engage moralistically in terms of guilt. Men also have to be brought to feel the reality of the pain. Working with men can involve connecting them to their own sufferings, rather than to assume that because men share in patriarchal power in relation to women, they are somehow not entitled to feel their own pain. This involves a careful balance, for this is in no sense to excuse or legitimate the sufferings they have caused. Sometimes this is the fear women have. Rather it is a matter of learning how best to work with men so that they learn to take more emotional responsibility for their actions.

Men, bodies and ethics

It is still too easy for men to trivialize women's experience and to assume that they maintain a right over women's bodies and sexualities. This is partly legitimated through the ways that the body and sexualities are already diminished and devalued within a dominant Christian culture. Within the West this denial was continued within modernity, which defined women's bodies as part of men's property and which defined men's freedom as a freedom to do whatever he will with property at his disposal. This vision of relationship as property is deeply embedded within notions of marriage. Traditionally it was felt that "she belongs to him" and it is her duty "to fulfil his sexual needs". This ethic still underpinned relationships in the 1950s, and so helped unconsciously to structure expectations into the present for many men.

A difficulty, when working with men, in identifying sex too exclusively with power is that we can unwittingly reproduce negative and guilt-ridden attitudes towards sex that have such long histories in the West. If we are not to reproduce the Cartesian notion that the body is not "part of" who we are, but is part of a despised "animal nature", then we have to revision an embodied ethics which is already gendered and aware of the integrity of sexual differences. We have to revision a sense of what it means to be "human", which does not identify the "sexual" with the "animal". Often these identifications are at work in prevailing discourses, so we fail to appreciate the ways we are already implicated in them.

It is partly because men grow up so estranged from their own bodies as sources of pleasure that they learn to look outside and beyond themselves for their happiness. This can encourage men to feel they are somehow entitled to expect women to make them happy, and women can grow up accepting that they are somehow responsible for the happiness of their partners. At one remove from their own bodies, men can be caught as observers of their own experience, as "voyeurs" of their own lives. This links to the control that men feel they need to have in relation to their own lives. They can also feel they need to control the lives of their partners and children.

With mass unemployment and the restructuring of the labour process, partly as a consequence of globalization, it is becoming harder for middle-class and working-class men to affirm their male identities through work. Traditional ways in which men sought to affirm their masculinities are blocked, so that the domestic sphere assumes a new significance for many men. This can reinforce the pressure and tension within relationships that are already unstable because of the renegotiation of gender relations, when domestic life becomes the site in which men feel forced to affirm their already threatened masculinities. At a time when women are also asserting their autonomy and independence, it easily becomes an arena of domestic harassment and violence.

But in the 1990s men have also withdrawn from relationships as a site which can feel too fraught with emotional intensities. Men have learnt to withdraw to the gym, often leaving women resentful and taken for granted, especially when they feel their partners are not pulling their weight at home. Men focus upon their bodies as the space upon which masculinities can be affirmed. There is a widespread ethic of the "hard" body and an identification with training as a way of proving yourself "man enough". Exercise becomes a matter of work and is structured into the week. Men become aware of their looks and this becomes a hope for relationships in the uncertain sexual worlds of the 1990s.

But the hardening of the body can further instrumentalize men's relationships with themselves. It can also make them less sensitive to their own emotions, as well as to the feelings of others. Men can feel locked into their bodies and into regimes of training, as if they will somehow provide solutions to the problems in their personal and intimate relationships. Men can feel that, as they demand so little for themselves emotionally, that their partners should do likewise. They should get on with their own lives and be less demanding of them emotionally. But at another level men can feel lost and isolated, unhappy with traditional masculinities, but unsure how to change. Unable to reach out to partners who are no longer so pre- pared to do the emotional work for them, they can take refuge in the gym or with their mates. They can at least feel that the gym provides them with an "escape" and that it can be a way of avoiding the drinks and drugs that so many of their friends seem to go for.

Working with men

Working with men can be difficult because men from different class backgrounds are so used to thinking that they ought to be able to deal with their problems on their own. Asking for help is so easily experienced as a sign of weakness that it is only going to make men feel worse about themselves. This has to be acknowledged in the ways men are approached, for they so easily feel that whatever they share is bound in some way to be used against them.

Often it is only in an extreme crisis, when things are out of control, that men will draw upon help that is available to them. This is echoed in the resistance men often feel in going to doctors. Often they will only present themselves when they are forced to do so by their partners. They will tend to minimize what is going on, assuming that if the symptoms came on their own, they might just go on their own.

Men are often so concerned with "losing face" in front of other men that they are likely to ask for help only if they are assured it is confidential. This can mean a preference to see someone on their own and a resistance to working in groups. There are particular fears that are related to groups, because of the threat of being made to feel small in front of others. This is what links many men to a feeling of privacy. Of course it also has to do with sustaining control, and many men found it difficult in the early years of the women's movement to realize that their partners might be talking about their relationship "in public". This was the source of a great deal of tension.

Often masculinities are so taken for granted and men feel caught in proving themselves in relation to them, that it can be difficult to recognize that men can behave quite differently in different societies or cultures. A sense that it is possible to deal with situations in different ways helps to create an emotional space for exploration. As men become more sensitive to how they have also had to harden themselves against the hurts and abuses of their own childhoods, a healing can begin to take place. This can help men to a sense of their own self-worth, rather than feeling they have constantly to prove themselves against other men, testing themselves against the achievements of others. Being so other-directed can make it difficult for men to appreciate themselves, for they are constantly judging themselves as lacking in relation to other men and then taking their frustration out on their partners.

If men can only feel good about themselves through feeling better than others, there is a constant pressure to devalue and discount the experience of their partners and their children. For, often it is difficult for men to acknowledge their own emotional needs without compromising a sense of male identity. To have needs is already to prove that you are "feminine", so you can resent others who might have more of their needs acknowledged and met. This can create an envy of children who can seem to be getting an attention from their mother that you did not get for yourself. Men can feel guilty for having needs at all, for there is a moralism which is often a price of male superiority. But this can make men hard on themselves and punishing on others.

As men begin to recognize some of the complexities in their relationship with their inherited masculinities and to appreciate that they live in a different world from their fathers, they might be more open to change. As men can accept more of their own vulnerability and recognize more of their emotional needs without feeling threatened, they can become a little less compulsive, less driven and less hard on themselves. But this is a process which takes time and it is not easy within a Protestant culture that devalues time spent on oneself as a form of self-indulgence. This makes it difficult for men to recognize that they can enjoy their pleasure, which does not have to be at the expense of others. Often it is pleasure, as Marcuse recognizes, that is feared (Marcuse 1968).

For men to recognize that not only can they give love but that they can also be lovable themselves is to question the terms of Protestant moral culture. For men to recognize that they can both give and receive love is also part of the process of undoing/deconstructing structures which sustain male violence. As men also begin to appreciate how they have also suffered violence at the hands of parents and teachers and how this went unacknowledged and unrecognized, they begin to voice some of the hurts they also carry. They realize how these brutalities went unnamed because they were an accepted part of what is involved in proving you were "man enough". If we are also to have zero tolerance of these forms of abuse, then we have to envision masculinities that name these violations for what they are.

This also involves men recognizing how insensitive and violent they can be with themselves, suppressing their vulnerability and feelings and unable to voice their emotions. This can help men to recognize the sufferings their violence does to women and to children. As men become slowly aware of how they project their feelings of inadequacy and feelings of not being good enough onto women, who are made to carry these unresolved feelings in the violence that is done to them. Max Weber understood the crucial relationship between the ways the Protestant ethic produces feelings of inadequacy and worthlessness and how this is related to the identification of a dominant masculinity with work within a capitalist society.

With the widespread changes in industrial societies and the mass unemployment in the 1990s these structures are broken and it is no longer possible for so many men to affirm their masculinities through work. In this crisis of traditional masculinities we can also see the resurgence of male violence in a period when women are seeking greater freedom and autonomy. I do not think it useful to image this in terms of a war between the sexes, but we have been forced to recognize the sufferings wrought by male violence. As more men engage in a process of change and develop more contact with their emotional lives they will begin to question their inherited masculinities. As men learn to satisfy more of their own needs, this should take some of the pressure off their relationships in which women were expected to do the emotional work. As men take more emotional responsibility, they can also challenge the violence of men around them, sharing ways of working on themselves.

Men will not easily give up the power they have inherited within a patriarchal society. But as men recognize what they will also gain from more equal and loving relationships, they hopefully will engage themselves in movements for social change. This involves challenging prevailing forms of philosophy and social theory which within modernity have identified "being human" with "being rational". We need new ways of thinking that can explore the ethics of relationships and recognize emotional and somatic life as sources of human dignity and well-being.

As gender relationships become more equal and as different sexualities are equally validated, we recognize not only the oppression of women, gays and lesbians but also the ways that men with diverse masculinities of class, "race" and ethnicities have in different ways been brutalized and made "less human". As Milosz recognizes, rather than take a humanity for granted, as men we also have to start the slow process of humanizing ourselves (Milosz 1991).

References

BLUM, L. & SEIDLER, V. J. (1989) *A truer liberty: Simone Weil and Marxism.* New York City & London: Routledge.

FOUCAULT, M. (1990) *Care of the self.* Harmondsworth: Penguin.

GILLIGAN C. (1982) *In a different voice: Psychological theory and women's development.* Cambridge MA: Harvard University Press.

KANT, I. (1948) *Groundwork to metaphysics of morals.* Trans. by H. J. Paton. Hutchinson: London.

MARCUSE, H. (1968) *Negations.* London: Allen Lane.

MILLER, J. B. (1976) *Towards a new psychology of women.* Harmondsworth: Penguin.

MILOSZ, C. (1991) *Beginning with my streets.* New York City: Farrar Strauss & Giroux.

SEIDLER, V. J. (1986) *Kant, respect and injustice: the limits of liberal moral theory.* London: Routledge.

SEIDLER, V. J. (1989) *Rediscovering masculinity: reason, language and sexuality.* London: Routledge.

SEIDLER, V. J. (1991) *Recreating sexual politics: men, feminism and politics.* London: Routledge.

SEIDLER, V. J. (1994) *Unreasonable men: masculinity and social theory.* London: Routledge.

SEIDLER, V.J. (1997) *Man enough: embodying masculinities.* London & Thousand Oaks CA.: Sage.

WEIL S. (1962) *Selected essays 1934–43.* S. R. REES (ed). Oxford: Oxford University Press.

Chapter Thirteen

Values and processes in groupwork with men

Malcolm Cowburn and Hilary Pengelly

Introduction

It is, doubtless, a laudable aspiration to wish to help men change. It can be argued that men bear a large part of the responsibility for much that is harmful in the world, and if we want the world to be a better and less harmful place men must change. However, in considering issues related to how groupwork initiatives may help men to change, more than rhetoric is required. This chapter considers issues relating to preparing groupwork programmes for men, focusing in particular on issues relating to the relationship between ideology and the processes of selecting men for groupwork programmes.

The problem of masculinity

Men are not a homogenous group and masculinities vary according to age, race, class, sexuality, and physical and learning abilities. However, in considering which men may benefit from groupwork programmes, it is important to be aware of the presence and influence of the "dominant" form of masculinity and consider how this relates to the groupwork.

In Western societies there appears to be a dominant (hegemonic) form of masculinity. Fielding notes the following features of this masculinity:

> ... (i) aggressive, physical action; (ii) a strong sense of competitiveness and preoccupation with the imagery of conflict; (iii) exaggerated hetero-sexual orientation, often articulated in terms of misogynistic and patri-archal attitudes towards women; and (iv) the operation of rigid in-group/out-group distinctions whose consequences are strongly exclusionary in the case of out-groups and strongly assertive of loyalty and affinity in the case of in-groups. (Fielding 1994: 47)

Similar constituents of this dominant form of masculinity have been observed by many commentators, including Mac An Ghaill, who noted that:

> . . . male students at Parnell School learn to be men in terms of three constitutive elements of compulsory heterosexuality, misogyny and homophobia. (Mac An Ghaill 1994: 96)

and Jackson:

> "Hard case" masculinity not only defines itself positively through assertiveness, virility, toughness, independence etc. but also negatively by defining itself in opposition to what it is not – feminine or homosexual. (Jackson 1990: 124)

Because of its dominance, this masculinity is often construed as being the "norm" or "natural", while other masculinities are construed as "abnormal" or "unnatural". This norm (and the "normal" man) is generally uncritically accepted.

And yet it is clear that dominant forms of masculinity are problematical – the two key components highlighted above, heterosexuality and violence, account for much male behaviour that is harmful and destructive. The problematic nature of hegemonic heterosexual masculinity is evidenced when we look at the research that has examined the attitudes about, and proclivities towards, sexual violence in populations of "normal" adult men (Kanin 1969, 1985; Malamuth 1981; Rapaport & Burkhart 1984; Muehlenhard & Linton 1987; Petty & Dawson 1989). Most of these studies have used college students. As the majority of students tend to have come from middle-class socio-economic groups, they cannot be regarded as representative of the general population. However, these studies demonstrate that a significant percentage of the "normal" male population believe it acceptable to carry out a sexual assault and report the likelihood of doing so if they could be assured of not being detected or punished. A percentage also report having actually carried out forced sexual assaults against both women and children. Within this context it is easy to understand why it has been the women's movement(s) that has called attention to harmful and dangerous aspects of male behaviour, and male-dominated institutions and organizations that have largely ignored these calls.

Men with problems, men as problems: values and groupwork

The influence of the dominant masculinity is crucial to how groupwork programmes define the target group of men they seek to recruit and the type of programme they offer. Until recently groupwork initiatives with men tended to ignore or reject hegemonic masculinity, recruiting men considered to be "deviant" or "abnormal" on the basis of psychiatric diagnoses, with a view to restoring their essential "normal" masculinity. Such labels ignored any critical focus on masculinities. But certain groupwork initiatives for men have targeted those men whose behaviour is characterized by what Jackson (1990) defines as "hard-case" masculinity. Rather than seeking to avoid this group of men, fearing that they may contaminate other group members, a number of groupwork initiatives have developed a critical questioning of this "hard-case masculinity", and have formulated programmes that both challenge it and offer alternatives to it. However, merely developing programmes that ignore the pervasive influences outside the group session does not effectively challenge hegemonic masculinity.

Many years ago one of the authors (M.C.) spent long hours in groups with men convicted of sexual offences, attempting to help them recognize the choices they made in the build up to and in the execution of sexual offences. The group programme also addressed issues of male behaviour, particularly those relating to sexuality and sexual behaviour, and highlighted sexist and oppressive aspects of men's behaviour – not just sex offenders but all men. At the end of each group session, group leaders watched as the group members went home with their tabloid newspapers – that depict women as sexual objects and men as sexually uncontrollable – uncommented on let alone challenged. Challenging aspects of the dominant masculinity, which initially may have appeared unrelated to the men's offending behaviour, was not and still is not easy. It was issues such as these, where the implicit values of the groupwork programme were clearly at odds with dominant understanding of male behaviour that helped push the group leaders into explicitly articulating the first value base to our groupwork initiative (Cowburn 1990). This value base sought to locate male sexual violence within a continuum of male sexual behaviours, it recognized that sexual violence was always harmful (something that is often denied by dominant forms of masculinity, e.g. myths that rape is enjoyed by women or that children forget and are not harmed by sexual activity with adults), and that men can control their response to sexual arousal (contradicting another myth about male sexual behaviour). Since then the value base has grown and changed (Cowburn et al. 1992; Cowburn & Modi 1995); however, by explicitly locating our practice within an ideological framework that saw male violence as being congruent with "normal" male behaviour, our practice was clearly and openly located in a critical relationship to dominant masculinities. Doing this enabled the groupwork programme to develop in a focused way that was led by research and *critical* thinking rather than the latest cognitive exercise. Male violence was seen not as the product of cognitive distortions, but as an extreme embodiment of the hegemonic masculinity. Thus, while the programme helped men identify ways of changing, it also highlighted the difficulty of doing so in a society that both covertly and not so covertly endorses some of their attitudes and actions.

How groups can help men to change

Recognizing the pervasive and dominant influence of hegemonic masculinity does not necessarily imply that all groups for men should be solely and actively deconstructing this masculinity. Similarly, it does not imply that all groups for men should be open to all men. While all groups are located within the ambit of hegemonic masculinity, "men's groups" vary considerably in origins, aims, membership, format/ programme and process. Some have been formed "voluntarily" and focus on personal growth and change; others, while also sharing similar foci, have been established by agencies for identified groups of men whom "society" thinks should change. According to where they locate themselves in relation to the dominant form of masculinity these groups exist on a continuum from those that seek to change what men do, to groups that seek to change how men feel and think about themselves and their relationships to others (Fig. 13.1). Obviously some groups will endeavour to incorporate more than one objective but there is usually a priority given to one of these. How a group is planned and, in particular, how its aims and objectives are articulated may determine the type of men it seeks to attract.

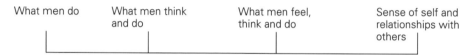

Figure 13.1 Objectives of men's groups: a continuum.

The terms "aims" and "objectives" are often used indiscriminately and interchangeably, and thus can lack sufficient focus both for the group leader attempting to run a programme and also for any observer attempting to learn from established initiatives. For the purposes of this paper the term "*aim*" will signify a distant goal that a programme may be attempting to achieve (e.g. the anti-sexist "enlightenment" of all group participants), whereas an "*objective*" represents one step on the way towards the overall aim – a limited goal (e.g. each group member will identify how sexist attitudes manifest themselves in his daily life). Thus, while a programme may have many *objectives* leading towards its *aim(s)*, it is unlikely that it will have more than one (or two) *aims*. Clarity of expression of aims and objectives may enable a programme to identify its target group for membership.

Recruiting the "right" men: screening and selecting

In considering recruitment of men to men's groups two processes need to be considered: *screening* and *selecting*. Occasionally the two terms are used interchangeably to signify the process by which a group membership is identified and established. However, the processes are not the same and the meanings of the words indicate very different approaches to recruiting group members. The *Shorter Oxford English Dictionary* describes the process of *screening* as: "to sift by passing through a 'screen'". The same dictionary describes a "screen", in this context as: "an apparatus used in the sifting of grain, coal, etc.". The word "*select*" is defined as meaning

"To choose or pick out in preference to another or others". A process of establishing selection criteria for men's groups is focused on identifying what and who is wanted in a group. A process of screening is concerned with specifically identifying what/whom is *not* wanted in a group, and also assumes that such can be identified.

To screen a man prior to allowing him to participate in a groupwork programme is to consider whether he is "suitable" for the programme. Unsuitable men are screened out – they are excluded. General justifications for screening of men for men's groups are located in three key areas:

- The protection of others, particularly vulnerable individuals such as women and children.
- To ensure a level of agency accountability for organizations responsible for setting up groups to work with men.
- To ensure that group dynamics are not adversely affected.

Recently, in Britain and the USA there have been concerns expressed in the media and by politicians about the presence of "known" sex offenders in local communities, and the consequent danger that they pose. There have been cries for the convicted sex offender to be identified publicly and to be excluded from all social space in which he may have access to children. The selecting of men to attend groupwork programmes may also be influenced by these cries. However well-intentioned the motives may be for identifying and excluding convicted sex offenders from groupwork programmes, the rationale underpinning them may be open to question. Those who would seek to "police the paedophile" out of social encounters with children say that doing so would make children safer. However, the number of offences that are never reported each year (discussed in most prevalence studies) must raise doubts as to whether merely identifying and excluding the convicted sex offender will do very much towards making society safer.

However, research with convicted sex offenders (Abel et al. 1987; Burdin & Johnson 1989; Conte et al. 1989; Colton & Vanstone 1996) has shown that some convicted sex offenders plan their offences in advance and have a range of strategies both to identify suitable victims and to create circumstances where they can commit offences without being disturbed. Thus it is reasonable that group leaders may have justifiable anxieties related to convicted sex offenders being in their group, particularly if the group is being held in premises that allow easy access to people who may be victimized. These anxieties will be exacerbated when taking into account the agency's responsibility to ensure the safety of the public – particularly in premises that the agency has a responsibility for.

Groups for men occur in a wide range of places and settings. In some of these there may be a range of other activities for other people happening at the same time. Thus men who have been identified as convicted sex offenders potentially pose a known risk to other members of the public if they attend groups in public places. The exact nature of that risk is unknowable, but should a convicted man offend against people in the setting where he is attending a group and it emerges that the organizers of the group knew of his convictions but did nothing to protect other members of the group or the public, the organizers may be deemed to be culpably negligent. Thus it may be wise for organizers of men's groups to make some efforts at establishing that none of their group members has a conviction for behaviours that may endanger the public. This is to ensure that the workers and their organization are seen to act responsibly rather than to guarantee safety.

A man may be excluded from a group for reasons related to how he would respond and react in a group setting. The following key information about potential group members may help workers identify and avoid some problems.

- *Motivation*: not all men seeking to join groups are motivated by a desire to change themselves. Sometimes their motivation may relate to circumstances outside the group programme agenda, and thus their participation within the group may be either nominal or actually disruptive. For example, a man who has been violent to his partner may have received an ultimatum that unless he "does something about his violence" the relationship will be terminated. He may, therefore, attend a group for men who wish to end their violence to their partners but only under duress from his partner. Lacking any personal motivation to change, he may resent both the group and the messages of the programme and seek to disrupt it. It is important to clarify the nature of a man's motivation before he joins the group.
- *Mental health*: a man's mental health may prevent him participating in a group programme or may mean that he potentially poses a threat to other group members. Some group programmes designed to help men change are very demanding – both cognitively and emotionally. This may adversely affect some men's ability to participate in them and may unwittingly provoke violent reaction. It is important to check whether potential group members have a recent psychiatric history (including whether they are currently receiving any medication) and if so to ascertain (with their permission) from their psychiatrist whether they are able to manage the stresses of the course. Additionally, however, it may be important to discover (from them and their consultant) how they are likely to react to pressures of groupwork, because their reactions may disrupt the programme of the group and pose a threat to others.
- *Substance abuse*: if a potential group member is currently abusing substances it is unlikely that he will be able to cope with the groupwork programme, and again this may pose serious difficulties for both other group members and the group leaders in running a programme effectively.

Considerations about how the man would behave and contribute to the group processes may influence group leaders in deciding to reject him from their group. This area is closely linked to the considerations of issues of selection insofar as issues related to "group performance" may be articulated as selection criteria rather than exclusion criteria.

The criteria influencing the recruitment and selection of group members are closely linked to both the aims and objectives of the group and also to the processes and style of the group. There is rarely only one criterion for selection to a group; often selection criteria link an external event and an internal (personal) response (e.g. the birth of a child and the feelings associated with that, perpetrating or being the victim of an assault and the feelings associated with that, etc.). However, to have experienced a particular event and to have had (or failed to have) a physiological, emotional and cognitive response is generally not enough to constitute selection criteria. In discussing how he chose men to participate in a group for sex offenders in prison, Perkins (1987: 198–99) commented that those whom he considered suitable for the group were able to specify problems and identify goals that they wanted to achieve through the programme, and were willing to take part in the activities of the group. Those whom he considered to be unsuitable for the group denied having committed offences or acknowledged the commission of offences but attributed them to other parties (i.e. asserting that there was nothing about their own behaviour or attitudes which needed changing) or felt they would not offend again (i.e. that the group was unnecessary).

Clearly identifying that potential group members perceive that there is something about themselves that they would like to explore and possibly change is important. As is ascertaining the level of commitment that potential group members have to working with other men in a group on an agreed subject. Ensuring that men have motivation in these areas may help to "select out" men who are either opposed to the objectives of the group or do not think that it would be helpful to them.

"Safe to participate in the programme": group processes and group leadership

While effective screening may help to exclude some men who could adversely affect the dynamic of a group programme, there are other considerations that need to be addressed which go beyond the individual circumstances and motivation; these are related to the well-being and effectiveness of the group as a whole. Generally they relate to the ability of all potential group members to participate equally and effectively and to feel safe while doing so.

Theorists of groupwork (Schutz 1966; Yalom 1970; Tuckman & Jensen 1977; Whitaker 1985) have identified various stages which groups go through in their development. These stages involve the group coming together, struggling to find an adequate means of working, working effectively and finishing. Tuckman & Jensen (1977) identify five stages of group development: forming, storming, norming, performing and adjourning.

They consider the *forming* phase of a group to be characterized by orientation, exploration and communication (with the worker and with each other). Group members have the opportunity to test out whether they belong in the group, and there may be the early stages of developing trust and a group bond. In this stage it is important for group leaders to establish the "ground rules" of the group. These relate to how group members behave with each other, and they may establish grounds for a group member being excluded from the group (these could be "offensive" words or behaviours such as racism, or they could relate to behaviours that the group is trying to help the men change, e.g. domestic or sexual violence).

A key aspect of ground rules that deserves separate mention is confidentiality. According to the type of group there may be total confidentiality or no confidentiality. An example of a group where confidentiality might be total would be a voluntarily run self-development group where men sought to help each other understand aspects of themselves, for example their sexual behaviour. Groups with either no or limited confidentiality are usually run by statutory and voluntary agencies where the agency's responsibility to the public is considered to be greater than their ability to maintain confidentiality – for example, no group in this context would be able to maintain as confidential a disclosure from a group member that he was committing acts of sexual abuse. It is important at the beginning of the group that group members are very clear as to the boundaries of confidentiality within their group, for this will significantly affect how the group runs. To facilitate this clarity some groups ask group members to sign a contract agreeing to the rules concerning confidentiality and the disclosure of information to third parties. Similarly, at the forming stage of the group it is important that group leaders mention to group members whether or not the groupwork programme is being evaluated, and if so how and what will be expected of group members. Evaluation is an increasingly commonplace feature in group work programmes; keeping group members informed about it is crucial to how safe group members feel in the group sessions.

The next stage of the development of a group identity is described by Tuckman & Jensen (1977) as *storming. Storming* is characterized by the formation of subgroups and pairings within the larger group, and consequent struggles for power and control. In this stage group members may be tested by other group members, and frailties and vulnerabilities may be exploited; black, gay and disabled group members may become either scapegoated or marginalized. This will be particularly so where they are either alone or in a substantial minority in the group. Ahmad (1992) makes the following comments about minority black participation in white dominated groups (and we think these comments are relevant to other oppressed groups):

> One of the major problems of "multi-racial" groupwork has been that "groups" are predominantly White, with one or two Black members. As a result, Black members, instead of gaining support and strength, instead of sharing common feelings and aspirations have found themselves even more isolated and sometimes in threatening situations . . . even in those groupwork settings, where there is numerical parity between Black and White members, there may be different perceptions about common issues that are difficult or impossible to share; there may be group dynamics that undermine Black members' experience and contributions, there may even be a clash of interests and priorities between Black and White members. "Multi-racial" groupwork needs to be prepared to deal with these shortcomings

and pitfalls. Otherwise, groupwork, however inadvertently, will just collude with the social control of Black clients even though in the disguise of groupwork (Ahmad 1992: 62)

In the *norming* and *performing* stages of the group the group develops a cohesion and is able to co-operate in performing the tasks of the group programme. This again may be problematic for the black, gay or disabled group member, who may experience difficulty in feeling part of a cohesive group, which is likely to be dominated by white heterosexual able-bodied men. The pressures to conform to the views and attitudes of either the group leaders or the dominant subgroup may lead others either to lose a sense of their identity or to abdicate from the processes of the group. Sensitive and skilful group leadership is essential to help the group in these stages.

No aspect of group leadership, and in particular confrontation, is value-free, and activities may be experienced differently by both worker and group member according to the gender, race, sexuality, age and physical and intellectual ability of both parties. It therefore requires the worker to examine his or her own value system. Ahmad (1992) states that confrontation (and we would add "group-leadership") in an aware and anti-oppressive manner "requires [both] confidence and competence". This, she argues, can only be gained when workers are continually "aware of their own perceptions and values" that may have oppressive connotations. A prerequisite for this is "an ongoing programme of self evaluation", and an essential prerequisite of an ongoing programme is self-evaluation and self-confrontation (Ahmad 1992: 35).

In working with men in groups there will inevitably be competitiveness and rivalries within the group and group members may challenge the authority of the group leaders. Group leaders need to clarify how they understand these behaviours of men in groups and also how they will respond to them in a way that does not duplicate the oppressiveness of hegemonic masculinity. And this, of course, takes us back to the importance of clarifying and making explicit the value base that underpins the groupwork initiative.

Conclusion

This chapter has endeavoured to draw out the links between values, programme planning and group processes in groupwork with men. It has suggested that values underpin all elements of groupwork programmes, and that if such programmes aspire to work with men in ways that are not oppressive, these values need to be explicit and open to challenge and change. A clearly thought out organizational infrastructure that identifies the men that it wishes to work with and the men with whom it cannot work is key to a programme being able to offer a safe environment for men to begin a process of change.

References

ABEL, G. G., J. V. BECKER, M. MITTELMAN, J. CUNNINGHAM-RATHNER, J. L. ROULEAN & W. D. MURPHY (1987) Self-reported sex crimes of non-incarcerated paraphiliacs. *Journal of Interpersonal Violence* **2**(1), 3–25.

AHMAD, B. (1992) *Black perspectives in social work.* Birmingham: Venture.

BURDIN, L. E. & C. F. JOHNSON (1989) Sex abuse prevention programs: offenders' attitudes about their efficacy. *Child Abuse and Neglect* **13**, 77–87.

COLTON, M. & M. VANSTONE (1996) *Betrayal of trust: Sexual abuse by men who work with children.* London: Free Association Books.

CONTE, J., S. WOLF & T. SMITH (1989) What sex offenders tell us about prevention strategies. *Child Abuse and Neglect* **13**, 293–301.

COWBURN, M. (1990) Work with male sex offenders in groups. *Groupwork* **3**(2), 157–71.

COWBURN, M. & P. MODI (1995) Justice in an unjust context: Implications for working with adult male sex offenders. In *Probation working for justice*, D. WARD & M. LACEY (eds), 185–207. London: Whiting & Birch.

COWBURN, M., C. WILSON & P. LOEWENSTEIN (eds) (1992) *Changing men: A practice guide to working with adult male sex offenders.* Nottingham: Nottinghamshire Probation Service.

FIELDING, N. (1994) Cop canteen culture. In *Just boys doing business? Men, masculinities and crime*, T. NEWBURN & E. A. STANKO (eds), 43–63. London: Routledge.

JACKSON, D. (1990) *Unmasking masculinity: A critical autobiography.* London: Unwin Hyman.

KANIN, E. (1969) Selected dyadic aspects of male sex aggression. *Journal of Sex Research* **5**, 12–28.

KANIN, E. J. (1985) Date rapists: differential sexual socialization and relative deprivation. *Archives of Sexual Behavior* **6**, 67–76.

MAC AN GHAILL, M. (1994) *The making of men: masculinities, sexualities, and schooling.* Buckingham: Open University.

MALAMUTH, N. M. (1981) Rape proclivity among males. *Journal of Social Issues* **37**, 138–57.

MUEHLENHARD, C. L. & M. A. LINTON (1987) Date rape and sexual aggression in dating situations: incidence and risk factors. *Journal of Counselling Psychology* **34**, 186–96.

PERKINS, D. (1987) A psychological treatment programme for sex offenders. In *Applying psychology to imprisonment*, B. McGURK, D. THORNTON & M. WILLIAMS (eds), 192–217. London: HMSO.

PETTY, G. M. & B. DAWSON (1989) Sexual aggression in normal men: incidence, beliefs and personality characteristics. *Personality and Individual Differences* **10**(3), 355–62.

RAPAPORT, K. & B. R. BURKHART (1984) Personality and attitudinal characteristics of sexually coercive college males. *Journal of Abnormal Psychology* **93**, 216–21.

SCHUTZ, W. C. (1966) *FIRO: The interpersonal underworld.* New York: Science and Behaviour Books.

TUCKMAN, B. W. & M. A. C. JENSEN (1977) Stages of small group development revisited. *Group and Organisation Studies* **2**(4), 481–99.

WHITAKER, D. S. (1985) *Using groups to help people.* London: Routledge & Kegan Paul.

YALOM, I. D. (1970) *The theory and practice of group psychotherapy.* New York: Basic.

Chapter Fourteen

Working with men for change: a sequential programme for men's development

Jim Wild

Men live with the interior knowledge, conscious or not, that by ruling, they are dominating someone, i.e., women. Since they live with/have to look at those with less privilege every day, they must develop a way of not really "seeing" them. Men know on some level they are not superior, and they know that this gender division is unjust – so the question becomes, how to live with it? The answer is, learn not to really "see" it. **Shere Hite,** Women as revolutionary agents of change, (1993)

Introduction

We now come to the practical section of the book. It offers a step-by-step programme, covering a wide variety of issues surrounding men and masculinity, designed to help men change.

The programme will be particularly relevant to:

- Social care workers.
- Groups of men in the community who are thinking of setting up a men's group and would like to have some structure to their meetings. These men may or may not already know each other.
- Groups of men in the workplace who see the benefits of such a group in terms of enhancing organizational culture and gender interaction.
- Men who would like to work through particular issues alone. However, I offer a word of caution here: it must be emphasized that this is a programme designed primarily for men who wish to make connections and to develop in a supportive environment. It is common for men to struggle with such issues when they are alone, so it is preferable to meet in a group.

I begin by presenting a model of adult learning that can be clearly understood and that is capable of application to the project of working with men for change. I go on to offer a programme of 29 exercises, drawing on a range of established techniques as well as on my own experiences as a facilitator of men's groups. The issues explored in these exercises are wide-ranging, though not exhaustive, and the exercises can easily be adapted to the needs of a wide variety of groups. My hope is that readers will let their enthusiasm and creativity develop and enhance the programme. Those with experience of facilitating men's groups may prefer simply to dip into the chapter for new techniques or different perspectives on a specific issue.

Throughout the chapter I use examples from my own life to illustrate the points I make. Self-disclosure is, I believe, a vital aspect of work with men. An understanding that others have shared the shame of being beaten by a parent, or humiliated by a bully at school, can be profoundly liberating. I would strongly encourage group-facilitators to use improvization and role playing to assist the sharing of histories and the development of an understanding of the way that we as men represent ourselves. Having said this, it must be made clear that with all disclosures there are risks, and that an important part of the work of a group is to support men through times when they are struggling and uncertain. The sequencing of this programme is thus designed with intent: no matter how well your group seems to be progressing it is vital not to explore areas that will cause anxiety too soon. Men will need time to feel grounded and comfortable within the group before they move on to deal with personal and political issues that may have been absent from their past.

This is essentially a practical programme and I have deliberately avoided the use of academic language or excessive references. However, I do provide a selective list of further reading at the end of the chapter.

Being clear about what your group is for

There are now a wide range of men's groups and organizations advocating and publicizing diverse stances on issues to do with men. Some would cast themselves as explicitly pro-feminist groups; others are protective of the traditional power privileges of men and hostile to feminist ideas and practice. Group agendas frequently emerge from personal experience. Some men may have had disputes in divorce proceedings and financial settlements made against them and are reacting to what they see as an injustice. Others may be defensive about increasing accusations of sexual abuse being made against men and have set up pressure groups concerned with challenging assumptions on such issues. Given the emergence of groups with such diverse interests it is important to be clear about what your group stands for and what it hopes to achieve. It is common for individuals starting men's groups to show great energy and commitment at the start of the project only to find that few men respond to the information provided. Unless you are clear about your strategy, potential participants will not understand the relevance to their own lives of participating in the group. I will return to this point under **Getting started** (below).

At this stage it is important that I outline the values and beliefs that have informed my own participation in and facilitation of men's groups, and that underlie the programme I present in this chapter. The key assumptions of this chapter are that from birth, we as men have experienced socialization and conditioning that may lead us to:

- have difficulties expressing a full range of emotions
- maintain an unfair share of power and privilege
- provide inadequate parenting to our children
- use conflict and violence to resolve differences
- abuse women, children and other men
- establish institutions and organize activities that exclude women.

Having stressed the importance of making clear the purpose and strategy of your group, I should note that you may alienate potential participants by promoting such ideas too forcefully in the early days. It is important to be subtle in promoting a group to men who may have little awareness of the effect of male power. If I were starting a group in a family centre I would be very cautious about presenting a view of men as potentially inadequate parents, for example. If, however, I were thinking about an activist group to raise issues in a local community, I would feel able to be more overt about a pro-feminist stance.

I would emphasize the need for a certain amount of screening of potential group members. If men have been referred to the group by an agency in a social care context you will need to now how and why they have become involved with that organization. You should also conduct initial interviews with applicants. For more guidance on this point you should consult Chapter 13 of this book. Your supervisor should be a vital source of support; if they are not experienced in this area you should obtain, with their agreement, a consultant with prior experience of working with men.

I have not discussed in depth in this chapter the problems for women running, or co-facilitating men's groups. Thoughts on this subject are given elsewhere in the book. My personal experience however is that, despite the excellent work being done by women in specialist areas – working with violent men or sex offenders for example – generic, non-specialist programmes work better when run by men. It is vital for men to see other men taking the initiative in this area.

Getting started

You might have a notion of the purpose and agenda of your group but no clear understanding of uptake. Your next task, therefore, is to begin marketing the programme. If your group is based within an organization you are likely to have automatic resource to the means of dissemination as well as in-house marketing and design expertise. If your group is community based, you will be reliant on newspapers and magazines, local radio and community notice boards or poster sites and on local organizations supportive of the issues. An excellent guide to getting publicity can be found in Boldt (1993). Those wishing to establish links with statutory and voluntary organizations in the UK should consult *The Social Services Yearbook*, published annually.

Though the debate concerning men and change has become much more mainstream in recent years, joining a men's group is still going against the grain. As a potential group-facilitator you are likely to encounter incomprehension and occasionally outright hostility at both the individual and the social level.

In the early 1980s I coordinated a left-of-centre community newspaper in a small town. We used the paper to publicize a men's group and to our surprise received about 20 calls. The following week the official local paper ran an interview with a local Conservative councillor who speculated about the group's activities, describing it as an "ominous" development. This had the effect of reducing prospective members to seven. With hindsight I would have approached the official paper for space to respond to the councillor's view, using his misrepresentations to develop a wider debate about men and change – and to get free publicity.

Hostility to the establishment of a new group need not take such a public form. Those trying to organize men's group within social care settings, have frequently found that that their chief obstacle is a well-established way of doing things and a lack of understanding about the purpose of a men's group. In the course of a research project on why men do not attend family centres I interviewed eight men, all of whom should have been attending the family centre on a regular basis but were never available. Their statements revealed that they saw the family centre as a place for women and children exclusively. Further investigation revealed that though these men certainly held traditional, patriarchal views about their role in child-care, their self-exclusion was mirrored in the attitude of staff and workers at the centre. Their unwelcoming attitude towards male participation exacerbated the men's uncertainties about how they would cope with responsibility for a crying baby or for changing a nappy.

It is clear that most men have hidden fears about being placed in situations where they are unskilled and inadequate. Though these fears may be misconceptions based on inexperience or prejudice they must be acknowledged as a powerful determinant in shaping men's attitudes, and in shaping the values of workers (especially male workers) in family centres and in social services departments. Such intransigent cultures can and must be challenged but they are hardly likely to be changed overnight.

Potential group-facilitators and group-members are also likely to face some hostility at an individual level. My own experience is of incomprehension from managers and colleagues alike, with responses to my involvement in men's issues ranging from the automatic assumption that I must be gay, to the advice I received from a training officer not to mention my involvement in pro-feminist men's development on my CV, to outright prejudice and hostility.

There is, without doubt, a downside to the decision to embark on such a journey, but I hope this chapter will begin to make clear the upside – of a rich emotional discovery in areas neglected and feared by too many men for too long.

Towards a model of understanding: the application of adult learning concepts to men, masculinity and change

The past thirty years have seen a considerable evolution in the theory and practice of adult learning, enabling educators and trainers to develop ever more effective methods of influencing behaviour and facilitating the process of change. The application of such methods however has been, in general, limited to management training. They have not, to my knowledge, been discussed in the context of work with men. My aim in this section is to introduce the reader to one of the ways in which management training conceptualizes the process of change, and to apply this model to the intense learning process experienced by men coming to terms with issues of masculinity and change.

Julie Hay (1994) develops a useful model, illustrated in Figure 14.1. I use each of the stages mapped out by Hay to discuss a standard learning curve experienced by men who have begun to think seriously about these issues.

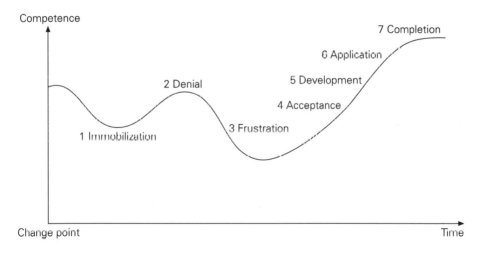

Figure 14.1   The process of development as proposed by Hay.

1. *Immobilization.* When men are confronted by aspects of themselves they have not explored or that they have avoided, they can feel overwhelmed by the implications. They may feel inadequate, or stupid. They may become confused, considering that the messages they received in childhood were wrong or that their

lives have been set on the wrong course. There may be enormous fear and uncertainty. Men may retreat to the security of what they have – power, control over their lives – and consider that this is acceptable.

2. *Denial.* Men are prone to consider the whole spectrum of emotions frightening, preferring to operate in the sphere of logic, control and reason. Consequently, following the immobilization phase, men are likely to deny that there is a problem, looking for reasoned arguments against change. Holding on to the safe haven of received notions of masculinity, they may argue that gender divisions are "natural".

3. *Frustration.* As men move on from denial and begin to feel confident in their explorations of what being a man is, there may be feelings of frustration. They may feel the need to change at a conscious level, but realize that they lack the experience or knowledge to do so. Most men are used to having instant answers, achieving results and getting things done – but forcing change in such a crucial area of identity can only lead to more frustration.

4. *Acceptance.* Men begin to understand that there are new and different agendas. This is an important time for many men as they look back, realizing perhaps that the "man" they have been is a fiction, not whole and not empathetic with others. This is the stage at which they prepare to move on and to test out new ways of being a man. The sense of new paths opening up may be mixed with the feeling of loss and even grief that accompanies the letting-go of old ways.

5. *Development.* At this stage men begin to formulate a clear understanding of new horizons. This is a period of energy and enthusiasm, in which masculinity ceases to be defined by traditional expectations and in which others begin to recognize the change that has occurred. Still the development is in need of anchorage as there is no longer a preconceived notion of what a man is, only a way of emerging from a history of false notions.

6. *Application.* Men are at ease with their developing exploration of what being a man is; willing and able to challenge old ways of relating to others.

7. *Completion.* Challenging patriarchy is never complete. All around are messages and received ideas that will attempt to force regression and question conclusions. At this stage however there is a strong sense of being "grounded" and a strength and confidence in understanding what was before and what is now.

Hay considers that it may take up to four years to successfully complete a major change. The programme that I describe below does not expect men to change overnight; indeed, I would suggest that our commitment in this area is lifelong. It is crucial that men should view the process as something to experience emotionally rather than to race through or to become competitive about. The struggle I describe above is, perhaps, the hardest most men will ever face, because:

- men are starting from a position of privilege and power
- this privilege and power is intergenerational and has huge legacies
- moving from an accepted masculine role towards a position that challenges that role will lead to re-evaluation on many levels
- patriarchy is everywhere and is constantly invasive.

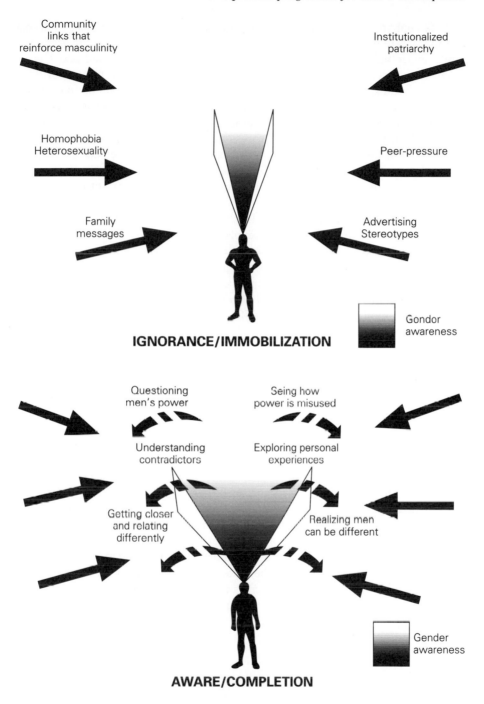

Figure 14.2 A visual representation of gender awareness in the first (immobilization) and last (completion) stages of the learning cycle.

In applying Hay's competence curve to the change process in men, I felt that her ideas were helpful in grasping how men react to pressures that put their masculinity under threat. I should stress, though, that learning to be anti-sexist is an immensely complex process – in my view qualitatively different from most other types of learning. If I learn to drive a car, I tend to keep that level of competence most of my life; learning to live in an anti-sexist way requires a constant process of reevaluation and re- learning. In order to make clearer the myriad of influences on gender identity at each stage in the process of development – influences that come from personal history, from close relationships and from outside sources – I have devised Figure 14.2. In this figure I present a visual representation of gender awareness in the first (immoblization) and last (completion) stages of Hay's learning cycle.

I hope that my interpretation of Hay's learning curve and the map of influences I provide in Figure 14.2 begin to explain both the degree of resistance and the poor motivation frequently experienced in the early stages of working with these issues. The programme that follows is designed to break down such resistance in a gradual and measured way, encouraging men to engage fully with the importance and the possibility of change. I would also point readers to a very useful book on the theme of motivation: Miller and Rollnick's *Motivational interviewing*.

The Programme

While I have suggested a structure for the first meeting of the group, I have not made specific recommendations for the number of exercises that might be included in each subsequent session. This is something for individual group facilitators to plan, depending on the composition of the group and the time available – the group you are running may be for a weekend, or for 12 months. However, the exercises are divided thematically, into ten sections. I give each exercise time limits, but these are not set in stone. There will be times when the group has the energy and enthusiasm for extended discussion and other occasions when the group (or its facilitator!) feels more flat. Be sure that men use "I" as opposed to "you" and "we" as this distances the speaker from their statement. You should also be careful to avoid situations that breakdown into cross talking or cliques.

You will need a flipchart, plenty of paper, pens, blu-tack™ and scissors.

Getting to know myself; getting to know each other

The opening session

Open the group with a personal introduction, some welcoming comments and a general affirmation of the group's purpose; something along the lines of what follows:

> I'd like to open the group by saying a little about myself and what we hope you will get out of the group. We are here because we understand that as men we need to change. We may not know a great deal about what this means at this moment, but we are curious and committed to looking at the idea of change within ourselves and within society at large. My name is ... I have been interested in the issues for. . . . years and I am very pleased to be welcoming you all to the group. To start, I would like each group member to say who you are and what led you to join the group.

It is important that everyone should have the chance to be heard, to claim space for themselves, without interruption or cross talking. This might seem obvious but remember that this may be the first time these men have ever met in such a context They may not be clear about how to "be", or whether previous ways of getting time in the company of men are acceptable.

Listed below are examples of the way men often are in the company of other men:

• competitive	• masterful
• loud	• powerful
• making jokes (at the expense of others)	• practical
• full of bravado	• sporty
• boastful	• emotionally safe
• talking across others	• superficial
• strong	• abusive.

An awareness of these points during the opening session will be useful in interpreting the dynamics of the group and in calling early attention to issues that may need particular attention. By the end of the first group meeting you should certainly be developing an understanding of the characteristics of individual group members, looking out for the following:

- who is establishing leadership
- who is quiet
- who doesn't speak at all

- who is the joker
- who wants to be known as having knowledge
- who uses words with care
- who seems frightened or anxious
- who takes up space (particularly when there is silence).

When the introductions are over, it is essential to spend some time setting out ground-rules for future sessions – a process I call "contracting". Any successful group needs a clear set of shared rules and a common understanding about boundaries. Listed below are some of the issues that have been included in contracting in previous groups I have run:

- confidentiality
- no violence
- no interruptions
- do not get into "putting women down"
- take risks
- contribute and learn
- remember that this is not therapy
- use the group meeting as a time to be different.

For contracting to work, it must be done collectively rather than imposed. I suggest asking participants to form smaller groups to brainstorm on "What I want out of this group" and "What I do not want". While the men are engaged in this exercise, you should make your own list of non-negotiable points (amongst mine would be the first four mentioned above). After 15 minutes, ask the groups to feed back while you write the findings on a flipchart. This list should be on display at each meeting.

You should complete the first session with a hand-out, and this is a good opportunity to introduce men to the competence curve discussed in the previous section of this chapter. If participants are willing you might also arrange for a group photograph.

Subsequent sessions

From the second session onwards you should start every meeting by "checking in": sharing news and asking participants to talk about "how I'm feeling". This should help you to gain an impression of whether there are likely to be any blocks for individuals, and to allocate time to men who have specific problems. It can be useful to create space for words of support from other group members in such cases. Be aware that some men may have problems that are beyond the scope of the group to deal with. Group meetings are not a substitute for specific counselling or therapy.

The news section should be a time for men to take a risk and mention anything that may be on their mind – whether a personal issue or a public event. In one of my groups the subject of the gun-man who had recently gone on the rampage at a school in Dunblane, in Scotland, came up. It was clearly a subject that was much more than an "opener", providing the group with important material. In such a situation I would go with the energy of the group, giving time to a situation that profiles a specific issue relating to men.

Exercises

Exercise 1: Why I joined this group
Ask the men to pair up and talk for 10 minutes each on "Why I joined this group". Encourage them to make notes and then to compile a list seeking out common themes or areas that seems interesting to explore further.

Exercise 2: This is me
Hand out a sheet of paper and a pen to each man and ask him to find a space in the room. Ask each man to draw a line, with one end marked "born" and the other marked "now", identifying key points in his life along the line. Participants should be told that the paper will be used in subsequent exercises. After 30 minutes ask the men to choose a partner and to share the information on their paper for five minutes each. Then ask the group to re-form, giving each pair a few minutes to comment on the exercise and their feelings about it.

Exercise 3: This is me, continued . . .
For this exercise group members should provide two photographs – one of themselves when young, and one recent picture. These photographs should be attached to the start and finish of the life-line produced in the previous exercise. Ask the group to consider the gender influences of family and friends. Who was the biggest influence? Ask them to sketch in names or events that had a gender issue attached and to try and map out the ways in which daily life and its structures had an impact on their gender identity. Give the group 20 minutes to do the exercise then get them into pairs, ideally with men they haven't worked with before, to feedback. After 10 minutes, move them into groups of four for a further 20 minutes, before getting the whole group together for a general discussion of gender influences.

Life-lines can bring up important and emotional material. For example, a man who has experienced physical abuse as a child may find the exercise especially difficult. There may be individuals who want to share everything in the first session – and this too can be cause for concern. Remember that these men do not know each other. In the early stages there is a need for balance in deciding what to share and what not to. Asking the facilitator to "hold back" from too much emotional intensity may seem ironic. Our culture is relentless in its desire for the instant response. I am convinced, however, that a gradual and deepening awareness is preferable to an initial abundance of uncharted emotional disclosure. Constantly remind the men to be gentle and nurturing in the way they reveal themselves to each other and in the way they make discoveries about themselves.

Exercise 4: Arguments for and against change
Reassemble the groups of four and, equipped with a sheet of large paper divided in half, ask the groups to "brainstorm" reasons for and against change. After 20 minutes, groups should feedback to the whole group, identifying common themes and differences. Be aware of men "distancing" themselves, or of wanting to use "we" or "us" statements. Asking "what does this mean to you?" is a good way of clarifying individual issues. This is a good point to resume discussion of the learning curve in Figure 14.1.

Images of men and women

The way we create an understanding of what is masculine and what is feminine is influenced by a myriad of circumstances and events – and in particular by the subtle interaction of accepted norms and our own daily response to them. The images we formulate may contain contradictions that lead to confusion or uncertainty, or that lead to the development of behaviour that is oppressive or dominating. We rarely see images of the gentle side of men, or of men seeking guidance or support from women. The consequence of this is that we inhabit and experience only particular aspects of ourselves and deny the wider range of emotions and responses of which we are capable. Similarly, our ability to conceptualise alternatives to the image of the white, able-bodied, heterosexual man as a "norm", is thwarted by powerful internal and external images that may lead us to marginalize others in abusive ways.

As a child I frequently went to the cinema with my father. This was at a time when James Bond films were at their height of popularity, and one of the films I remember most vividly was *You only live twice*, starring Sean Connery. At one stage there is an aerial view of Bond running across the roof of a high-rise building. He holds an iron bar in his hand. Several men move towards him, attempting to thwart his escape. To the sound of fast-paced music, he smashes them all to the ground. As our hero makes his escape the men he has attacked are lying unconscious on the roof-top. I clearly recall the thoughts in my mind as I watched this sequence: "I want to be like that."

There are many ways that this personal disclosure could be analyzed within the context of a group. We might choose to look at the ways in which such violent images legitimize male violence, at the heroic personality of James Bond and his appeal to men, at the film's portrayal of women, or indeed at my father's motives for taking me to see the film.

Exercise 5: Heroes from childhood

Ask the group to form pairs and to spend 10 minutes considering their heroes from childhood, concentrating especially on those that provided strong images of masculinity for them. You might encourage discussion by showing video clips of the exploits of heroic figures from well-known films. Make sure that each man has his space to say why the hero was important to them. This exercise generally leads to animated discussion as group members "tap-into" their childhood feelings of excitement. If this happens it is well worth sharing the experience in the general discussion which follows as it may lead to more insight about collective experiences of masculinity. Be prepared for other responses; some men may not share the feeling of bonding. Black men are likely to have had difficulty in identifying with the heroes of white culture; and gay men who were aware of their sexual orientation in childhood may find this a difficult exercise. Take care to give space for diversity and to acknowledge the problem of the male imagery that was missing.

In drawing up these lists and discussing what they meant to developing boys, try to seek out the common themes. It is likely they will be about men being in control, men winning wars, men being violent, men being irresistible to women. Use a discussion of such themes to make links to the next exercise.

Exercise 6: Troubled men

In the film *South Pacific* there is a wonderful scene which sums up the image of masculinity in the movies. Two of the male leads are talking about a dilemma one of them has with a woman. In this unusually vulnerable moment, one gives the other some supportive advice: "When I have problems I often find going hunting helps".

Exercise 6 uses the same material as Exercise 5 to look at the opposite end of the scale. Group members are asked to think of a man they admired on film or TV, and to try and recollect a time when he was:

- crying
- vulnerable
- seeking help from another man
- seeking help from a woman.

This will be a difficult exercise but give 10 minutes regardless of the silence before moving the group together for discussion. You will find that this exercise frequently deflates men. There are several reasons for this. They find themselves unable to find enough examples and, not having "the answer", become confused or uncertain about the exercise, seeking to rationalize. Or they many have begun to make contact with the pain and anguish of being forced away from enriching emotional expression. If this happens it is important to acknowledge it and to remind the group of the model of change illustrated earlier. Men need to know that the insecurity they feel is quite natural – if they can do this, it will be a growth point for the group.

Exercise 7: Images of women

Using a similar format to that of the last two exercises, Exercise 7 explores the role of women in the eyes of boys and developing adolescents. Ask the men to think back to the women they liked or fantasized about and about those women whom, in hindsight, they had particular misconceptions. Women have so often been seen in the cinema as platforms for the maintenance of and adornment of men. This exercise should explore the marginal effect of female characters in popular films on the lives of men: looking at their responsibility for home, children and domestic arrangements. The aim is to highlight the superficiality of men's understanding of women by comparing their recollections of female characters with their energized recollections about male heroes. Ask for feedback after 10 minutes, drawing out discussion about the image of women as "being there for men", and the ramifications of this inequality.

Exercise 8: Powerful women

Again in small groups, ask the men to recollect women they saw as powerful or influential in their childhood, discussing the ways in which these characteristics were demonstrated. In drawing out the issues, ask the men to consider the effect such images had on their relationships with their mothers and sisters. Again, men may struggle with this exercise as they fail in their ability to make an adequate list along the lines prescribed.

Exploration of these themes can be continued if the group continues to find it useful. A next step might be to look at the construction of less stereotypical images of men and women. You could split the group into two, asking each to present a role play or a reinterpretation of a well known film: James Bond failing with a woman or crying because he can't take the pressure of being a spy, for example. Such an exercise relies on considerable trust between members of the group and it is important to "debrief" when it is finished.

Exercise 9: Present day reflections of gender and power

For this exercise you will need the following:

- a video tape containing a complete section of an evening news programme
- a quality (broadsheet) newspaper
- a fast-sell (tabloid) newspaper
- a financial paper.

Assemble the group into four smaller groups and for 30 minutes ask them to analyze the news in relation to gender. Each group should be given a piece of paper for each different news source; dividing it into two, with columns marked "men" and "women". Hand out news pages (rather than features pages) from the papers, asking the groups to record a tick in the appropriate box each time someone speaks on the news programme, and each time someone is quoted or mentioned in the news article being analyzed. They should also do a count of pictures of men and women in the papers. Then ask for feedback. What you will find is that, on the television news, men outnumber the women by about eight to one; in the papers it will be more. This exercise provides a simple illustration of the fact that much of what we call news is about men making decisions and that many of these are connected to war and conflict – between men. The discussion that follows should consider the power men have in all spheres of activity that influence or control other people. This exercise can be related to the previous explorations of images of men and women. At this stage I would recommend selecting an article for men to read that looks at different cultures and shows that history does not always state that men have been in control forever. Good books you might use include Miles' *The women's history of the world* and Coontz and Henderson's *Women's work – men's property*.

Me, now and change

By this time the group will be well established and facilitators should have a clear notion of how it is gelling. Despite the focus of the group there will, inevitably, be men who attempt to dominate the proceedings, who must be carefully handled. Unspoken rules and guidelines, not in the original "contract", may have become a part of the group's life. Remind the group of its "task", to explore the possibilities of being a man, but do also recognize that each group has a unique identity and cohesiveness, which should, by this stage, provide a supportive and safe enough environment to allow men to start venturing into more ambitious and uncertain territory.

By now, group members will have started to consider issues that relate to their lives and identities, but they have yet to constitute a firm personal agenda for change. The first step is to help them identify ways in which they would like to be different. The key questions to reflect on are identified by Jeff Hearn on page 10 of this book. To his questions I have added three of my own. I recommend giving group members a list of these questions before you begin work on this section, suggesting that they might talk them through with a close friend or partner:

- How important to me is changing myself and other men?
- How much effort should put into this?
- Do I want this to be a fundamental part of my life?
- In what ways do I like being a man and in what ways do I not like being a man?

- In what ways do I feel ambivalent about change?
- What are the implications of this change?
- What internal and external pressures exist to help or hinder my ability to change?
- Am I able to identify support systems to help me?

Exercise 10: Clarifying my intentions

Group members should provide a photograph of themselves for this exercise, and the facilitator will need to provide felt-tip pens and sheets of paper large enough to contain a life-sized body outline. Each man should ask another to draw around him to create an outline; then he should attach his photograph to the centre of the sheet. Some time will be spent working the outline, so ask participants not to damage or discard the sheets.

Begin by asking the men to write on the figure all the phrases or words that come to mind when they think of themselves. Ask them to write in a different colour what others would say about them, or what they imagine they would say. Then assemble the group for feedback.

Next, hand out sheets of A4 paper, preferably of a different colour to the sheet that contains the body outline and, asking the men to work alone, give them 10 minutes per question to consider each of the questions listed above. If this exercise is to be effective group members should have had a chance to think about the list of questions prior to the session. Both question and answer should be written on the same sheet of paper, and participants should be encouraged to spend a few minutes discussing their answer with another man before the group is reassembled for general discussion. When each question has been considered, direct the men to stick the smaller paper containing their answers to the larger paper containing the body outline. They can then circulate and observe the responses of others.

In my experience this is a very emotional moment for the group, at which men develop a sense of mutual support and a realization that they are all on a similar journey. You should try to make this realization part of the exercise. If the atmosphere invites intimacy, ask the group to form a circle and encourage each man to make a short statement of affirmation, starting with your own:

I feel very moved and touched by what I've seen here today. I feel a sense of commitment to being different though I know that it will take courage to face that journey.

Some will experience this as a moment of great joy in the face of a hard and relentless struggle and will come to subsequent sessions with a feeling of optimism. Others may experience a renewed realization that a commitment to be different will cause problems ahead. They may be struggling with contradictory messages from childhood or from present-day issues with partners or friends. They may be unable to identify how they feel. Making sure that you "check in" at the start of each session, will help you understand more fully what is going on for each man.

Schooldays

Schooldays may be a time that group members remember as a great period in their lives, but they may also have been a time of conformity, peer pressure and bullying. The schoolyard culture is one of rigid norms and great anxiety. For boys, traditional masculinity is seen as the only possible way of being. Alternatives are ridiculed and often savagely attacked. Minorities are frequently victimized, with racism and homophobia widespread. Boys who, for whatever reason, are seen not to fit in or who let their guard down, might just as easily find themselves a target. The result of being isolated, singled out or scapegoated in this way is to make boys feel small, insignificant, weak and ashamed.

Such victimization is not always limited to relationships between peers. It is frequently part of the institutional set-up of the school. During my own schooldays we had a sports teacher, a large and aggressive man, who would use peer pressure to obtain control and conformity. He loved rugby and would generally start the lesson by shouting out to the group of boys he was teaching: "Right then, we'll have the men who want to play rugby to the left of me and the girls who want to play soccer to the right." He would choose a handful of the soccer players to make up the numbers for rugby and at the end of the rugby game suggest to a group of the larger boys that they should take the cleanest would-be soccer player for a good roll in the mud, which often meant a kicking. The implications of this punishment were clear: be tough, get stuck in, or else.

This section invites men to recall, in the case of some, what it felt like to be part of the violent majority; and in the case of others what it felt like to be on the receiving end of violence or intimidation. Group members are asked to reflect on ways in which pressure is used to obtain conformity, both at school and in society at large.

Exercise 11: Boys and girls

School is usually the first place where boys and girls are brought face to face in an institutional context. Even at the age of five they rarely mix in the playground. By the time children reach secondary school, separation along gender lines has led to ignorance and fantasy. A vivid memory from my own schooldays is that of an older boy who would talk to us about girls while we waited for the school bus: "Don't forget the three Fs", he would say. "Find them, fuck them and forget them."

Divide the group into pairs to recall what boys did and what girls did at school. In the discussion that develops it is important to make the link between the ways in which boys and girls become isolated and the long-term consequences for gender relations. You might pose the following questions:

- What would have been the implications of playing together?
- Are there any examples of what happened to boys/girls if they did?
- What did boys know about girls?
- Where did boys get messages about girls?

There is likely to be some confusion about the reasons for these questions. However, it seems to me to be vital, at this stage, for men to begin to question the way in which our institutions are organized. This exercise should encourage them to think about the damage patriarchy does to men and women, boys and girls, from a very early age – abusing and damaging our ability to understand and relate to others.

Introjects

I introduce a Gestalt term to the programme at this stage, because it seems to me a powerful way of understanding ourselves, our motivations and our prejudices. The term *introject* refers to the powerful messages boys and girls receive from external influences from the moment they are born. The pressure to conform to a socially acceptable norm is intense. Parents fear boys being too soft and girls too masculine and the need to please our parents is immense. We can all point to examples in our everyday lives. I recently visited my sister's house for tea and her three year old son had a friend round to play. They ran round the house holding hands. My sister noticed this, took her son's hand and smacked him hard: "Little boys do not hold hands", she told him.

Introjects are the source of our internalizing of masculinity and femininity. We live in a culture that exploits these powerful notions to encourage consumption. Thus, personal interactions interface with institutionalized patriarchy to saturate us in subtle or blatant ways at all levels of our daily lives.

I should make clear that introjects are not always harsh and they do not always enforce stereotyping or prejudice. Clearly, we also take in good things from family and from those around us. However, in societies characterized by such polarization of the sexes, we are rarely unblemished by the gender messages and restrictions that are constantly reinforced by those with influence upon us. The crucial issue is how we undo the damage done by our internalization of a lifetime of introjects about our gender roles. The first step is to examine the origin, purpose and mechanism of the introjects we have received. We are then more able to distinguish those introjects that affirm aspects of ourselves we value from those that reinforce prejudice. The exercises I present below aim to begin this important and valuable work.

Those wishing to know more about Gestalt therapy should read Latner's useful handbook: *The Gestalt therapy book.*

Exercise 12: Brainstorming introjects
Divide the group into subgroups of about four men. Give them at least 50 sheets of paper, half of which are blue (for introjects that relate to men) and half of which are pink (for introjects that relate to women). Ask each group to brainstorm for 15

minutes, coming up with as many common social and personal introjects as they can. Examples would include "boys don't cry", or "dolls are for girls". All of the lists should be stuck to a wall – with the blue on one side of the room and the pink on the other. Each group member should read through the lists of introjects, choosing one in particular that has importance to him. Then the group should be reassembled and each man given time to talk about the statement he chose.

I find this an immensely powerful exercise, especially with a group of more than 12. The wall of introjects is a powerful and often shocking illustration of the cumulative process by which we absorb ideas about how we should be. Seeing so many of these statements together reveals how bizarre they can be.

You may wish to extend the work on introjects by dividing the group into two and, choosing an introject for each person, invite them to work on a role play to illustrate or to parody its message. This is an exercise that can produce moments to savour!

Exercise 13: Messages my father gave me

This is a further exercise on the theme of introjects. Divide the group into pairs to explore messages or advice they received from their fathers. Take care to include those who were fatherless and suggest that they reflect on male influences within the family, at school or in the community. As an example from my own life: my father would, usually after a spell of drinking, give me advice about women: "James: you will learn that a man takes and a woman gives." He would not expand on this statement, only qualifying it with the words: "You'll learn."

Here are some examples of introjects relating to the messages our fathers give us, from participants on workshops I have facilitated:

- That's women's work.
- Women are emotional creatures.
- Never show your emotions in public.
- Never let your feelings get in the way.
- You must never show weakness.
- There's only one thing women are good for.
- You can't hold my hand (father to son).

At this stage I should say that when I run gender issues workshops and men's programmes the hurt and disappointment in men's feelings about their fathers is a common theme. I recall one man talking about his father's tendency to hide behind a newspaper. Only when the son made excessive demands would the drawbridge be lowered for a few moments to allow the brief interjection of a harsh comment, before it rose again. Was he so terrified or incapable of relating to his son that the newspaper was his only source of defence?

Exercise 14: What my father was like, and what I would have liked him to be like
Divide the group into pairs and ask them to write on one side of a sheet of paper what their fathers were like, and on the other side what their ideal father would have been like. Each pair should share these thoughts with the group to allow common themes to emerge. As I have mentioned above, it is common for men to respond to recollections of the relationship with their father with great emotion and often with anger. As the facilitator you will need to manage this without letting men become overwhelmed. You may find it useful to encourage participants to shout their anguish out loud, or alternatively to seek a supportive hug. Do not underestimate the preparation time required for this exercise or the extent to which participants will rely on you, as facilitator for support. You should also encourage them to seek support in each other. While the feelings that emerge in this session may be therapeutic, do remember that this is not a therapy group. Some men may need support outside the group from a trained and experienced counsellor.

Support and vulnerability

Questioning ways of thinking and behaving that have governed our lives since childhood can lead to pain and inner turmoil. Men will often resist attempts to challenge deeply-rooted aspects of their behaviour by withdrawing or by rationalizing what is good about the way things were. At this stage what is most needed is support, from family, from friends and from other members of the group.

However, it is also true that one of the key components of "traditional" masculinity is to be seen to be strong, and to be able to reach answers to problems alone. "Real" men never show vulnerability and do not seek help. Though we read a lot about men being "in crisis" in the late twentieth century – with women replacing men in the workplace and boys less academically successful than girls – this sense of crisis is rarely overtly articulated by men on an individual basis.

By now, the men in your group should feel grounded enough to allow them to explore their vulnerability and to reach out to each other for support.

Exercise 15: A time I needed support and didn't get it
Split the group into pairs and ask them to spend 15 minutes considering the above question. Make it clear that it is not necessary to consider "big" issues; that examples from everyday life are fine. It might be useful to provide an example from your own life: perhaps a decision you are having difficulty making and have spent some time debating internally. When the group reconvenes the task of the facilitator is to identify the reasons why men were not able to obtain the support they

needed, looking for common themes, and leading on to a general discussion about the origins of men's difficulty in both asking for and finding adequate support networks.

Exercise 16: Mapping out a support system

This exercise aims to help men identify what support systems they already have. This can be a problematic exercise for more isolated men who may feel embarrassed by their lack of support.

Each man writes his name in the middle of a sheet of paper, surrounding it with the names of those he receives support from. This map becomes the focus for exploring his satisfaction with the resources he can draw on for support. A useful extension of this exercise is to draw a second map, supplementing unsatisfactory networks with an "ideal" and making commitments to get more support.

Notice how many men put the group on their map. By this time the group should be seen as a validating and important meeting point, and it is a good idea to affirm its importance at the end of the exercise.

Support needs a definition, which should be discussed in the general feedback session following the exercise. It is not about meeting with mates and talking in superficial terms about "safe" subjects, such as work or sport. It is about being in need, about realizing that you don't always have solutions, but that you can rely on empathy and warmth from another person. There are complexities to seeking and to giving support. Men need to be confident that the support they are offered is genuine and that their vulnerability will not be exploited. Those seeking support must learn to clarify what they need, and who might be best placed to help them. Role-play is an excellent way of exploring these issues within the group.

As discussions on the subject of support proceed, there is much to be gained from inviting participants to speak about their dilemmas and problems and to practise reaching out to other group members for support. For this to be effective the facilitator should help the group understand that giving direct advice or attempting to find a solution is not always the most helpful way forward. In order to clarify this point it is helpful to explain the different vocabularies of advice and support:

Advice

- I had that problem and I found that if I . . .
- What you are really saying is . . .
- I think that what you need to do is . . .

Support

- It is terrible that you are in such a dilemma . . .
- I can see the pain you are going through . . .

227

- I'm wondering if there is anything you want of me . . .
- I want you to know that I'm here to give you support if you want it . . .

Homophobia

Men's fear of vulnerability, of intimacy and of seeking support, is part of the larger problem of men denying their emotional closeness to other men. Such denial is frequently rooted in a prejudice against, or fear of, men who love men. The homophobia of individual men is normalized and exacerbated within our society by the history of criminalization of homosexual sex and the labelling of homosexuality as a psychiatric condition that still persists in some schools of thought. It is, sadly, still the case that many gay men live in fear of both physical violence and discrimination: fearing that coming out at work may lead to discrimination, and that coming out to parents and siblings may lead to family crisis.

I have personal experience of the latter. My older brother told my entire family that he was gay, except my father. My father's well-known tendency to refer to homosexuals as "poofs", "benders", or "arsehole bandits" made the prospect of coming out to him an especially daunting one. When my brother finally decided to tell him, my father stormed off in great despair, arriving home hours later to sit, immobile and trembling, in his armchair. I made him a cup of tea and went to talk to him. He reached out his hand to me with a look of absolute tragedy: "It's your brother", he said, "he's bent". My reply, "Oh, is that all: we've known for years", threw him completely. He was shocked out of his despair and sought clarification. His biggest fear had been that the family would share his despair and would never survive the news.

As Mac An Ghaill demonstrates with great clarity in *The making of men: masculinities, sexualities and schooling*, boys are constantly policing their own and other's sexuality. Many teenagers who attempt to be openly gay do so in an oppressive and abusive environment, often suffering verbal and physical abuse, which can result in depression or even attempted suicide. Homosexuality represents a challenge to male heterosexuality on an individual level, as well as to hegemonic masculinity and to institutionalized patriarchy. Being different can take tremendous courage.

Exercise 17: Exclusion and closeness
Ask the group to form pairs to discuss how school subculture, supported by traditional masculine antagonism, regulated those they saw as deviant. After reporting back to the larger group, each pair should explore the level of closeness they experienced at school with a particular "mate". How was that closeness played out?

In the larger group, seek to identify common themes and discuss the notion of what "closeness" means. *Note*: there may be men in the group who are gay and have not been able to explore this. As the facilitator you must make certain that should this be the case, and should they wish to use the opportunity to come out, the group should provide a "safe place" for them to do so.

Exercise 18: Men as friends

This is a similar exercise to the last one, but it seeks to explore men and friendship now. Ask participants to talk about a friend in their adult life, and about what that friendship means to them.

Some important questions to consider:

- Do you talk openly to each other about your feelings?
- Do you talk about your fears?
- What do you define as intimacy?
- How do you validate your friendship in a non-verbal way?
- What is it like to be touched by your friend?
- When do you feel anxious about your closeness?

Some of the above questions are safe, others may produce (and are designed to produce!) anxiety. The hope is that men will realize the tragedy of what has been "knocked out of them" if they crossed the defined boundaries of male intimacy during childhood or early adulthood.

Exercise 19: Touch

Ask the men to pair up and to spend five minutes simply looking at each others' face, in silence. Then ask for feedback. Ask them to repeat the exercise holding hands, again reassembling for feedback after five minutes.

I recommend ending this session with a relaxation tape. Men may well have uncomfortable feelings about this session, whether it is sexual attraction or repulsion that has emanated into their consciousness. Ending with a session of relaxation is a good way of inducing a calming effect. Suggest to the men at the end of the previous session that they should bring a sleeping bag, so that they can lie down comfortably for 20 minutes while the tape is playing. End with another session of feedback.

Men, power, control and abuse

Exercise 20: Issues of violence

For this exercise you will need to set up the room before the group arrives. Do not mention what the subject will be during the preceding session.

The box below contains a list of facts and figures about men, violence and abuse.

Almost half of all murders of women in the UK are killings by a current or former partner

In London, 100,000 women each year seek treatment for violent injuries received in the home

61% of rapes in England are committed indoors, usually in the victim's home

Domestic violence in the UK accounts for a quarter of all reported violent crime

70% of women in Britain say they are worried most by the possibility of being raped

Four in ten homeless women in the UK left home as a result of abuse

Almost two thirds of men believe that they would respond violently to their partner in certain situations

Boys are more accepting of violence against women than are girls

A majority of 70% of boys felt that there was some likelihood of their using violence in future relationships

(*Source*: Zero Tolerance Association of London Authorities)

A survey carried out in Pakistan revealed that 99% of married women and 77% of working women were regularly beaten by their husbands

In Spain there were 15,888 reports of conjugal violence in 1992

In Denmark, 25% of women point to violence as their reason for divorce

In ex-Yugoslavia, it is estimated that women and children account for over 70% of the total number of murdered people, and that there have been over 35,000 cases of rape

It is estimated that over 24.3% of the displaced Salvadorian women were assaulted and in fear of their lives during their journey into exile

Over 90 million African women and girls are victims of genital mutilation

(*Source*: International Workers' Aid, Germany)

> **It is estimated that there are 70,000 child prostitutes in Zambia**
> **and 500,000 child prostitutes in India. The Netherlands is**
> **thought to have 1000 child prostitutes**
>
> **In Britain one in four children have been sexually abused**
>
> (*Source*: Campaign against Pornography)

I suggest typing out each of these statements, centred and in bold, and then enlarging the words on to sheets of different coloured A3 paper. You might supplement them with enlarged newspaper headlines, detailing atrocities committed by men and with photographs of men at war or otherwise engaged in violence. You will need at least 70 posters for them to have their full impact. In addition, make about eight copies of the competence curve (Figure 14.1), also as large as possible, on A3 paper. Put up all the posters around one-half of the room.

As the men arrive, invite them to mill around and take in what the posters, photos and headlines say. Most men become very defensive when confronted with statements of this kind and their attempts to distance themselves from such behaviour should form part of the opening discussion of the session. Make a note of what they say on the flipchart.

Here are comments from some of my previous groups:

- I think some of these statistics are wrong. (*Denial*)
- I don't do that sort of thing. (*Abdication*)
- The sort of men who do this are monsters. (*Distancing*)
- I don't feel good about being a man. (*Guilt*)
- I'm sick of women blaming men for everything. (*Deflection/avoidance*)
- Women can be violent too. (*Defensiveness*)

The problem with comments of this nature is that they are not constructive and they cannot motivate men who have become depressed or who feel guilty, inadequate, overwhelmed, or immobilized. Sometimes men's responses reflect their own experience of being abused. While a recognition of this experience can be an important growth point, the purpose of this exercise is to force participants into a recognition of their own potential for violence and abuse. It is important to make it clear that however overwhelmed and frightened men are made to feel by being confronted with such testimonies of abuse and violence, this bears no relation to the suffering experienced by those to whom the posters refer. With this feeling of uncertainty we move on to the next exercise.

Exercise 21: Activism and commitment

This exercise aims to encourage the group to consider the ways in which we as individuals "buy in" to the system of domination and control and the ways in which, in not challenging it, we support and strengthen it. Men are asked to look at the possibilities for challenging the system on a variety of levels. They are reminded that, though individuals may make decisions to campaign or to explore personal growth through a men's group, challenging male power is not something that can be done for a couple of hours once a week.

Ask the men to attach to the empty walls the body outlines they produced in Exercise 10. Divide them in to groups of four and ask them to consider the questions below:

- How can I help to stop male violence?
- In what ways can I become more active to help change things?

Ask participants to list the personal and political activities that they *could* engage in, rather than the things they necessarily will do. Invite them to be as creative as possible in their ideas. Collect the ideas on sheets of A3 paper and attach them to the wall containing the body outlines. Then ask the men to circulate, considering the posters on both sides of the room, and reassemble the whole group for discussion.

This will be a tough session for most men, but their development over previous weeks and months and the growing support of the group should help to make it a rewarding one.

Childcare

Over the past decade I have worked in child protection, a field which is very much concerned with work with violent and abusive men. This period has seen an increased understanding of the violence adults can do to children and of society's tendency to deny abuse or to brush it aside (for example, by repeated "humorous" references to "dirty old men", who may in fact be chronic abusers). Second-wave feminism has played its part, both in highlighting abuse and its causes and in making demands of men to work against abuse.

Exercise 22: Abuse and parenting
Divide the men into two separate groups: one group to define abuse in terms of childcare, and the other to define good parenting. Ask the two groups to share their ideas with the group as a whole, drawing out important points. *Note*: it is essential to have a clear and non-abusive understanding of what positive parenting is. You may need to supplement the group's ideas on this point.

Exercise 23: Men with children
For this exercise you will need to ask friends to do a little acting for you. Using a video camera, record a scenario in which a man reluctantly takes a child for a walk

in a pushchair. He should be doing this in a way that makes his reluctance very clear – wheeling the pushchair with one hand, clearly detached from the experience. He walks past a pub where some male friends are drinking and they make jibes about the job he is doing. At this stage, stop the video and ask the men to state what happens next. An alternative is to provide a pushchair and a doll and to ask two groups to role-play the same scenario. Ask them to work out a conflict outcome ("Fuck off you bastards or I'll knock you through!"); a collusive outcome ("Oh yeah, come and take over so I can have a sip on that pint, then!"); and an outcome that actually challenges the taunts ("Yes, I'm out with my kid. You know, I never knew my old man and I made a promise to myself that I would always be there for my kid. Beats being in the pub any day!").

Exercise 24: Fathering
In the past six months I have spent a lot of time with my two-year-old daughter. It has been incredibly hard work: demanding of my time, energy and patience. I have often noticed men in the park, who, while they are playing with children, are not necessarily "in contact" with the experience. Often they seem very self conscious or remote. Or they give the impression that something simple, such as pushing a child on a swing, is an onerous task.

Ask the men to pair up and discuss:

- what sort of father they are, or think they would be, or
- why they can't, or don't wish to be a father.

In the general discussion, try to explore the importance and profundity of being openly available to and emotionally connecting with a child, in a way that involves no ulterior motives. Remember, though, that this could be a problematic exercise for men who are not able to father and for those who are separated from their children.

Men's work/women's work

I find it useful to run the three exercises that follow in one session. They juxtapose the need men feel to have an impact on the world, to conquer or control their environment, with an area many men trivialize by referring to it "women's work" – childcare and housework. The contrasting of these areas of activity provides an excellent opportunity for discussion about men's priorities.

Exercise 25: Men's impact on the world
Divide the men into small groups and ask them to make a list of the words they associate with men's need to succeed, to control or to dominate. Look especially

for words that hold the same associations in a variety of contexts. For example, some British men have recently broken the world land speed record in a car called "thrust" – the name of which clearly denotes a specifically male activity! You could make a videotape of television advertising and discuss which gender the consumer item is aimed at by reference to the words used. Advertising is an excellent example of the way in which the use of specific words removes men from domesticity, into action, competition or domination. The message is that they should get out of the house and get into more "important" things.

Exercise 26: Priorities
Ask the men to enact a role-play, in pairs. One man plays the part of a racing driver and the other a sponsor of "Thrust 2". The racing driver has been asked to go to the USA for three months testing and trialling of the new car. He is about to turn the sponsor down because his partner is planning to start a new job and he has agreed to stay at home to look after the children. The sponsor does all he can to convince the driver to leave his family and to take up the challenge. This exercise could also be done in the form of writing a letter.

Exercise 27: Housework
Again in pairs, ask participants to draw up a list of points in favour of doing domestic work and points in favour of escaping into a hobby or activity. Inevitably, most men find it very difficult to find positives connected to domestic activity. Playing or watching rugby, cricket, football, or drinking down the pub are generally seen as preferable to childcare, cooking and cleaning. Use this exercise to lead into a more general discussion about relationships, equality and what men find hard to change about themselves. In particular it will be interesting to discuss who did what in the childhood home, and to compare the arrangements with present-day tensions over men and women's roles within the household. Encourage the group to make connections between men's conception of their domestic role and their fear of emotional closeness. Can our hobbies be seen as a structure designed to divert us from intimacy? What would it be like to be so emotionally close that all other distractions – sport, drinking and even work, seemed unimportant? This is indeed a subversive and even a revolutionary suggestion.

Relationship with women

By this stage in the programme, the men will be ready to discuss their personal relationships with women, and to explore the ways in which those relationships should be re-evaluated in terms of the work they have done. The key questions to consider are as follows:

- How do men perceive women?
- How do we work with women as colleagues?
- How should we love them?
- How can we work out conflicts?
- Can men and women really be friends?

Exercise 28: Relating to women

Ask the men to divide into pairs and to work through the following list of questions:

- What sort of relationships do I want with women?
- What are the potential barriers?
- How can I relate to women differently?
- Do I have women as friends?
- If I am in a relationship with a woman, what does this mean?
- How do I use my power when with women?
- What areas do I need to work on practically, domestically and emotionally to effect change?

Reassemble the group for discussion and to explore commonalities and differences. You should try to place the discussion within the context of the work that has been done in previous exercises, focusing on men's historical relationship with women, and on how individual relationships have developed since childhood and its embargos against friendship with women.

Endings and making commitments

The group will have been meeting for some time and participants will have experienced, perhaps for the first time, a way of relating to other men in a qualitatively different way. This is, in itself, something profound, significant and mould-breaking.

Here are some comments made by men from groups I have run:

- I never fully realized what it meant to be a man. Now I know that I have been living a lie, hiding from myself and from others . . .
- For so long I have been tough, hard and self reliant. I am finding it hard to be different, but I know this is what I want to be. I've felt different feelings. That sounds strange to say and its been frightening, but I want to be a different man, a better partner and want my kids to know me . . .
- Everywhere I look I now see gender issues, power and exploitation. It's making me dizzy and angry. I want things to change . . .

Exercise 29: Ending
Ask each man to talk in turn, within in the group as a whole, about:

- what they now feel differently about.
- how they will sustain these changes.
- how they will get support of the sort they have had from the group.
- what are their plans to keep going.

A good way of bringing the work done so far to completion is for each man to share something with the group, whether of his own creation or simply his own selection. This might be a poem, a painting, a favourite piece of music or a reading from a book. A final, formal goodbye is the appreciation exercise, in which the men circulate and say something positive to everyone in the group. It is crucial not to rush this exercise so that each man has time to talk to everyone.

The best we can hope for is that men will move forward with the enthusiasm to continue the process of personal change and with a commitment to activism. This is a very different process for men than it is for women. Reclaiming power can be energizing, but in giving up power there is a different dynamic at work. Beyond the initial feelings of immobilization and denial there is unmapped ground for men to "expand" into. This is a terrain of new emotional experience, that leads to a profound change in how we view the world. Once men reach this stage, we really can be hopeful of change, in ourselves and in society at large.

References

BOLDT, L. G. (1993) *Zen in the art of making a living: A practical guide to creative career design.* Harmondsworth: Penguin.

BROOKFIELD, D. S. (1987) *Developing critical thinkers.* Oxford: Oxford University Press.

HAY, J. (1992) *Transactional analysis for trainers.* New York: McGraw-Hill.

MAC AN GHAILL, M. (1994) *The making of men: masculinities, sexualities and schooling.* Oxford: Oxford University Press.

MILLER, W. R. & ROLLNICK, S. (1991) *Motivational interviewing: preparing people for change.* New York: Guilford.

The Social Services Yearbook. Harlow: Longman. [Published annually.]

Suggested Reading

APPLEBY, S. (1994) *Men, the truth.* London: Bloomsbury.

BROOKFIELD, S. D. (1994) *Understanding and facilitating adult learning.* Milton Keynes: Open University Press.

CAVANAGH, K. & CREE, V. E. (eds) (1996) *Working with men: Feminism and social work. Children & violence* – London: Gulbenkian Foundation.

CONNELL, R. W. (1995) *Masculinities.* Oxford: Polity.

COONTZ, S. & HENDERSON, P. (1986) *Women's work – men's property: The origins of gender and class.* London: Verso.

FRENCH, M. (1992) *The war against women.* Harmondsworth: Hamish Hamilton.

HESTER, KELLY & RADFORD (eds) (1996) *Women, violence and male power.* Oxford: Oxford University Press.

HITE, S. (1993) *Women as revolutionary agents of change.* London: Sceptre.

JENKINS, A. (1993) *Invitation to responsibility.* Dulwich Centre Publications.

LATNER, J. (1990) *The Gestalt therapy book.* Highland, New York: The Gestalt Journal.

LEVANT & POLLACK (eds) (1995) *A new psychology of men.* New York: Basic Books.

MILES, R. (1993) *Women's history of the world.* London: HarperCollins.

MULLENDER, A. & MORLEY, S. (eds) (1994) *Children living with domestic violence.* London: Whiting & Birch.

PERELBERG & MILLER (eds) (1990) *Gender and power in families.* London: Routledge.

PHILLIPS, A. (1991) *Engendering democracy.* Oxford: Polity.

PRINGLE, K. *Men, masculinities and social welfare.* London: UCL Press.

ROWAN, J. (1987) *The horned god.* London: Routledge.

RUTHERFORD, J. (1997) *Forever England.* London: Lawrence & Wishart.

SEIDLER, V. (1997) *Man enough.* London: Sage.

WALSH, R. (ed.) (1997) *Women, men and gender: Ongoing debates.* New Haven, Connecticut: Yale University Press.

Index

abuse, *see* child abuse; sexual abuse; violence
acceptance, in change process 212
accountability 154
    see also responsibility
Adler, A. 81
adult learning model 211–14
Africentric success 65–6
Aggleton, P. 102
aggregation 89
aggression
    nature of 135–9
    see also violence
Ahmad, B. 204–5
alcohol consumption 170–1
application, in change process 212
assertion
    and HIV prevention 104
    nature of 135–9
attachment, in group therapy 89–90

batterer groups
    organizational safety 164–5
    structure of 155–6
    women's work with 153–5
        problems of 156–65
Bednar, R. 106
Bennett, M. 75
Berne, E. 104
black feminism 20, 33–5
black men
    and change 59–61, 69–70
    definition of success 65–6

in groups 204–5
in HIV workshops 114–15, 124
masculinity of 62–5
political critiques 6
research with 61–2, 70
survival strategies 63–5
violence against women 34
voices of empowerment 68–9
voices of hope 67–8
voices of resistance 66–7
body
    control of women's 192–3
    and ethics 193–4
    and masculinity 50–1, 193–4
bonding 89, 164
Bonnell, C. 101
boys
    emergence of masculinity
        188–9
    and gender stereotypes 39, 40
    as gendered other 42
    see also childhood

caring
    as arena for change 7–8
    exploring in groups 33, 232–3
    men's role in 21, 33, 179
change
    features of 6, 74, 78–9, 93–4
    Orbach's views on 43–5
    relating to women 6, 39
    see also employment

239